Thank You, Brain, For All You Remember.

What You Forgot Was My Fault.

Thank You, Brain, For All You Remember.

What You Forgot Was My Fault.

by

W. R. (Bill) Klemm, D.V.M., Ph.D.
Professor of Neuroscience
Texas A&M University
College Station, TX

*In a time of drastic change,
the learners will inherit the future*
– Eric Hoffer

Thank You, Brain, For All You Remember.
What You Forgot Was My Fault

First Edition
Published by Benecton Press, 9001 Grassbur Road, Bryan, Tx 77808
Printed by Goose River Press, 3400 Friendship Road, Waldoboro, ME 04572, U.S.A.

Copyright © 2004, W. R. Klemm

All rights reserved. No part of this book may be reproduced, stored in a retrieval system, or transmitted in any form by any means without the prior written permission of the author.

Library of Congress Cataloging-in-Publication Data

Library of Congress Control Number: 2003195005

Klemm, W. R.
    Thank you, brain, for all you remember. What you forgot was my fault.
Includes bibliographic references and index.

ISBN 1-930648-82-0

Dedication

To my grandchildren: Kelley, Rachael, Stephen, David, Mason, Michael, Benjamin, Allison, and Annabelle. May you all grow up to have super (and happy) memories.

Books by Bill Klemm

Animal Electroencephalography
Applied Electronics for Veterinary Medicine and Animal Physiology (edited)
Science, The Brain and Our Future
Discovery Processes in Modern Biology (edited)
Brainstem Mechanisms of Behavior (co-edited)
Understanding Neuroscience
Global Peace Through The Global University System (co-edited)

How To Contact the Author

Bill Klemm is available to provide speeches and seminars for selected businesses, associations, or other organizations. Readers are also encouraged to contact him to suggest ideas for future editions. He may be reached at:

Dr. W. R. Klemm
Dept. VAPH, Mail Stop 4458
Texas A&M University
College Station, TX 77843-4458

Web site: http://www.cvm.tamu.edu/wklemm

Contents

Introduction, 1

My Memory is O.K. Your Memory is O. K., 7

Why Your Teacher Always Bugged You to Pay Attention, 37

Memories Hang Out With the Right Crowd, 67

Catch It While You Can, 109

We Get Emotional About Our Memories, 147

It's In There Somewhere. I Just Can't Find It, 185

Memories That Lie, 215

Sleep: Perchance to Dream. Perchance to Remember, 245

Why Old Dogs Can't Learn New Tricks (Or Can They?), 271

Untie That String On Your Finger, 303

Index, 309

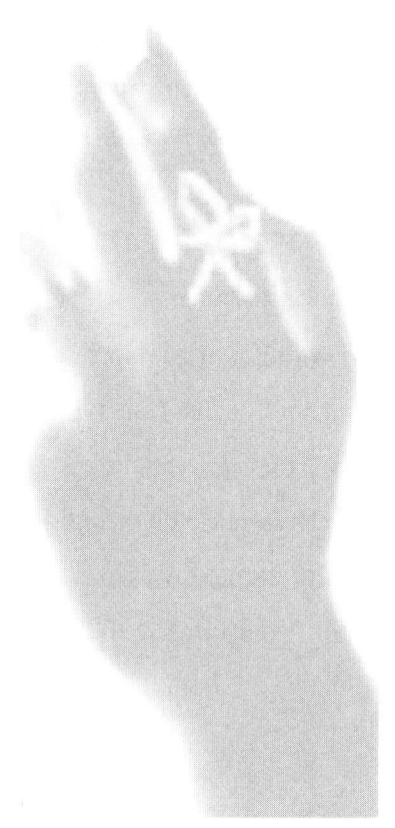

Introduction

Remember those kids in grade school who always shot up their hands when the teacher asked a question? Those kids always seemed to have the answers. They thought they were so smart - and you thought so too, especially if you were also one of those with hands up in the air all the time. Though we envy and sometimes even dislike such smart people, most of us really would like to be smarter - to make better grades if we are in school, or to impress our supervisors, or to be more competent and successful at whatever it is we do.

But what is smart? Technically, being smart is having problem-solving skills that are measured on IQ tests. There are other kinds of intelligence, such as innate social skills and emotional intelligence. But these don't concern us here. What we are talking about here is basic competency that depends on knowing a lot of "stuff." Unless you are doing something such as solving differential equations every day, being smart to most people means knowing a lot. And how much you know depends on how well you can remember.

The good news is that everybody can learn how to remember things better, even if they can't raise their IQ score. Even in a school setting, I have concluded after 40 years as a college professor, that the single most important thing about success as a student is not IQ but how much a student remembers from the instruction. Poor students invariably signal their problem with such complaints as:

- *I read this chapter over and over and still can't remember what it says.*
- *Look at how much I highlighted this text. I knew all the right parts to study.*
- *You have no idea how hard I worked in preparing for this examination!*
- *This test is not representative of what I know. I learned a lot more than that.*

Introduction

Good students don't experience this angst, because they remember most of what was presented in class, with only a few short study periods to refresh their memories. It is not fair, you say. Hogwash, I say. Poor students are typically poor students because they don't know how to memorize efficiently. That is a skill that can be learned - which is the point of this book.

If you are reading this, you probably want to improve your memory. Guess what? I did the research on this book, because I too want to improve my memory. Everybody I know has an imperfect memory. The subtitle of this book, "What You Forgot Was my Fault," is not meant to make us feel guilty. It is to emphasize that our mind (the "my" in "my fault") has the power to mess up the brain's memory systems. These systems operate mostly in the background of the unconscious mind, interacting with the effort you make consciously. No grounds for feeling guilty exist if you haven't read the more than 150 key ways to improve your memory that are described in this book. But if your memory has not improved after reading this book, then be my guest: feel guilty. You will have deserved it.

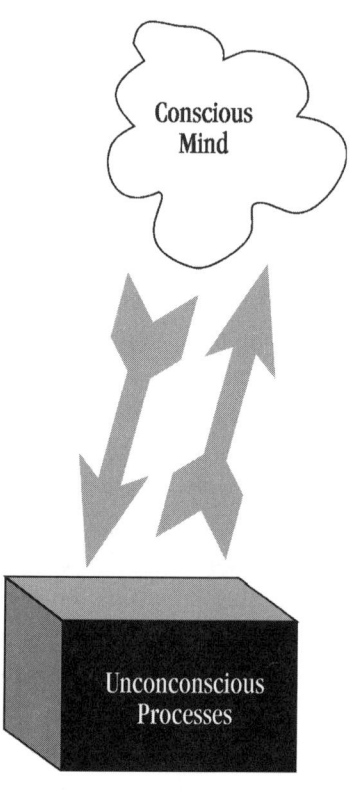

All of us, even if we are not students, have compelling reasons to learn how to remember better. A good memory impresses people. It suggests that we are smart, even if all we have done is learned more than other people. A good memory helps us tell jokes and stories, recall the news, remember phone numbers, and recall names and faces. A good memory makes us more competent in our jobs, because we remember how to do things without having to look up information all the time. A good memory saves time and makes us more efficient. A good memory also helps us to be smarter, because it gives us more information with which to reason.

A good memory also provides crucial support for creativeness. This is especially noticeable among scientists, who often make associations among multiple research reports to generate new hypotheses and theories. They have to remember the essence of these papers in order to think of new ways of putting the information together or viewing the information in ways that had not been done before. Notable among scientists for a remarkable memory is David Baltimore, a Nobel laureate biochemist and President of Cal Tech. A colleague says that Baltimore "can startle people by bringing up points they made months before. He remembers other people's research better than the people themselves do." This memory ability has another advantage. Another colleague observed, "Because he's very confident in what he knows, he's confident in what he doesn't know."[1]

Before the printing press, a great premium was placed on good memory. Not only did everyday business affairs depend on memory, but entire cultures were passed down by oral histories. In modern times, when information is freely available all around us, memory skills have atrophied. Television, radio, newspapers, books, and other media have made us lazy in our memory skills. Information comes to us without any effort on our part. If we had to work to get information, we would surely remember more of it.

Biomedical and psychological research have revealed a great deal about the mechanisms of memory. There are over 50 scientific journals that publish articles on memory research. Numerous books have attempted to summarize the discoveries for researchers. Many of these discoveries have been made in the last ten years. But even older research has often failed to find its way into practical applications. Scholars study memory for its own sake and to learn how the brain does things. Scientific papers commonly fail to point out the significance of the findings for everyday living. That is where this book

3

Introduction

comes in.

What we all want is the ability to make the right things memorable. Mom wants to know how to remember where she put the car keys. Dad wants to remember what it was he was supposed to pick up at the grocery store on the way home. He also wishes he could remember the jokes he wants to tell at coffee break at work. The kids want to know how to remember school work on test day. The whole family worries about Grandma's getting so forgetful that she needs a full-time caretaker. In the business world, advertisers want to create ads that make their product memorable, salesmen want to remember all the facts about their products and those of the competition, investment advisers want to remember what's hot and what's not. Everybody has real-world memory problems every day.

There is much a-do these days about educational reform. Politicians and parents are demanding newer schools, parental choice of schools, smaller class sizes, more emphasis on science and technology, and a host of other reforms. If we just spent more money, education would improve. The facts of many studies fail to confirm this assumption. What do we know about how kids learn and how to help them learn better? How kids learn involves a huge component of remembering. Good memory builds competence, self-esteem, and ambition for kids to strive for greater achievement. *So, why don't schools teach kids how to develop their memories?* Probably, it is because most teachers don't know what it takes to have a good memory. Nobody told them either.

In the adult world, good memory serves one well and usually helps determine the upper limit for success in life. In giving speeches or making presentations, people with a good memory give the impression of being informed, even of being intelligent. People who remember anecdotes and jokes are a people magnet. Socially, remembering names and faces ranks at the top of admired social skills. As Dale Carnegie said in, *How To Win Friends and Influence People*, the most important words in any language to every person is that person's name. Don't you always feel a glow when you enter a store and the clerk greets you by name?

Introduction

One measure of how much we value memory is the existence of numerous books on how to improve your memory. Memory books are as ubiquitous as cook books. Memory books fall into two classes, neither of which is completely satisfying to the general public. The more popular memory books teach memory gimmicks. These devices include special techniques to help you memorize lists of items or to associate names and faces. While these techniques are handy (I use them myself), they do not convey much understanding about human memory nor do they help much in improving memory capabilities without the use of gimmicks. The other category of books includes those written by scientists for each other. Not only are such books hard to read for non-scientists, but typically such books are written to serve the authors' own professional agenda, not to help people improve their memory.

This book is different, because it goes beyond tricks and gimmicks to get at the scientific basis for good memory. This present book reveals the principles that underlie the memory tricks and gimmicks. By reviewing in plain language what scientific research has shown about memory, I hope you will find here many memory improvement ideas. To make sure you don't miss any of the core ideas, I explicitly identify them at the end of each chapter. They total over 150. That's the good news. The bad news is that for best memory you have to remember over 150 ideas. While in the process of learning these ideas, you might want to put a sticky note at the end of each chapter for quick review of the key ideas.

This chance to create a different kind of memory book was the main reason I wrote this book. This writing was my first major enterprise as I entered semi-retirement from a 40+ year career as a neuroscientist. This book has given me a chance to "keep my hand in" research. Secondly, I have always been interested in learning and the question of why people differ so vastly in their ability to learn. As a life-long learner myself, I am convinced that good learners are good because they go about learning in right ways.

As a professor most of my adult life, I have encountered hundreds of students who were poor students because they used poor learning

Introduction

strategies and techniques. Even as a college student, I was so struck by the ineffective learning attempts by many fellow students that I wrote a pamphlet on how to make good grades that was distributed by the fraternities and sororities.

I now realize more completely how important learning is for everyone. All of us see in others, and perhaps in ourselves, many opportunities that were lost because of not knowing enough. What a waste it is when we fail to "be all we can be" when it comes to learning. This need is magnified as we move into the Information Age, where success in life is increasingly determined by how much we know. In case you missed it, please read again Eric Hoffer's quote on the title page.

I hope that you will find here many memory improvement ideas that will help enrich your life. Let us proceed.

Bill Klemm

1. Hyman, K. 2003. David Baltimore's redeeming presidency. The Scientist. April 23, p. 48-50.

Memory Makes Us Who We Are

The Role for Science

Memory in Everyday Life

The Memorable and the Forgettable

How the Ancients Did It

To Train in Spain is Mainly in the Brain

The Rich Get Richer and the Poor Get Poorer

Memory Kinds

Underground Memories

Schools Teach Kids *What* to Learn. Who Teaches Them *How* To Learn?

Getting Better at Memory

My Memory Is O.K.

Your Memory Is O.K.

Memory is a net: one finds it full of fish when he takes it from the brook. But a dozen miles of water have run through it without sticking.

– Oliver Wendell Homes Sr.

7

Memory Makes Us Who We Are

We are what we remember - including what we know that we don't know we know. Without memory, we would not know who we are. We would not remember our name, our addresses, our loved ones, or anything about the events that have shaped our lives. Who we are reflects what we have learned, whether learned consciously and unconsciously, remembered explicitly and implicitly, and learned on purpose or by accident. In his book, *The Created Self,*[1] Robert Weber makes this point as follows: "We see that memory itself is an important selector, definer, and preserver that goes far beyond sheer storage as it exercises its preferences and aversions. What memory selects to encode and value serves to define the self." Weber goes on to explain that there are at least three ways that our memories "define the self." First, we interpret our current experiences based on the store of memories that have created our biases, emotions, and storehouse of knowledge. Second, a similar role for memory occurs with the interpretation that we give to already existing memories. Third, we sculpt our personality, attitudes, and competencies by deciding what we want to remember and what we want to forget.

The Role for Science

What does research offer in the way of improving memory? ... a great deal, as I hope to show in this book. You may not think of science as the route to a better memory, but it is. Science has been teaching us how to improve our memory for almost a hundred years - ever since Pavlov showed us that dogs were four-footed furballs of conditioned reflexes. The problem is that a lot of scientific research on memory is buried in arcane scholarly journals. Applications to everyday life are seldom mentioned in research journals.

Much of that research is not performed with practical aims in mind. Scientists conduct experiments to test theories and hypotheses about how things work - in both normal people and those who have some kind of memory disorder. Nonetheless, what scientists discover in their memory research very often does have practical applications. The purpose of this book is to examine the results of many experiments and glean from them the applications for everyday memory requirements.

In addition to the specific memory aids that have been discovered through experimentation, science continues to reveal just how marvelous our brains are. Our brains have somewhere on the order of a hundred thousand million cells (that is 100,000,000,000). Each nerve cell (called a neuron) may make contact with hundreds of other cells. Since memory is contained in the electrical patterns of activity among all these connections, it should be evident that our theoretical capacity to remember is almost limitless.

The human brain is a great learning machine. The connections between and among nerve cells are sculpted by experience. Learning experiences cause neurons to organize themselves in multiple circuits, providing multiple ways to learn, memorize, and recall information. New junctions (synapses) are routinely created by the main cell type in the brain, called glia, which outnumber neurons by 10 to 1.

Consider the circuitry in the cerebral cortex (the outer surface of the brain) that is devoted to processing sensory experiences from the arm. We know about this area because experimenters have placed electrodes over different cortical areas in anesthetized monkeys and recorded electrical responses of cortical tissue to electrical stimulation of the various nerves in the arm. The arm has three main nerves (radial, median, and ulnar), and specific cells in the cortex respond to electrical stimulation of each of these nerves. Experiments by Dr. Merzenech and colleagues[2] in monkeys show that cutting the median nerve causes a functional shriveling of the amount of cortex that normally responds to median nerve stimulation. That is, since these cells are no longer needed for the input from the median nerve, they get recruited into circuitry used by input from radial and ulnar nerves. We know that this occurs because the amount of cortical tissue that responds to sensory input from radial and ulnar nerves expands greatly with time after the median nerve is cut.

Thus, the brain is a computer that can build and program itself. The capacity to learn is built in. The main cause of learning and remembering deficiencies lies elsewhere.

Memory in Everyday Life

"Mommy, grandma can't find where she left her glasses. Have you seen them?"

"I know we have met somewhere. I'm sorry, but I can't remember your name."

"I walked into den the other day and suddenly realized that I did not know why I went in there."

"Professor, I studied for this test like a demon. What do I have to do to make a better grade?"

Millions of dollars are spent each year on herbs, vitamins, and books to improve memory. This interest is growing as more and more Baby Boomers come to the age when forgetting normally becomes a problem for most people. Maybe you have reached this stage of life and that is why you have sought out this book. Maybe your work requires you to have a good memory, and you are not advancing in your career because of memory limitations. Maybe you are a student trying to make better grades.

Let's be honest. The vast majority of us have problems with our memory. Politicians who must remember lots of people, especially benefactors, know this. Businessmen who must remember key details about their clients know this. Housewives who forget to pick up certain groceries know this. Professional football players know how hard it is to memorize the play book. Students who have to prepare for exams know this.

When I was younger, competing for good grades in school, and later competing to get into and succeeding in veterinary school, I quickly learned that I had to work on improving my memory. Now that I am getting older, it is apparent that I have lost some of the memory capability of my youth. But also, as a practicing neuroscientist for about 40 years, I have learned that memory has been the object of much scientific study, and that much has been learned that goes without widespread practical application.

Given all this evidence of a widespread need for better memory, how do I dare assert that my memory is o.k. and that yours is too? Well, the point is that for most of us there is nothing fundamentally wrong with our memory. Whatever memory failings we have are due to failure to use our innate memory capabilities to their full potential. It is a mostly a matter of faulty education, not a matter of faulty biology. In some cases we have been told erroneous things about memory. But for the most part, we haven't been taught much about memory at all.

This book will show readers that there are many things they never have been told about how to remember. It will help bridge the chasm between memory research and memory application. I will try not to make any glib promises, but this book will give you fresh insights into making your memory better. Hopefully, you will have learned some neat things in addition to gaining memory skills. Also, you will discover that each small step in raising your memory capacity makes it easier to advance to the next level of memory competency.

The Memorable and the Forgettable

We forget more than we remember. Moreover, most of that forgetting occurs soon after learning. For example, in the late 19th century Hermann Ebbinghaus studied the recall of strings of nonsense syllables (example, xatch, obcur, votuf, etc.). He noted that memory fell off dramatically with time after learning. Within the first few minutes, less than half of the items could be remembered. By 10 minutes later, only slightly more than one third could be remembered, and this level of error persisted out to a month after learning.

What is memorable and what is not? As I write this, I am recalling a radio advertisement that I heard about two hours ago. Normally, radio ads are not memorable, much to the dismay of advertising agencies and the sponsors. The whole advertising industry is created to grab your attention and make you remember products and why you should buy a particular item or brand. Anyway, the radio ad went like this:

"There are two things every man should know:

1. How to watch two ball games at the same time
2. How to drive without asking directions
....
....
.... **this part I don't remember**
....
....
....
...... *Be a man, but ask your wife for permission first."*

Two hours later, I remember the ad word for word, except for the part that matters most to the sponsor. I don't remember anything about the product being advertised, the product name, or why I should buy it. Why? Because the memorable part was what was so attention grabbing, clever, and funny, I remembered that part of the ad, not the part that advertisers wanted me to remember. Here is a case of an ad being so clever, it was stupid - from the sponsor's point of view.

Why can't we remember better? Maybe it is more useful to ask, what makes things memorable? We all remember the day John Kennedy was shot. Many people say they remember what they were doing at that exact moment that the news was announced. We remember the picture of Neil Armstrong's "one small step for man, one giant leap for mankind" as he stepped onto the moon. We remember what we were doing on 9/11 when the World Trade Center was destroyed. We remember these things because they had impact. They were important intellectually and emotionally. They grabbed our attention and evoked vivid imagery.

But remembering phone numbers, grocery items, and the like is hardly captivating. However, such mundane information can be made captivating, and thus become memorable, but we have to contrive ways to make it so, as we will discuss later in the book.

Failure to remember much about our childhood is more complex. Some of that faulty or incomplete memory is perhaps due to repression. That is, according to the cornerstone of Freud's beliefs, unpleasant events are suppressed by the conscious mind. But also, some of such memories can't be retrieved because the contextual cues that were originally associated with the events are no longer available. You can test this for yourself by going back to a childhood home, discovering a flood of memories and feelings that had been long "forgotten." There is yet another explanation for faulty childhood memories that I have never heard or read about, but is certain to be true. This explanation holds that many childhood memories no longer exist because the brain has re-wired itself in the process of growing up. The brain of a child is being continually re-built in terms of connections among neurons, the chemical and hormonal sensitivities of neurons, numbers of neurons (at least in a few brain areas), and the number of supporting cells known as glial cells. The circuitry that supports memory is continually sculpted by new experience. Such sculpting must certainly carve away some of the circuitry needed to support certain old memories.

In this book, our focus will be on *how* memory works and how that understanding can help us reduce the amount of memory failure. Much of the information here is not found in other books, because they are not based on research and what scientists have learned about memory.

How the Ancients Did It

Before the advent of the written language and means of large-scale printing, whole cultures were transmitted from generation to generation by prodigious feats of memory. Extraordinary memory was exhibited even in everyday life. Greek orators, for example, are said to have been able to memorize speeches lasting seven hours or more.

A common way the ancients memorized so much was to create mental pictures instead of trying to memorize words or abstract ideas as such. The trick was to create mental images that represented the words and ideas to be memorized. To remember my name, Bill Klemm, for example, you would visualize a baseball umpire (if you knew about the famous Bill Clem, the umpire) being presented a bill at home plate. If you don't have the umpire as a frame of reference, you might make up a picture of a clam (Klemm) spitting out a bill for the pearl that it is selling to you. If you wanted to remember that I am the author of this book on memory, you would picture the clam containing the memory book instead of a pearl.

The basic idea has been implemented in several ways. One way is the well-known FIG system, which stands for File, Image, Glue. The idea is that you begin with some place to file the memory, a peg to hang it on so to speak. Then you make a picture of what it is you want to remember, and then associate (glue) it with the peg. Peg systems of various sorts have been developed. One involves body parts: toes, feet, ankles, calves, thighs, buttocks, stomach, etc. Because you already know the body parts and their sequence, you don't even have to memorize the pegs. Memorizing a grocery list of "marshmallows, candy, peanuts, milk, squash, and beans" might be accomplished as follows: you picture marshmallows between your toes. They keep popping out as you walk and you have to stop and put them back in. Then you imagine seeing an anklet bracelet made of candy bars. You want one, but you can't have one because you would have to tear up the anklet. Next you visualize a bag of peanuts stuck in the calf-high stocking. The bag keeps banging into your other leg, and every once and awhile you have to stop and put the bag back in the stocking. For the milk, you see your self standing in a huge carton of milk, up to your thighs. You can't get out, because the top of the container is to high to reach by jumping. Every time you jump, you fall back in, up to your thighs. Next you remember squash because you see yourself sitting down on squash, squashing it with your butt. Finally, you remember beans, because you see beans (navy, naval) squirting out the navel in your stomach. Well, we could go on and on, but you get the idea. You don't need a whole book to elaborate the idea with examples, which is what most memory books do.

Another technique elaborated by most memory books is the room method. You use familiar objects in a room to serve as memory pegs, again creating mental images for each item to be memorized and then sticking it onto the peg. The approach can be extended to all the rooms in your house or objects in your car, or any structure.

Yet another approach is to memorize a list of pegs that are associated with numbers. For instance, 1 could be associated with "tree," because a tree trunk looks like a 1. Two could be associated with a pair (of anything). And so on. Most books on improving memory present such lists, which after you memorize them, can create 100 or more pegs for items to be memorized.

One problem, not easily solved, is how to unremember what is on the pegs. After all, you use the pegs over and over again for different items. Clearly, this system works best only for items that you just want to remember for a short while, like grocery lists. The chapter on association will elaborate these peg methods.

To build a comprehensive memory capability requires much more than using the FIG gimmicks. And that, dear reader, is what this book should help you do.

Your Memory is O.K.

To Train in Spain is Mainly in the Brain

Memory arises from our minds and from our brains. Mind changes how the brain thinks, what it thinks about, and what it remembers and what it forgets. Remembering and forgetting involve many of the same brain/mind processes. They are like two sides of the same coin.

MEMORY

Neural processes ← ↕ → Mental processes

Brain gives rise to mind. Mind alters the way the brain thinks, what it thinks about, and what it remembers. Thus, memory has both mental and neural foundations. In other words, memory can involve both conscious and unconscious processes.

We train our brain. Commonly, this is done by conscious effort, wherein our mind decides what we want to expose our brain to and what we want to learn. Our unconscious mind also programs our brain, causing the brain to learn things that we may not know we are learning. So, the point is that whatever your brain is exposed to, it has the potential to learn it, whether you want to learn it or not. Even so, you will remember better if you consciously want to remember.

Basic Memory Processes

Here is how many scientists think memory works. Information comes in (from the bottom in the following diagram) and gets "written" on a scratch pad, which forms the basis for so-called "short-term memory." This short-term memory is immediately accessible, but it is also vulnerable to erasure by such things as sensory distractions, other thoughts, or drugs. The process of manipulating what is on that scratch pad requires first that it be compared with what has already been remembered and then assessed for relevance and importance. Next, the new learning information has to be assessed for importance (saliency). This assessment may also require comparison with what is already in long-term memory storage. Information that passes muster for saliency gets passed into processes that consolidate the information into long-term storage.

You might ask, "Why do we remember so much trivia that is hardly relevant to anything?" My answer to that is that the information WAS salient to your brain - for reasons that your conscious mind may not recognize or appreciate.

Your Memory is O.K.

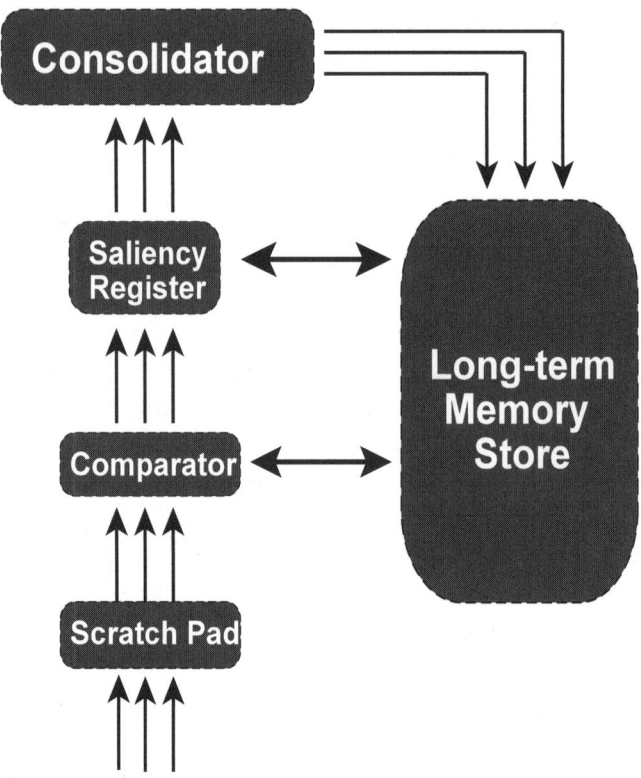

Even In Rats, The Rich Get Richer and the Poor Get Poorer

By "rich" I mean culturally and emotionally rich, not financially. It is common experience in public schools that, statistically speaking, children from low-income, culturally deprived, families do less well in school. Some social observers believe that this reflects the role of genetics in personal achievement. That is, people with the lesser genetic endowment will of necessity have lower incomes and deprive themselves of cultural enrichment. Other social observers claim that this vicious cycle is passed on through the generations, not by genes, but by poor upbringing.

Here is not the place for the old "nature vs. nurture" arguments. But this is a good place to consider whatever role environmental enrichment might have in memory. Some classic experiments in rats reveal that the environment during early development affects the ability to learn at later ages. Mark Rosenzweig and colleagues reported a series of experiments on young rats that showed many beneficial effects on brain development from raising rats in environments that were stimulating. Brains developed better when rats had opportunities to explore novel objects, to exercise, to live in social groups, and to "play." In terms of memory performance, such rats had better ability to solve difficult memory problems such as mazes and visual discrimination reversal.[3]

Memory Kinds

Scientists admit that they really don't know how the brain stores and retrieves memory. We know that our conscious minds perceive memories in terms of pictures and sounds, especially language. But brains operate with neurons that code information as electrical discharges. Neurons speak "neuronese," as Owen Flanagan[4] says in his book on the mind. Some process in our brain has to translate neuronese to pictures or sound and vice versa. Nobody knows how that is done. Fortunately we do not need to know how that is done for the practical purpose of learning how to improve our memory. As an analogy, we don't have to know how computer chips work in order to make computers work for us.

It is not enough to say that we have a good (or bad) memory. People can be good at memorizing some things and not at others. Memory improvement often needs to be focused on specific memory problems rather than some vague notion about memory capacity in general. Many amnesic patients have shown that there are different kinds of memory and the brain accomplishes some of them in different ways. A person can have perfectly normal memory for certain kinds of things and terrible memory for others.

There are new memories and old memories. New memories relate to creating a memory for recent experiences, while old memories refer to old, well-remembered experiences. Memories for facts and memories for skills appear to involve different processes and parts of the brain.

Remember when you were in school, and the teacher asked you a question about a homework problem? Whether you got the answer right or not, you were consciously trying to recall the answer and provide it to the teacher. In such cases you were declaring, either orally or in writing or some equivalent way, what you had remembered. This kind of memory is called "declarative" memory. It is also useful to call this "explicit" memory. Such memory typically deals with facts and events of which a person is consciously aware.

Multiple Memory Systems

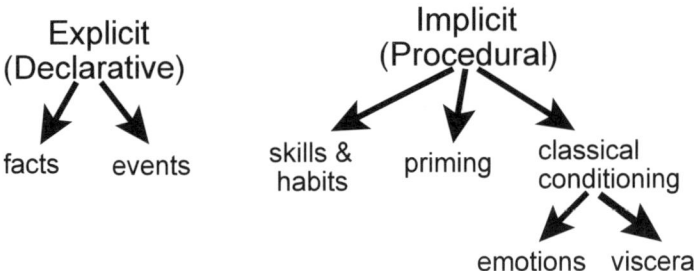

There is another category of memory in which recall is implicit; that is, you remember, but you do not consciously know that you are remembering. Knowledge without awareness, it has been called. Scientists have known for many years that certain stimuli that do not register in the conscious mind can still evoke brain electrical responses. More recently, the same thing has been seen in studies using magnetic resonance imaging.[5] You might call these "underground memories," because they are buried beneath the level of consciousness.

Underground Memories

When such memories are unearthed, they prove that you can learn without knowing that you learned. This unconscious learning is the kind that just sinks in while you are thinking about something else. The idea is that implicit learning is performed by the unconscious mind, which acts sort of as a black box that does the learning in some mysterious way. It then makes the memory of that learning available for action, many times by the black box itself, without awareness in the consciousness.

This is reminiscent of Freud's ideas about consciousness and unconsciousness. If he hadn't been so hung up on sex, he might have formulated the modern ideas about thinking and unconscious processing. Nonetheless, Freud got a bad rap, because it was he above all people who got scientists thinking about dual minds, conscious and unconscious. He also showed that many repressed and unexpressed memories lie buried in the unconscious, while still capable of influencing our attitudes, beliefs, emotions, and actions.

Implicit learning has been demonstrated in many laboratories. For example, Antonio Damasio[6] and colleagues at the University of Iowa asked volunteers to draw cards from any of four decks of cards. Each card was marked with a dollar amount "won" or "lost." The subjects did not know that if cards were drawn consistently from two of the decks it would create a net yield of a loss. The other two decks, if drawn from consistently, yielded a net gain. Most of the subjects eventually began drawing from the two net-gain decks, even though they could not say why nor did they recognize consciously that these decks were more likely to yield a gain. Their unconscious brain knew what was going on, even if the conscious brain didn't have a clue. Whenever they drew from the two bad decks, the skin conductance measurements which were continuously monitoring sweat (and thus stress levels) indicated that this was a bad choice, even though the final proof that this was a bad choice was not available. Their nervous systems were learning the rules implicitly. Nobody was aware of any rules. They just seemed to know what to expect intuitively.

What's the point of unconscious learning? Why learn things if you don't know you know them? Freud would have argued that the unconscious brain learns things so it can hide them from the conscious mind. Now, neuroscientists are starting to think that unconscious memories are formed because that is more efficient or at least provides a duplicate, parallel path for learning so that more total learning can occur. Also likely, the interactions between conscious and unconscious minds reinforce the memory processes of both (more about that later). Though I generally hate to use computer analogies, here is one that seems apt: the brain processes so much information that it needs to use both brains (conscious and unconscious). It is like a computer that runs on machine language that is essential, but that no one wants to see on the monitor.

So what is consciousness for? The traditional view is that the conscious mind exerts direction and influence over the unconscious. It has "veto power" and, short of that, can guide the unconscious's unthinking processes. It should also be obvious that the conscious mind programs the unconscious mind by the choices made consciously. Conscious thinking can also provide a starting point for learning, and with rehearsal, can drive that learning into an automated underground where the task can be performed without "thinking."

Do you touch type? Remember how you learned? Some teaching systems have you memorize, consciously, the location of the keys: A, S, D, F, G on the middle row for the left hand and H, J, K, L on the middle row for the right hand. Then after you deliberate on these locations and practice them until your mind and your fingers know where the right keys are, the teaching strategy moves to left hand keys on the top row and right hand keys on the top row. When this is learned, you consciously learn the location of left hand and right hand keys on the bottom row. After you have practiced these key strokes for many months, the process becomes automated - implicit. Ask most typists to describe the keyboard layout and they can't tell you. The brain just knows (and doesn't bother to tell them about it). This is really what it means to say that "practice makes perfect." Well-learned skills and habits of all kinds (such as riding a bicycle, swimming, hitting a golf ball, or dancing) fall into this implicit category, which is also often called "procedural," because it often involves movement procedures.

Remembering motor skills is greatly influenced by the first few hours after learning. Practice may make perfect when it comes to skills involving movement and coordination, but a more critical factor appears to be the simple passage of time. The first six hours after learning a motor skill, such as riding a bicycle, comprise a window of vulnerability during which the skill can be impaired or even lost by attempting to learn a second motor task[7]. During those hours, researchers from the University of Maryland School of Medicine and Johns Hopkins University School of Medicine say, the central nervous system is consolidating a pattern of neural pathways that control performance of the task, moving them from one part of the brain to others in the process.

They tested the idea that the neural representation of a motor task might change with time in the absence of practice. Using positron emission tomography (PET) imaging to monitor changes in cerebral blood flow, the researchers taught study participants a new skill involving rapid, accurate movements of a motorized robotic arm. They found that during the critical first five to six hours, the neural links that form the brain's internal model of the task shift from the prefrontal regions of the cerebral cortex to the premotor, posterior parietal and cerebellar areas.

Even without practice, after five or six hours, the recipe for the task is virtually hardwired into the brain. This makes it easier to understand why an adult who learned to ride a bicycle as a child can go through several decades of adult life without riding a bike and still be able to ride without falling.

During this 5-6 hour "re-wiring" interval, memory for the task is vulnerable. Trying to learn something else, especially another motor task, is likely to undo the learning that has taken place. This possibility could have enormous implications for the way skills training is conducted in educational, industrial, and athletic settings. Take the training of a football quarterback, for example. If you want him to work on his passing, a coach should probably confine a given workout to just that, and not end the passing workout with lessons on how to run the option.

Another kind of implicit memory is spatial memory. That is, your brain knows where you are in space but you may not call that information up into conscious awareness. A common test of implicit spatial memory involves a radial maze foraging task for rodents. The apparatus commonly used contains 8 arms that radiate from a central start chamber. A hungry rat naturally runs up and down the arms looking for food, which the experimenter places at the ends of the arms in a way that the rat cannot see if food is there.

There are several variants of how this test is run. In one scenario, each arm is baited with food (cheese, for example) and the rat runs up and down the arms and learns not to run up arms already visited (lower left in diagram). The learning task is to remember which arms have been visited, so that the rat does not re-visit any arm. What is remembered are the visual cues in the room around the maze. If the part of the brain known as the hippocampus is damaged, the rat never learns this task, but keeps running up arms that have already been visited.

Another scenario is to bait only certain arms, and now the learning task is to remember which arms can contain bait and which will never have bait (lower right in figure). A normal rat learns this task, but a rat with damage to the hippocampus has problems. Rats with the lesion remember which arms have no bait, but they can't remember which baited arms they visited that no longer have bait. Clearly, this is a short-term memory deficit.

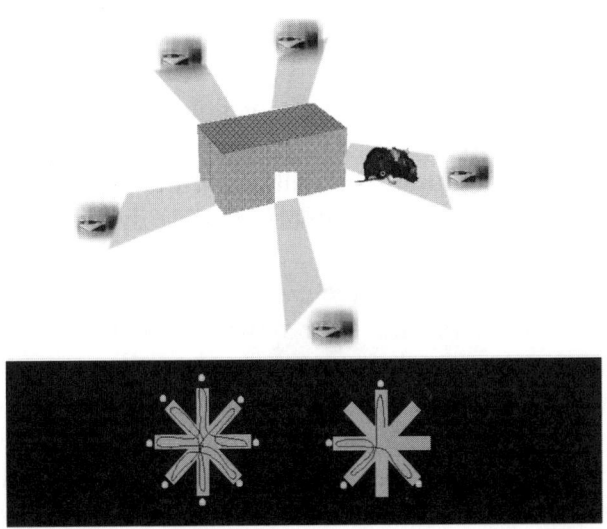

Eight-arm radial mazes are used to test working memory in rodents. A rat foraging for food in baited ends of the maze has to remember which arms have already been visited.

How spatial memory works was elucidated in the early 1970s when several different labs showed that certain neurons in the hippocampus are "place" cells. That is, they discharge only when the rat is located at certain places in space. Spatial learning seems to take place via the hippocampal cells, because their space fields vary with learning experience.

Some implicit memory is not restricted to movement or motor skills. One sub-type is priming. After studying a list of words (example: *garage*), most people correctly complete the correct word when they are asked to state the first word that comes to mind when they hear the stem, *gar*.

Another sub-type of implicit memory involves many kinds of Pavlovian conditioning. This kind of remembering develops when a pair of stimuli are presented together. One stimulus always elicits a response, even in the absence of learning. In the case of Pavlov's dogs, the stimulus was the sight and smell of food which made the dogs salivate and want to eat. Such a stimulus is called an *unconditioned stimulus*, abbreviated UCS. But if a bell tone is turned on before the UCS and left on during that interval, the dogs will eventually start salivating before they see and smell food. That is, they have learned (i.e., have been conditioned) to expect food when they hear the tone. The tone in this case is called the *conditioning stimulus*, because that is the stimulus that conditions the learning.

Typically, most people have problems with explicit memory, for reasons that we explore later. For now, let us focus on the role of attentiveness, because explicit memories benefit from paying better attention to what needs to be remembered. Even in implicit learning, attentiveness is beneficial. For example, in the word priming task mentioned above, the magnitude of the word-priming effect is greatest when the experimental subjects become aware during the test that they are producing words from the list seen during the study session.[8]

A more radical view of how we remember is that none of it is done in the conscious mind. According to this view, all our memories are retained in the unconscious, and the black box that runs these operations will sometimes let our conscious mind in on what is going on. Many scientists believe that the brain does most of its business underneath the radar of our consciousness. Some scientists go so far as to say that hidden functions and implicit memories are the fundamental mode of the brain's operation. Consciousness is an "add on," useful only for providing a kind of feedback to brain that is added to sensory feedback. Scientists get such ideas from observing lower animals, whose brains serve them quite well, even though there is little likelihood that such brains can generate conscious awareness. While this idea is a current hot topic in neuroscience, it was expressed as early as the late 1800s by Thomas Huxley - maybe others thought of it before him. Actually, I think this theory undervalues consciousness, but this is a topic for another book I am planning, a sequel of sorts. I think I will call it "Bad Brains" and explore the issue of free will and personal responsibility when life hands you a "bad brain."

Schools Teach Kids *What* to Learn. Who Teaches Them *How* to Learn?

Astonishingly, we can go through 12 years of primary and secondary schooling, then college and even graduate school, with very little explicit instruction in how to get our memories to work at their natural capacity level. What we learn about "learning how to learn" occurs haphazardly, often by accident.

There is much a-do these days about educational reform. Especially in the U.S., it is now abundantly clear from test scores and basic skills tests that U.S. students rank near the bottom of industrialized countries. Dire economic consequences of our poor K-12 education are certain, as Lester Thurow explains in his book on the economic battle between the U.S., Japan, Germany, and the European Union[9]. Even if some improvement is occurring in the U.S. schools, improvement in foreign schools is increasing faster. The U.S. is unique among industrial nations in not having an organized post-secondary educational system for the non-college bound. While some intellectuals think that everybody should be given government support to go to college, the fact is that many students are not interested in or capable of college work. Moreover, as Thurow argues, what the U.S. workforce needs is not more college students but better trained non-college students. Thurow cites a study that showed that for every dollar that is spent on non-college bound, we spend $55 for the college bound. This is not only patently unfair; it is bad economics.

Britain, Spain, and France spend more than twice as much as the U.S. does on non-college bound. Germany spends three times as much. Sweden spends SIX times as much. The Germans do not even consider the U.S. as a competitor for the future. Their sights are on Japan and South Korea. Germany has evolved the old Guild system into a world-class apprentice system for the non-college bound, and the system ensures that they have a well-trained work force that can move their economy into the post-industrial age.

U.S. politicians and parents are demanding newer schools, smaller class sizes, more emphasis on science and technology, and a host of other reforms. Worthy as these aims may seem, they miss the larger point. What do we know about how kids learn and how to make them learn better? How kids learn includes a huge component of remembering. Precious little about learning how to remember is provided in the classroom.

Why are so many children slow in school? It isn't because they are stupid. It is because they don't remember what they read or hear. I have even had Honors classes in a university where they students could not recall something I had just said a minute before. So memory or lack thereof is not a matter of intelligence. It is a matter of not knowing how to memorize.

Getting Better at Memory

The first step toward a better memory is to recognize what causes memory problems. Increasing age is of course part of the problem (see this book's last chapter on aging). But other reasons apply that are independent of age. Reporter Nora Zamichow conducted a series of interviews with memory experts that identified four major causes of forgetting. The experts identified four causes as information overload, multi-tasking, stress, and lack of sleep.[10] Information overload and multi-tasking make it hard to pay attention and concentrate, and we explain how to cope with those problems in our next chapter involving attention. These two problems also create interference effects, which we explain in our chapter on how memories are consolidated (that is, converted from temporary to permanent form). We explain how stress impairs memory in our chapter on emotions. And we explain why insufficient sleep impairs memory in our chapter on sleep.

An underlying theme emerged from all of the Zamichow interviewees: have a healthy lifestyle. Not only should you eat well and exercise regularly (particularly aerobic exercise), but mental exercise seems to be crucial. Read, think, solve problems, Work crossword puzzles. Play chess - anything that challenges and stretches your brain function. I never made a formal study of this, but the group of 80 - 90 year old practicing scientists I know seem to have much better memories than people in the general population of comparable age. And think about all the aged comedians (Bob Hope, Red Skelton, George Burns, Milton Berle, and others) who even at 85+ were still memorizing hundreds if not thousands of jokes and could still sustain 15-min monologs of jokes.

You can train yourself to become a better memorizer. Indeed, that is what the rest of this book is about. Some memory training occurs more or less naturally as we get older and develop better learning strategies through brain maturation and cumulative experience. For example, recalling a series of items (like dog, car, apple, dress, house) is accomplished much better by older children than younger children. When psychologists investigated the reason that older children do better, it became clear that older children cumulatively rehearse the study items as they are presented. Thus, we could hypothesize that if younger children were trained to rehearse as items are presented, their performance would improve.

Relevant experiments have been performed by several groups. The studies by Brown's group[11] provide some useful examples. They used a "keeping track" task in which a child was shown, in a pre-determined order, a number of items that belong to different categories. For example, a food item was followed by an animal, an article of clothing, and a vehicle. A series of such trials was presented in which the same categories were used, but in different order and with different exemplars. The task was to identify the name of the last item seen in a category selected by the experimenter. The table below shows some specific test items.

Trial	Items				Category Questions
1	apple	dress	car	dog	What was the last *food*?
2	airplane	cake	mouse	pants	What was the last *animal*?

3	shoe	car	rabbit	bread	What was the last *food*?
4	cow	pants	airplane	cookie	What was the last *clothing*?
5	car	cat	apple	coat	What was the last *vehicle*?

Previous studies of this kind had shown that adults and older children performed well on such tasks, but preschool children did not. These younger children required fewer instances of each category; that is, they needed fewer items in each series.

Retarded adolescents had the same problem as younger children. Brown and colleagues surmised that younger children and retardates had a *strategy* deficit. They could have been searching through their memory for all the instances of a category, looking for the one they saw most recently. However, a better strategy would be to rehearse just the four items on each trial, and selecting the one that fits the category asked for by the experimenter. To test this possibility, two groups of poor learners were compared. One of the groups was given explicit instruction to rehearse just the four items on each trial as it is presented. Performance was evaluated on how many category items in a series could be processed correctly. Subjects whose performance declined as the number of items in a trial series was increased were presumed to be using the inefficient strategy of searching through all the presented members of a category for the most recently seen instance. Subjects who were unaffected by the number of items presented were presumed to be cumulatively rehearsing each trial as it was presented.

Results were dramatic. Subjects who were explicitly trained to cumulatively rehearse performed more accurately than the control subjects and were not adversely affected by the number of instances in a category. But this was not the case with untrained subjects. For example, they performed more poorly on one category with six instances than on the two categories with four, and their performance on these two categories was worse than on the single two-instance category.

Brown's group also showed that they could mess up the performance of good learners. They tested ninth graders of normal IQ in the keeping track test. But for half of the subjects the experimenters tried to block the cumulative rehearsal that was assumed to be the unconscious strategy of ninth graders. To distract their rehearsal, students were required to verbally repeat the name of the last-displayed item until the next item appeared. Under these conditions, the normal IQ students performed like untrained retardates. The poor performance degraded further as the number of category instances in a series increased.

* * * * *

The purpose of this chapter is to emphasize that for most normal people memory failures are their own fault. Their brains work just fine. In other words, forgetting is usually *your* fault, not your brain's fault. The brain is a marvelous organ, and it works well if you help it along and don't throw obstacles in its path.

You CAN learn to improve your memory. One of the keys is to BELIEVE you can improve your memory. Learn to trust your memory. Too many people with poor memories use crutches (for example, reminders on sticky notes, or placing reminder objects in places where you can't avoid seeing them). While such gimmicks may have their place, as for example in keeping an appointment calendar, too much reliance on crutches keeps your memory crippled. You need to train your memory, and then learn to trust it, to have confidence in your brain's ability to remember. If you promise yourself that you will remember a certain item or task, you will devote enough effort to assure the memory. And as you learn to fulfill your memory promises to yourself, you will learn to trust your brain to remember what you want.

Scientific research has and is disclosing a great deal about how the brain does it memory chores, but the discoveries don't always become widely known. A major purpose of the rest of this book is to make practical applications of this information. A total of over 150 specific ideas for improving memory are explored herein. These ideas are presented at the end of each chapter in which they are discussed. You may find it helpful to put a sticky note at these places in the book to make review handy.

The implications of these ideas are enormous. If the ideas could find their way into public school systems, educational reform would become a reality. Adults would find their lives simpler, more productive, and less of a hassle. A poor memory comes at a high cost. The good news is that you can train yourself to have a superior memory. That is what the rest of this book is about. Let us proceed to find out how to get that superior memory.

Key Ideas:

1. Memory counts. Improving your memory should be a continuous priority.

2. You remember best things that are important and/or have great emotional impact.

3. We can contrive ways to create impact for boring things we have to remember.

4. Research has revealed a great deal about memory, and many of the findings have practical applications.

5. Live well, in mentally stimulating environments - especially when you are young.

6. For learning movement skills, work on one skill at a time. Allow a 5-6 hour interval between practicing different movement skills.

7. "A picture is worth a thousand words" applies especially to memorizing.

8. Peg systems, such as FIG (file, image, glue) work, but are more of a band-aid for weak memory than a fundamental solution.

9. You can develop memory skills.

10. Cumulatively rehearse a series of items to remember them as they are being presented.

11. Distractions or interruptions of cumulative rehearsal will impair remembering.

12. Two basic kinds of memory are explicit and implicit. They use different processes.

13. Paying attention helps both explicit and implicit memory.

14. Priming can expedite implicit remembering

15. Associating what is to be learned with something that does not require learning is a fundamental way to remember.

16. We need to teach kids *how* to learn as well as *what* to learn.

17. Rote-memory rehearsal is a poor and inefficient way to remember.

18. Reduce information over-load and multi-tasking.

19. Reduce stress in your life and develop stress-coping skills.

18. Get lots of sleep.

19. Eat well (i.e. eat your veggies).

20. Exercise regularly, particularly aerobic exercise.

21. Be mentally active. Challenge your mind.

22. Believe you can improve your memory. Once believing, trust your memory.

23. Make memory promises to yourself and keep them.

Sources:

1. Weber, Robert J. 2000. The Created Self. W. W. Norton, New York, N.Y.

2. Merzenich, M. et al. 1983. Progression of change following median nerve section in the cortical representation of the hand in areas 3b and 1 in adult owl and squirrel monkeys. Neuroscience. 10: 39-665. references.

3. Renner, M. J., and Rosenzweig, M. R. 1987. Enriched and Impoverished Environments: Effects on Brain and Behavior. Springer-Verlag, New York.

4. Flanagan, Owen. 1991. Second Edition. The Science of Mind. M.I.T. Press, Cambridge, Mass, p. 175-177.

5. Blankenburg, F., Taski, B., Ruben, J. et al. 2003. Imperceptible stimuli and sensory processing impediment. Science 299: 1864-1865.

6. Bechara A, Damasio H, Tranel D, Damasio AR (1997) Deciding advantageously before knowing the advantageous strategy. Science 275:1293-1295.

7. Holcomb, H. H., and Shadmehr, R. 1997. Neural correlates of motor memory consolidation. Science. 277: 821-825.

8. Bowers, J., and Schacter, D. L. 1984. J.. Psychol. Learn. Mem. Cogn. 10: 164.

9. Thurow, L. 1993. Head to Head. Warner Books. New York, N.Y.

10. Zamichow, Nora. 2003. Faced with the fear of growing forgetful, baby boomers are turning to mental aerobics to train the brain to remember. Los Angeles Times, June 16, pg.1 (Health).

11. Brown, A. L., Campione, J. C., Bray, N. W., and Wilcox, B.L. 1973. Keeping track of changing variables: effects of rehearsal training and rehearsal prevention in normal and retarded adolescents. J. Exp. Psychology. 101: 123-131.

Why Your Teacher Always Bugged You to Pay Attention

- Grabbing Your Attention
- You Have to Pay Attention Even to the Simple Stuff
- Talking and Driving Don't Mix
- Possible Paradoxical Exceptions
- Memory Pills - Rx for Memory
- Making Yourself Pay Attention

The easiest way to get a kid's attention is to stand in front of the TV set.
— From 14,000 Quips & Quotes. Crown Publishers

Can you draw a picture of both sides of a penny? Probably not. At least the typical person cannot do it, as was established in a study by Raymond Nickerson and Marilyn Adams[1]. They found that although many people remembered a picture of Abraham Lincoln on one side and a Greek-architecture building on the other side, they had very poor recollections of any details. Strange, isn't it, that we remember so poorly something that we see several times a day, day after day, year after year? The explanation lies in the fact that we don't really see the details. We don't attend to such details because they seem irrelevant. All we need to remember is enough information to be able to distinguish a penny from a dime and from other coins. The size and copper color suffice. Thus, it is a wonder that we remember anything else. We remember Abe and the Lincoln memorial on the back simply because they are the largest and most conspicuous markings on the coin. We fail to remember much else because there is no need to. The moral of this example is that to improve memory, identify and reinforce the *need* to remember. If there is a need, we will pay attention, and if we pay attention we have a much better chance of remembering.

Failure to pay attention impedes memory because it is the encoding stage of memory that drives all other aspects of memory formation. Without encoding, memories do not form. Paying attention is important in memory formation, because it enhances encoding.

To remember anything, it has to register. For it to register, you have to pay attention. Recall all those parties you have been to where a bunch of people introduced themselves and now you can't remember their names? The problem here is that their names never registered. When people introduce themselves, we are often thinking, "Oh my, she is drop-dead gorgeous!" or "This guy looks like a real bore." or "What should I say to impress this man. He is important, and I want to make a good impression." In short, we may be thinking about dozens of things, none of which have anything to do with the person's name. And this problem only gets compounded when several people are being introduced at more or less the same time.

The registration step is key to the whole memory process. The diagram below shows the relationships. Note that registration can trigger immediate retrieval (working memory) or, with rehearsal, lead to longer lasting memory.

Basic memory process. To be remembered, a stimulus or learning event has to register in the nervous system. The memory is temporarily available as working or "scratch-pad" memory. With rehearsal, the memory becomes progressively more lasting, as "short-term" memory and perhaps even as long-term or permanent memory.

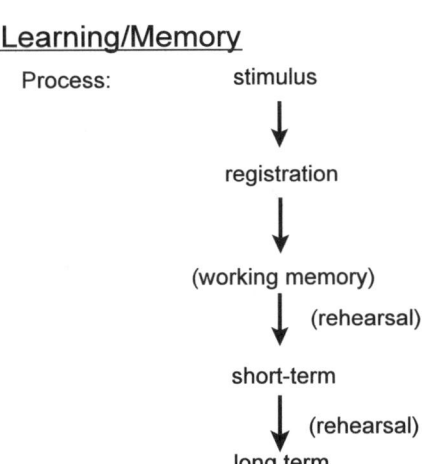

Grabbing Your Attention

Certainly there are people at parties whose names you DO remember. These are the people who for one reason or another grabbed your attention - there was something unique or especially significant about them.

I call this event-dependent memory. What you remember can depend on how well you directed your attention to the event and its meaning. Numerous studies in animals have shown that their nerve cells fire impulses much more vigorously when an animal is alert and presumably paying better attention to stimuli.

I remember some of my early experiments with trying to teach rats to remember something in just one trial. The task involved having the rat step off an elevated, safe-island platform on to an electrified grid. I would place the rat on the safe-platform that was located in the center of a large open area surrounded by walls. Instinctively, the rat stepped off the platform, because rats like to be near walls, not stranded out in the open. Of course, stepping off exposed the rat to foot shock from the electric grid. I would then take the rat off the grid. The next day I would put the rat back on the platform to see if he remembered not to step off. How well the rats remembered depended greatly on how intense the foot shock was or how long they were left on the grid. A strong foot shock was remembered so well, even with just this one trial, that nothing I did could prevent the memory formation. For example, I would use electroconvulsive shock (ECS) to wipe out memory - but it did not! (Human psychiatric patients who are given ECS do not remember what happened just before the ECS; therefore ECS is a common tool for studying memory in experimental animals).

A well-known example of event dependency occurs in the wild. People who try to poison rats in their homes or office buildings often learn to their dismay that some rats are not killed. If they survive eating the poison, their extreme sickness serves as an intense learning experience that causes them to remember not to eat poisoned bait again. Exterminators call this "bait shyness." I call it super-duper one-trial learning.

In our opening quip about getting a kid's attention, kids attend to TV when some interesting cartoon or show is on. What does one do about memorizing things that are not naturally compelling, that do not naturally grab your attention? First, you have to make the effort to pay attention. You must consciously tell yourself, "I am going to remember this." As you read through the manual on how to program a VCR or read a book chapter for an exam, you must tell yourself "I must – and will – remember this." To help that effort to concentrate, you must make learning conscious and deliberate. For example, when parking the car in a large parking lot, you should make a conscious effort to locate a conspicuous landmark near your car and memorize it on your way into the mall, stadium, or whatever. Focus needs to be sustained and information rehearsed in memory. Do not overload your circuits with *other* information or sensory input at the same time.

I should caution, however, that just because an event is arresting doesn't mean you will remember it correctly. Rebecca Rupp, in her book *Committed to Memory*,[2] relates two experiments that reinforce this point. In one study at Emory University, the students were asked immediately after the Challenger explosion to write accounts of where they were when the explosion occurred and how they heard about it. Three years later, only 7% of the students could match their original descriptions - 25% got everything wrong, even though the event was still vivid in their minds. In another study at Baylor University, students were asked to fill out a questionnaire about where they were when they first heard about the bombing that started the 1991 Persian Gulf war. When quizzed about their recollections three months later, most of the memory was inaccurate, getting more inaccurate with time as students were influenced by new information about the war. This effect is akin to deterioration of eye-witness memories in response to after-the-fact input. In all likelihood, students were not consciously attending the information, because they did not know they would be asked to remember it. Sloppy attention leads to lack of remembering or remembering falsely (see also this book's chapter on "Memories That Lie").

Another aspect of attention's role in memory is the so-called "serial position effect." If you are trying to memorize a list of items, you will tend to remember the first and last items in the list. The practical implication is, of course, that you have to pay attention more and work harder to memorize items in the middle of the list.

The well-known decline of memory with age seems to be caused by a decrease in encoding capability, and perhaps that is due to failing capacity to pay attention. An interesting experiment[3] has been performed at the National Institutes of Health intramural laboratories. These studies showed that older people have more difficulty encoding information than do younger people. Investigators measured brain blood flow in 10 young people (average age of 25) and in 10 older people (average age of 69) while they were performing a learning task. The task consisted of trying to memorize pictures of 32 unfamiliar faces, shown for 4 seconds. They repeated the task three times, each time with a scrambled sequence of the pictures. This was the encoding stage of the task. Then they were given a recognition task in which they were presented pictures of faces that were not in the memorized set. The new picture was paired with a picture from the memorized set, and the subject was to indicate which of the two had been seen before. This constituted the recognition phase of the memory task. Brain scans during the encoding and recognition stages showed clear age-related differences. During encoding, young people showed increased blood flow (reflecting increased activity of nerve cells) in certain parts of the cerebral cortex, and people in the older group did not show this sign of activation during encoding. Oldsters did have the same pattern of blood flow activation as the young people during the recognition stage of the task.

A large part of the trick of improving encoding is to make yourself pay more attention to your senses. Sensory stimuli, such as sights, sounds, odors, and touch serve as cues for memory. Hearing an old song may bring back memories of when you were dating your first love. Certain sights produce *déjà vu*, that is the feeling that you have experienced something like this before. Odors have an especially profound influence on memory. Think of all the memories that flood your brain when you smell the odors of Christmas (odors that emanate from the Christmas tree, apple cider, egg nog, candles). The reason that odors can be such profound memory cues is that the odor detectors in the nose go directly to the brain regions that process memory formation. Unfortunately, we don't usually pay close attention to the odors associated with events to be remembered. Thus, the memories are not registered explicitly and are hard to dig up from their burial grounds.

You Have to Pay Attention Even to the Simple Stuff

A basic mode of operation of all animals, even lower animals, is the phenomenon known as habituation. That is when a novel learning event is presented on a continuous basis, you get used to it and start to ignore it. You get in the "habit" (i.e. habituation) of no longer paying attention. Actually, you are learning to unlearn. Numerous animal experiments have clearly shown that learning ceases when habituation sets in. If the stimulus is changed, then "dishabituation" can occur, and you may start paying attention again. The practical application for memorization is that you may have to refresh continually the information you are trying to remember, such as thinking about it in different ways or applying it to different situations.

The most primitive form of attending to stimuli that become remembered is what has been called classical conditioning. This form of learning was popularized by Pavlov and his salivating dogs. That is, he showed that training dogs to associate a bell ringing with subsequent delivery of food caused them to learn that bell and food go together. Even worms can learn this way. If you give a mild electric shock to a worm, it contracts, because the electricity activates its muscles. Flashing a light just before the electric shock is given will eventually (after hundreds of training trials) cause the worm to contract as soon as the light flashes and BEFORE the electric shock is delivered.

Of course we don't know how or if worms "pay attention," but the role of attention in classical conditioning has recently been tested in humans by Robert Clark and Larry Squire,[4] at the University of California, San Diego in La Jolla, California. They tested both normal humans and those with severe amnesia in a conditioned eye-blink test. Here a sound tone is presented just before a puff of air is blown into the eye. The tone persists during the air puff. and these stimuli terminate together. An important variant of this standard approach, so-called trace conditioning, the subject only gets a "trace" of the learning cue in that the cue ends about 1/2 to 1 second before the air puff.

The investigators knew from similar animal studies that animals with damage to the hippocampus could not learn in the trace conditioning protocol. It was as if their working memory could not keep track of the tone cue during the interval between the end of the conditioning cue and the onset of the air puff, and thus the association between cue and stimulus was lost. In a similar way, the amnesic humans that Clark and Squire tested failed to learn with trace conditioning methods, but they did learn just as well as normal humans in the standard protocol where the cue stays on throughout the whole trial. With trace conditioning, the brain has to be aware during the interval between the brief cue and the air puff of the relationship of the two events and their time lag. The amnesic patients were amnesic because they had hippocampal damage from assorted diseases. Their failure in trace conditioning trials is entirely consistent with their other memory deficits, such as holding information in working memory.

Even the normal subjects had difficulty in trace conditioning if they were not aware of the time lag between the cue and air puff. They had to pay attention consciously to the learning situation and notice that the sound cue stopped, followed by a brief delay before the air puff. Then and only then did many repeated trials result in an automatic eyeblink in response to the sound and before the air puff.

Several practical implications follow. It appears that items to be learned are more difficult to learn if they are separated in time. Further, if they are separated in time, remembering is easier if you are consciously aware of their separation in time.

Speaking of the problem of remembering items separated in time, have you noticed how many television programs refresh the story line after commercial breaks? Script writers intuitively know that the commercial distracts one's attention from the story line and that the viewer has to be given some reminders.

And speaking of television, has anyone considered fully why television is a bad idea for kids? I mean, in addition to the usual argument about filling their minds with mush. As a university teacher, I have noticed in the last decade or so that many students cannot sustain attention for more than a few minutes. During a lecture or even class discussion, it is as if they are waiting for the commercial break. The problem is that years of television watching have conditioned them to expect a break every few minutes. Such breaks, if a professor indulges in them, mainly serve to distract attention and reduce retention of what went on before the break. Also, frequent breaks do not help students learn how to sustain attention.

In short, I am saying that we are raising a generation of kids with attention deficits. Television is training their minds NOT to sustain attention and focus.

Talking and Driving Don't Mix

Whenever I drive somewhere with my wife and start talking, she always complains that I slow down (we are often late because of you know who). It is not just my brain that has trouble doing two or more things at once. It is basic biology for all of us. The brain seems to operate best if it can focus.

Recently there has been a big flap about more car accidents being caused by cell phone users. As of this writing, 11 state and local governments have made it illegal to talk on a cell phone while driving. The problem is that the brain has to divide its resources for the separate tasks of talking and driving. Scientists have actually seen this effect by using brain imaging studies. In one study[5] the brain was scanned while volunteers performed two tasks separately and when they performed the two simultaneously. During separate-task performance, the task that was verbal lit up the image over the lateral part of the cortex (that is, there was more blood supply there because cells in that area process language). Then during a visual task, the back of the brain lit up (vision is processed in the rear of the brain). But when both tasks were performed at the same time the amount of activity in the verbal area and the vision area were both suppressed. In other words, the brain just could not respond optimally to both tasks at the same time.

So the implications for memory are obvious. If you want to memorize something, do one thing at a time. Focus, focus, focus.

Students often do several things that violate the focus principle. One has to do with note taking during lectures. Some students feel obliged to write everything down or write down so much during a lecture that they can't think about what is being said. A good student will attempt to make mental pictures and associations during the lecture itself, so that memorization is occurring throughout the lecture. Notes are important, but there may be other ways to deal with that issue. Many professors hand out typed lecture notes in advance of the lecture so that students can think more about the lecture and less about note taking. I always preferred to hand out what I called "skeleton notes" that merely provided a grand outline and required students to "fill in the blanks" during lecture. If a professor does not hand out notes, a better tactic might be to tape record the lecture and construct the notes later. If notes are taken during lecture, learning is enhanced if a student re-organizes the notes later. It goes without saying that words in the lecture should be translated as much as possible to pictures and diagrams, because these are so much easier to remember.

Another error that many students make is in the way they read. Almost all students use highlighter pens to identify key parts of a text. But many students either highlight too much or highlight the wrong things. They become so preoccupied in marking up the book that they don't pay enough attention to what they are reading. A better approach is to highlight just a few key words on a page and spend a few seconds after reading a page translating the message into linked mental pictures, followed by quizzing yourself on those pictures (see the next chapter, "Memories Hang Out with the Right Crowd"). The highlighted key words, if used as a starting point for mental pictures, then become very useful in reviewing the book for a test. One only has to spot the key words and think of the associated mental images.

So the point to remember is not just that paying attention is important to memory. What is crucial is paying attention to the right things in the right way.

Possible Paradoxical Exceptions

According to folk wisdom, chewing gum is supposed to help you concentrate. If so, then chewing gum ought to help you remember. Now, this idea has been formally tested in experiment at a university in England[6]. Keith Wesnes and his colleagues tested three groups of young adults on a battery of tests. Subjects were divided into three groups: 1) gum chewing, 2) sham gum chewing (pretended to chew gum by making the appropriate jaw movements, and 3) control, where no chewing or chewing movements were performed.

Subjects were tested for picture recall, spatial working memory, numerical working memory, delayed word recall, word recognition.

Several measures of attention were also assessed to check for evidence that gum chewing improved attentiveness. These tests included a simple reaction time test, a choice reaction time test, a digit vigilance test, and heart rate measurement. A cognitive load test was also conducted in which subjects subtracted by threes (repeated subtraction of three from a randomly generated starting number) and by sevens.

Researchers found no evidence for improved attentiveness. In fact, the sham chewing group revealed an impaired simple reaction time score, compared to the control and the gum chewing group. Presumably, this reflects a need for the sham chewers to think about making the sham movements, which diverted some brain resources from participating in the reaction-time response.

Heart rate was elevated during all task performance in each group. However, the rate was significantly higher for all tasks in the gum chewing group.

The memory-test data showed a clear improvement of gum chewing on spatial working memory, numeric working memory, and longer-term memory involving immediate and delayed recall. The authors have no explanation for these results. They suggest that perhaps the increased heart rate of the gum chewers increased blood flow to the brain. Another group of investigators had reported earlier that chewing increased blood flow to the fronto-temporal regions of the cortex that are involved in memory tasks. It is also possible that gum chewing increases insulin release, which perhaps could affect the availability of glucose to brain cells.

The improvements are small, though definitely significant statistically. We do not know the extent to which the gum chewing generalizes to other kinds of learning tasks and situations. Nonetheless, here is at least one example where trying to do more than one thing at a time can be done as well or better than doing one at a time.

What about listening to music while trying to memorize? I can't seem to find definitive research, but we all know that students like to listen to music while studying. There is a Web site[7] that gives an overview of what little research has been done. There has been interest in the so-called "Mozart effect" in which listening to classical music is supposed to help memory. The results are conflicting.

Whether or not music helps memory is surely a function of whether or not the music is distracting. If one pays attention to the music, then it would interfere with memory. Music with a lot of lyrics is probably bad for memorizing, because the words would interfere with the words you are trying to remember. Instrumental music played as background might help memorizing because it puts you in a good mood. I recall as a veterinary medical student listening to jazz while memorizing the enormous amount of material thrown at us by the professors. For me, it worked. Maybe the rhythmic beat of the music is akin to the rhythm of gum chewing. I don't know if I could recommend listening to music with strong rhythm is for everybody. The matter should probably be formally investigated.

Memory Pills – R_x for Memory

We know that some drugs can enhance arousal and attentiveness. Most of us know from common experience that stimulants, such as caffeine, can make us more alert and thus able to remember better because we are more alert and pay better attention. Nicotine may help memory in the same way. Conversely, sedatives, such as alcohol, and tranquilizers interfere with memory if for no other reason that they make us less alert and less focused.

Here, I am raising the possibility of new drugs that may have specific memory-enhancing effects. There are reports that a few drugs may help memory, such as flumazenil, beta-carbolines, and D-cycloserine. These drugs cause anxiety, and the memory effect may be due to heightened attentiveness and sensitivity to learning events that accompany anxiety (see the chapter on "We Get Emotional About Our Memories").

Drugs of abuse (alcohol, barbiturates, tranquilizers, marijuana and others) typically cause major impairment of memory formation. Even drugs that are used for legitimate medical purposes can impair memory. For example, a drug (haloperidol) often used to treat schizophrenia diminishes symptoms because it interferes with the function of certain dopamine-responsive cells, which unfortunately also participate in memory formation.

Let me emphasize that common prescription drugs or drugs of abuse either have no effect on memory or impair it. Some drugs are said to cause anterograde amnesia; that is, they cause memory failure even if you give it *before* the learning experience. Such drugs include benzodiazepine tranquilizers (such as Valium), barbiturates (such as sleeping pills), ethanol, and even beta-adrenergic blockers that are used to treat high blood pressure. Many other drugs cause retrograde amnesia; that is, they cause memory failure when given shortly after a learning experience. No doubt, many of the drugs also interfere with retrieval.

I remember when I was in graduate school a fellow graduate student who was so nervous about taking his oral preliminary examinations that he took a tranquilizer beforehand. The examining professors later told me that this student was a zombie - couldn't answer anything. Before the exam was well underway, they canceled it and told the student to reschedule. Some of these professors had this student in class and they knew he knew more than he was able to remember at the exam.

Alcohol. Alcohol is commonly used and abused. Alcohol can be very devastating to memory of young people. A magnetic resonance imaging (MRI) imaging study at the Pittsburg Medical Center[8] compared the brains of 14-21 year-olds who had abused alcohol with those in that same age group who did not abuse alcohol. The hippocampi of the drinkers was 10% smaller. Though that percentage may not seem large, we are talking about a loss of many thousands of neurons.

Another study at the University of California, San Diego[9] compared heavy-drinking 15 and 16 year-olds with normal kids the same age. In this study, a two-hour battery of tests was given to both groups, and in the drinking group, the test was given three weeks after the drinkers had abstained for three weeks. The drinker group had more trouble in remembering material they had learned just 20 minutes before, even though there was no alcohol in their system at the time. The possibility is that physical damage in the brain was created by earlier drinking.

An example of physical damage was given in a study of rats by Aaron White and colleagues at Duke University[10]. White gave large amounts of alcohol every other day for 20 days to two groups of rats, one adolescent, one adult. Rats were tested in a maze. Adolescent rats were tested after they had reached adulthood. When tested sober, both groups performed equally well on the working-memory maze test. But when intoxicated, those that had binged while adolescents performed much worse than the rats that had binged only as adults. Thus, it seems that binging during adolescence produces long-lasting impairment of working memory that does not occur with the same degree of binging as that of an adult. One interpretation is that the adolescent bingers lost so many neurons that they could not compensate for intoxication but not so many neurons that they could not perform all right without alcohol.

Nicotine. Another commonly abused addictive drug is nicotine, which people self-administer in the form of tobacco smoking, chewing, and snuffing. There is little doubt that nicotine stimulates the brain (indeed, many of the synapses in the brain are called "nicotinic," because they respond to nicotine with an excitatory response).

We have all known smokers who say that their normal mental performance depends on smoking. This includes memory. Certainly, smokers who have gone too long without smoking cannot perform well mentally. Outwardly, they tremble and become agitated. Inwardly, their minds are so possessed with the desire to satisfy the craving for nicotine that they can't pay attention to much else.

Nicotine is a powerful positive reinforcer. That is, it makes us feel good, and people willingly self-administer it. The role of positive reinforcement in memory is elaborated in the book's chapter, "We Get Emotional About Our Memories." But for now, let us remember that smoking makes us feel good, especially when we are reminded by things that we have learned to associate with smoking. For example, smokers commonly have a cigarette right after awakening in the morning. Naturally, the coffee they drink comes to be associated not only with the pleasure of coffee (which contains addicting caffeine) but also with smoking. Thus, the aroma of a fresh cup of coffee commonly triggers the desire to smoke. I quit smoking over 35 years ago, yet I still sometimes get an urge to smoke a cigarette with my morning coffee.

Scientists can study some of the effects that nicotine has on memory by using a so-called place-conditioning paradigm. The idea is that an animal, for example a rat, will spend more time in the compartment of an alley that was previously paired with a reward, such as food, morphine, amphetamine, or with subcortical injections of opioids and opioid peptides. They remember places and environments in which they experienced good feelings. Likewise, rats avoid compartments previously paired with depressing or unpleasant substances such as opiate antagonists, ethanol, or sedatives.

As an example of animals learning to remember the environment in which rewarding drugs are given, consider the experiments with nicotine by Edgar Iwamoto and colleagues at the Tobacco Health Research Institute at the University of Kentucky.[11] They tested rats in place-preference a test in which they could choose whether to spend their time in a dark chamber or a light chamber. Test rats were injected with nicotine via chronically implanted cannulas that delivered the drug (or saline in control groups) into the cerebrospinal fluid. Rats were then placed in one of the chambers. The next day, each rat was given the opposite treatment and placed in the opposite chamber. On the third day, each rat was given free choice to spend as much time as it wanted in either chamber. The baseline bias was for the black compartment, but nicotine treatment given when in the black compartment increased the preference for that compartment. When rats were given nicotine when in the white compartment, they developed an unnatural preference for the white compartment. This is the rat equivalent of the morning-coffee cigarette, where having coffee in the morning triggers overwhelming memories in a smoker of the rewarding effects of cigarettes. The rat had learned to associate a given item (place in this case) with pleasure (nicotine injection).

Why is nicotine rewarding? The usual answer is that it activates the brain's reward system, which can be activated by electrical stimulation of a bundle of fibers that pass through the hypothalamus. This bundle, called the medial forebrain bundle, includes fibers that release the neurotransmitter dopamine, and dopamine has been implicated in reward phenomena. Presumably, nicotine activates pathways that trigger release of dopamine. Also, nicotine is a mental stimulant, and the brain becomes more attentive to the environment and memory cues.

One reason that it is hard to quit smoking is that smokers are constantly reminded of the pleasures of smoking in certain environments: the pool hall, the bar, after-dinner dessert, after sex, etc. The situations themselves are positive reinforcers and they may act synergistically with the pleasures of cigarette smoking to make smoking seem more even more pleasurable than it would otherwise be.

In another study, this same research team showed that nicotine can impair memory. Rats were trained to touch a lever each time it was inserted into the rat's chamber. A food reward served to reinforce the behavior. Ten lever presentations were given in each session and sessions were repeated daily. Within 10 days, saline-injected rats were performing at 100% levels, but learning the association between touching the lever and food reward was impaired in a dose-dependent way by nicotine injection just prior to each session.

However, the conclusion that nicotine impaired memory could be be wrong. What about the possibility that nicotine substituted for the reinforcing properties of food? Maybe the nicotine-injected rats lost their appetite and thus were less motivated to touch the lever in exchange for food reward. Most human smokers lose weight because their appetite is suppressed by nicotine. You don't have to be a scientist to know that tests of nicotine effects on memory should be conducted in several ways, none of which use reinforcers that could be substituted for nicotine.

It is easy to suspect that nicotine assists memory. For example, we all know about smokers who seem to perform best mentally when smoking. But it is still not clear whether this is a direct effect of the nicotine in smoke or the indirect effect of the heightened mental arousal and physiological calm that is restored by smoking in a nicotine addict. The nicotine addict cannot concentrate, read, think, or memorize normally when in the throes of nicotine withdrawal. Addicts pay attention to their drug withdrawal agony and are less able to pay attention to anything else.

Cholinesterase Inhibitors. For people with brain diseases that impair memory there is one class of drugs that seems to help memory: "nerve gas." Actually, nerve gas, such as Sarin, which has been used by Sadam Hussein and by religious-cult terrorists in Japan, is a more potent form of the same class of drugs that is used medically and as insecticides. These compounds, called cholinesterase inhibitors, magnify the normal function of the neurotransmitter, acetylcholine, which makes the brain more alert and attentive. Unfortunately, over-stimulating this system is fatal. Memory improvement does not benefit the dead.

Drugs in this chemical class, such as Aricept (donepezil), do seem to help memory of Alzheimer's patients. Memory improvement is not usually dramatic nor sustained. The improvement that does occur is probably due to heightened alertness, attention, and conscious awareness.

Ritalin. There is one study showing a partly beneficial effect on working memory by Ritalin, the drug used to treat Attention Deficit/Hyperactivity Disorder.[12] This study was conducted on normal adult males, averaging 35 years of age. Experimental subjects were seen on two occasions, two weeks apart. On each occasion they were given either 40 mg of methyphenidate (Ritalin) or a placebo and given several neuropsychological tests as well as a brain scan (positron emission tomography, PET scan) to measure cerebral blood flow.

For the task conditions, subjects were presented either six ("easy") or twelve ("difficult") red circles on a touch-sensitive computer screen suspended above the scanner. For each problem, subjects were required to search through the array of red circles for blue tokens by touching each one to reveal its contents. The goal was to find all of the blue tokens, which were hidden behind the red circles. The key instruction was that, once a blue token had been found behind a particular red circle, that circle would not be used again to hide a token. Each circle was only used once to hide a token, and therefore two types of error were possible. A between-search error occurred when a subject returned to a circle in which they had previously found a blue token, and a within-search error occurred when a subject returned to a circle within the same search.

Under Ritalin, subjects made fewer search errors compared to the placebo control (average of 11.5 errors versus 16.1 errors). This confirmed an earlier report that Ritalin improved this kind of working memory. For a given subject, the degree of improvement was greatest for those subjects with the least baseline capability for this task. A task-related decrease in cerebral blood flow was seen in major areas of the cerebral cortex. Perhaps this served to suppress activity in cortical areas that otherwise would interfere with this kind of working memory. The drug did increase blood pressure, as this drug is known to do. Thus, the practical application may be quite limited in older men especially, even if it could be demonstrated that the drug's benefit extends to other kinds of memory.

Antidepressants. Drugs such as Prozac may improve memory in depressed people, if the drugs relieve the depression, which itself impairs memory. Recent research in an animal model of depression[13] showed that stressed mice show depression-like symptoms. When given antidepressant drug, the mice start within a few days to make thousands of new brain cells, in parallel with behavioral changes indicative of recovery from depression. They recover their interest in grooming and eating, and their memory improves. Notably, one of the few places in the brain where new brain cells can appear is in the hippocampus, which is instrumental in memory formation. The need for growth of new brain cells can explain why it takes several days or weeks for antidepressants to start having a psychological and behavioral effect. The role of these drugs in memory has received little attention, but we could expect that depressed people have memory problems in part because they are less motivated and aroused to pay attention. There is no reason, however, to expect memory improvement in normal people if they took antidepressants.

Supplements and Vitamins. Some people think that the crushed leaves from the *Ginkgo biloba* trees help memory, and it is widely prescribed in Europe. However, its usefulness is not borne out by controlled experiments. Dr. Paul Solomon and colleagues at Williams College and a memory clinic in Bennington, Vermont, tested 230 healthy volunteers, all over 60.[14] Each took a pill of either 40 mg of ginkgo or a placebo, three times daily for six weeks. Neither subjects nor investigators knew who was getting the treatment and who got the placebo. A series of tests for concentration, learning, and memory ability revealed no difference between the groups.

"Eat your blueberries," my grandmother used to say. Of course, that was no problem when the berries were in grandma's scrumptious pies. Now, it appears that grandma knew what she was talking about. Scientists at a USDA research center at Tufts University have reported an experiment that shows that blueberries help memory.[15] Rats were fed the human equivalent of one cup a day of blueberries for two months. Then they were required to swim through a maze. After 5 days, the blueberry-fed rats were making only half the mistakes of the control rats that had not been fed blueberries. The researchers even found evidence for more new neurons in the blueberry-fed rats. Injection of a dye that marked newborn neurons revealed new neurons in the hippocampus, whereas no new neurons were found in the control rats.

There was good reason to study blueberries, because they are well known to have an unusual amount of antioxidant chemicals, which can protect the brain from the wear and tear of routine metabolism. Also, blueberries are rich in flavinoids, which are thought to be anti-inflammatory. Other fruits are also being studied at the USDA center, but so far the blueberries show the most promise. Because we can find out which specific antioxidants or flavinoids are most potent and presumably can be made synthetically, the promise of "memory pills" may yet be realized.

In theory, taking the anti-oxidant vitamins C and E should help memory, because they protect nerve cells from damage from the highly toxic free radicals produced normally by bodily metabolism. The cumulative effect of free radicals over many years is probably one reason that so many brain cells die as we age.

There is some evidence that elderly people with poor memories might be helped by vitamin E and by certain drugs that increase cerebral blood flow. These matters are discussed in the final chapter on memory in the elderly.

Physicians and nutritionists have known for many years that

vitamin B deficiencies can cause nervous system impairment, including memory difficulty. If you are not deficient, taking B vitamins won't help memory, and some of them can even be toxic in large doses. Niacin (B3), B12, folic acid, and choline deficiencies are known to impair memory. In the case of B12, you may have enough in the diet but lose ability to absorb it as aging occurs. Do you know the good dietary sources of B vitamins? They include beans, peas, green leafy vegetables, and orange juice.

A recent study of mice has shown that vitamin A deficiency impairs memory.[16] The impairment is reversed in as little as two days of dietary supplement. This finding may have great practical significance, inasmuch as vitamin A deficiency occurs in millions of children in Third World countries where rice and wheat are the main basis of the diet.

Most minerals don't seem to help memory. But zinc is of special interest, because it is uniquely concentrated in the hippocampus, which is so important to memory. Several studies have shown that zinc deficiency does indeed impair memory. But don't run down to the drug store to buy zinc tablets. Tommie Turner and Magdi Soliman at Florida A&M fed large amounts of zinc to rats for 15 days and found *impaired* memory performance in a water-maze learning task.[17] Another mineral that may be important in memory is magnesium, because magnesium has many important functions in nervous tissue. This mineral has not been studied much in the context of memory, but many diets are deficient in magnesium.

So, the upshot of what we know about supplements and vitamins is that though advertising claims abound, there is no good evidence that any supplement, not even the highly touted herbal remedies such as ginko biloba, helps memory in normal people. If you were grossly under-nourished, vitamins and certain supplements would help memory and brain function in general and might have a secondary beneficial effect on memory.

Drugs On the Horizon. A new generation of enhancers is under development by at least two companies, Memory Pharmaceuticals and NeuroLogic.[18] The drugs being developed target intracellular molecules that modify responsivity of neuronal junctions or that affect genetic expression inside nerve cells.

Helicon Therapeutics and Memory Pharmaceutical companies are working on a class of drugs that affect memory by activating a chemical that, when it binds to neuronal DNA, switches on dozens of genes that make the proteins that underlie the representation of memory. The first neuroscience Nobel Prize of the 21st Century was given for the discovery of this switching system.[19] Here is the story:[20]

In the 1960s and 1970s, scientists discovered that new proteins were synthesized during the formation of permanent memories. Some of the experiments showed, for example, that blocking protein synthesis by certain chemicals would prevent the long-term formation of memories, even though the experimental animals could learn and hold memory in temporary form.

Clearly, the genes that make memory proteins have to be switched on. Search for such genes began with the observation in studies of invertebrates that learning was mediated by a molecular signally system, called the cyclic AMP pathway. Memory requires activation of the compound, cyclic AMP. The early studies were done in different labs, one which used the mollusc, Aplysia, and the other using the fruit fly.

What does activated AMP do? One of the things is that it binds to a protein (called protein kinase), causing part of the protein's subunits to be liberated. The liberated components move to the neuron's nucleus, where they bind to another protein, called CREB. Activated CREB then binds to the memory genes, switching them on. Research on drugs affecting this cyclic AMP and CREB system is exciting, and it may lead to a memory pill.

Incentives for a "memory pill" are huge. Obviously, students and workers with heavy memory demands would like any help they can get. The Department of Defense, in particular its Defense Advance Research Programs Agency, wants to enhance memory capabilities of its troops, particularly under conditions of stress or of long periods where troops are sleep-deprived.

There are some things to worry about any new "memory pill." First, as with any drug, you can expect side effects. There may be addictive properties. Such drugs could confer competitive advantages, to schoolchildren, for example, who want better grades or to workers who are competing for a better job. Not everybody will be able to afford such pills, and we have to ask, "Is it fair to deprive these children of entry into the better schools or earlier graduation, or to delay or diminish the careers of workers?" Secondly, is super-memory really desirable? People who have "photographic" memories are typically overwhelmed with so much information that they find it difficult to make decisions. Also, some things *need* to be forgotten, for emotional or social reasons. Finally, memory pills may only work in the short run, and the long-term effect might be undesirable. For most of us, the brain works quite well with the molecular signaling machinery that produces cyclic AMP, CREBs, enzymes, and neurotransmitters. Normally, the control systems provide robust buffering against any increase or decrease in brain biochemistry.

A much less problematic approach to better memory is to forget biochemistry and work on human cognition directly. Memory skills provide the major route to a better memory. There is much we know how to do to improve memory skills. Why don't we work on that? To illustrate, practice (rote-memory rehearsal) alone does not guarantee memory improvement, unlike the improvement in bodily strength that one gets from physical exercise. Even when remote memory works, it is hardly efficient. I, and many other professors, continually run into students who complain about their test scores when they diligently studied the material over and over again. Such students don't have a clue about how to memorize. They were never shown how the application of good techniques and strategies can have profound influences on memory capabilities.

Good students typically memorize the required information in only one or a few attempts. Most of them do not have any systematic approach. They have accidentally stumbled on some useful habits of learning. Good students can become even better students if they know what they were doing right.

Making Yourself Pay Attention

It is not enough to say we need to pay attention better to remember better. The trick is in learning how to focus and be more observant. Below is a list of things we can do to help. Many of these are elaborated at various other places in the book.

- Assign importance to remembering. If you don't think something is important, your brain won't commit its circuits to handling the information.
- Be interested and curious about what you need to learn. Don't let it be boring. Boring is a state of mind that you can do something about.
- Expect and demand of yourself successful remembering. Make failure unacceptable.
- Get engaged with the material. Ask yourself or others questions about it. Think about it in different ways.
- Make associations with the material to be remembered. Make mental pictures to represent the information (see chapter on "Memories Hang Out With the Right Crowd").
- Try to stay rested, alert, and sharp. Nobody focuses well when they are tired.

* * * * *

You can't learn anything if the information never registers. Paying attention helps registration to occur. Anybody can pay attention to strong stimuli or profound events, and thus remember them. The trick is to learn to pay attention to weak stimuli and events that do not "grab you by the throat" to make you remember them.

Modern culture is conditioning people to become easily distracted, by TV commercials, cell phone interruptions, Web browsing, and other components of our hectic lifestyles. The price we pay for all these distractions is the loss of skill in sustaining focused and intense attention. Memory ability suffers as a consequence. Multi-tasking is in; focus is out.

Most drugs that people take, such as alcohol or nicotine, affect attention. Tranquilizers, sedatives, and alcohol depress attentiveness and thus impair memory. Nicotine does stimulate the brain, but attentiveness diminishes markedly to below normal when nicotine levels fall, as in long intervals between cigarettes. There are some drugs on the horizon that may be clinically useful. However, healthy diets are needed to help the brain operate at full attention. Most vitamins are important to good memory, but only vitamin E and C supplements are likely to have any positive effect in people who eat a balanced diet.

In short, the best way to pay attention is through force of will. To remember, you have to want to remember and accordingly force yourself to pay attention to what is to be remembered.

Key Ideas:

1. Identify and reinforce the *need* to remember. If there is a need, we will pay attention, and if we pay attention we have a much better chance of remembering.

2. Pay attention to what you want to remember. Make certain that it registers.

3. Pay attention to the meaning of the event, not just its appearance or descriptors.

4. But do pay attention also to the event's appearance or descriptors. Things that are associated with the event help to learn the event and act as cues later when you want to recall it. Pay attention to the learning situation.

5. When trying to remember a series of items, pay attention to items in the middle. These require more attention to be remembered.

6. Things you associate with the main learning event should be contiguous, not separated in time.

7. Be more aware of the sensations (smells, sounds, images, touch) that accompany items to be remembered. These associated sensations can serve as cues to help you retrieve buried memories.

8. Rehearse while you are paying attention, stretching out the time and effort you spend attending to the event.

9. Reinforce attending by changing the way you think about or apply the items to be memorized. This will prevent habituation and loss of attentiveness.

10. Work on your attention span. Years of TV watching, with all of its breaks for commercials, has probably conditioned you to have a short attention span.

11. Simplify what you are trying to memorize so that it will be easier to focus attention.

12. Focus, focus, focus. Don't try to learn too many things at once. Performing two tasks at once degrades the performance of both. Chewing gum and listening to jazz or classical instrumental music might be exceptions.

13. Don't do drugs. All the common drugs of abuse degrade memory formation. Binge drinking of alcohol can cause permanent damage to brain and memory capability.

14. Try to create a pleasant rewarding environment when you are trying to learn something. Positive emotions help you concentrate.

15. Eat your blueberries and other sources of antioxidants. Vitamins C and E may help.

16. A and B vitamins help memory, but only if you are deficient. Large doses can impair memory.

17. No drug has been proven to be a practical way to improve memory in healthy people. Research in this area, however, is promising

18. Memory skills provide the major route to a better memory.

19. You CAN train yourself to be more attentive.

Sources:

1. Nickerson, R. S., and Adams, M. J. 1979. Long-term memory for a common object. Cognitive Psychology. 11: 287-307.

2. Rupp, Rebecca. 1998. Committed to Memory. How We Remember and Why We Forget. Crown Publishers, New York, N.Y.

3. Grady, C. L., McIntosh, A. R., Horwitz, B. et al. (1995). Age-related reductions in human recognition memory due to impaired encoding. Science. 269: 218-221.

4. Clark, R. E., and Squire, L. R. 1998. Classical conditioning and brain systems: the role of awareness. Science. 280: 77-81.

5. Just, Marcel et al. 2001. Interdependence of non-overlapping cortical systems in dual cognitive tasks. NeuroImage. August 14.

6. Wilkinson, L., Scholey, A., and Wesnes, K. 2002. Chewing gum selectively improves aspects of memory in healthy volunteers. Appetite. 38: 235-236.

7. http://faculty.washington.edu/chudler/music.html#mem

8. DeBellis, M. D., Clark, D. B., Beers, S. R., Soloff, P. H., Boring,, A. M., Hall, J., Kersh, A., and Keshavan, M. S. 2000. Hippocampal

volume in adolescent-onset alcohol use disorders. Am. J. Psychiatry. 157 (5): 820-821.

9. Brown, S. A., Tapert, S. F., Granholm, E., and Delis, D. C. 2000. Neurocognitive functioning of adolescents: effects of protracted alcohol use. Alcohol Clin. Exp. Research. 24: 164-171.

10. White, A. M.., Ghia, A. J., Levin, E. D., Swartzwelder, H. S. 2000. Binge pattern ethanol exposure in adolescent and adult rats: differential impact on subsequent responsiveness to ethanol. Alc. Clin. Exp. Res. 24 (8): 1251-1256.

11. Iwamoto, Edgar T. 1990. Nicotine conditions place preferences after intracerebral administration in rats. Psychopharmacology. 100: 251-257.

12. Mehta, M. A., Owen, A. M., Sahakian, B. J., Mavaddat, N., Pickard, J. D., and Robbins, T. W. 2000. Methylphenidate enhances working memory by modulating discrete frontal and parietal regions in the human brain. J. Neurosci. 20: RC 65: 1-6.

13. Santarelli, L., et al. 2003. Requirement of hippocampal neurogenesis for the behavioral effects of antidepressants. Science. 301:805-809.

14. Solomon, Paul R., Adams, F., Silver, A., Zimmer, J., DeVeaux, R. 2002. Ginkgo for memory enhancement. A randomized controlled trial. JAMA. 288: 835-840.

15. Casadesus, G. et al. 2002. The Brain in the News. Nov. 15, p. 4.

16. Ristine, J. 2000. Study links vitamin A, brain chemistry. The San Diego Union-Tribune. Nov. M8. Pg. B3.

17. Turner, T. Y., and Soliman, M. R. I. 2000. Effects of zinc on spatial reference memory and brain dopamine (D1) receptor binding kinetics in rats. Prog. Neuro-Psychopharmacol. & Biol. Psychiat. 24: 1203-1217.

18. Russo, E. 2002. Seeking smart drugs. The Scientist. October 28, p. 27-28.

19. Rourtchouladze, R. 2002. Memories Are Made of This: How Memory Works in Humans and Animals. Columbia University Press, N.Y., N.Y.

Why Your Teacher Always Bugged You To Pay Attention

Memories Hang Out With the Right Crowd

- Association is the Basis for Memory Gimmicks
- Memorable Writing
- Pavlov's Dogs
- Associations Causing Maladaptive Behavior
- How the Brain Does It
- Pigeon Holes in the Brain
- Learning to Learn
- State-dependent Learning
- Remembering What You Read
- Remembering What You Hear

"Iron rusts from disuse, stagnant water loses its purity, and in cold weather becomes frozen; even so does inaction sap the vigors of the mind"

— Leonardo da Vinci

Memories Hang Out With the Right Crowd

Think of the last time you went to the movie. Is the movie the only thing you remembered? Or do you remember the refreshment stand? Or perhaps that you spilled your cola? Or had a problem finding a parking place? Or having to go to the restroom in the middle of the picture? Or maybe the flat tire on your car when the movie was over? The point is, we don't remember things in isolation. Memories are linked by associations. That linkage can help us remember.

A compelling example of the power of association is provided by Harry Lorayne in his book, *How to Develop a Super Power Memory*.[1] He asks the reader to draw a map of England, or of China, or Czechoslovakia. Most people can't come close. But if asked to draw Italy, most people draw a close approximation, because they know that Italy is shaped like a boot.

Many students that I encounter try to learn by rote memory. This is a terribly inefficient and ineffective way to remember. Perhaps you have discovered this with phone numbers. You look up a phone number and rehearse it several times so that you will have it available for dialing. You dial the number. It is busy. You have to dial again. Do you still remember the number? ... probably not, because you don't have anything to associate with the number.

Many teachers will tell you that students learn best if they can learn by "hands on" doing. "Doing" doesn't cause the learning, but it provides more associations for the object of memory. In fact, a well established principle of remembering is to couple a short period of study followed immediately by a short period of applying that information in some "hands on" way. Ten minutes for each study period seems to provide maximum efficiency, because we humans have short attention spans. For example, if you are trying to learn a computer program, spend 10 minutes reading about a certain operation, and then follow that with 10 minutes of actually doing the operation. How to do that becomes obvious for most learning that involves motor skills, such as piano playing, shooting a basketball, riding a bicycle, and the like. If the learning material is abstract, application may have to be limited to diagraming, drawing, or creating notes. But find some way to operate on the information in a way that differs from the way it was presented.

Association is the Basis for Memory Gimmicks

When I was a teenager, my dad was an enthusiast for the Dale Carnegie leadership and personal development course. Part of the training in that course involved how to memorize. The leaders used me to help recruit enrollees. My job was to attend the first meeting and put on a memory demonstration. Before the meeting started, they would hand me a magazine, such as the *Saturday Evening Post*. The audience was told that at the end of the one hour meeting that they could quiz me to see how much I remembered. At the end of the meeting, the magazine would be passed around the room and people would ask me such questions as "Billy, what is on page 44 or what page has the story about Elvis Presley or what did the Elvis story have to say?" I would amaze the audience by answering all their questions in great detail. I knew the essence of what was on every page, pictures and text. How did I pull off such amazing feats? It is not that I had a photographic memory in the sense that most people think of photographic memory. But I did create pictures in my mind that represented what was on each page. These pictures were associated with pictures that corresponded to numbers. Page 11, for example, was coded as a goalpost, because 11 looks like a goal post. Then the contents of page 11 were linked in picture form to my image of a goalpost. If the page was about Elvis' childhood in Mississippi, I would picture Elvis in a cotton field on the Mississippi delta, with the cotton field laid out like a football field with goal posts at each end. Other details on the page would be plugged into this visual scene.

This is the kind of memory gimmick that is advocated in many memory books.[1] The key element of the gimmick is the making of associations of visual images. All such books stress the importance of *thinking* about what you want to remember. Think about how it sounds, or smells, or picture it. Also, think about the meaning and the meaning of any associated events or items.

The most effective way to remember is to think in mental pictures. One experiment with college students[2] has documented that they learn chemistry better if the instruction is provided in picture form than if done verbally.

Why are pictures so effective? The explanation lies in the fact that the sensory systems and brain devote far more nerve cells to vision than to any other sense. To compare vision and sound, scientists have counted the number of fibers in the nerves that convey vision (optic nerve) and sound (auditory nerve) in humans. The estimates for the optic nerve range from 730,000 to 1,700,000, whereas the estimates for auditory nerve fibers only range from 28,000 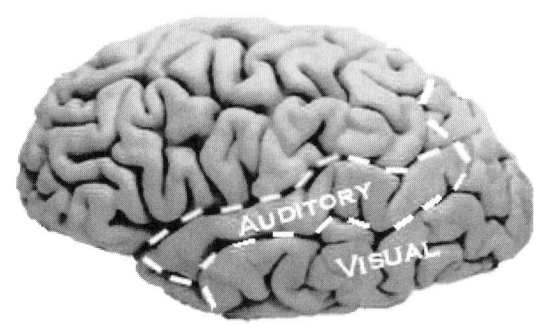 to 30,000. The counts are estimates based on hand counts of samples of each nerve under a microscope. At a minimum, 24 to 57 times as many nerve fibers are devoted for vision than for sound. No wonder we remember pictures best! They provide us with the richest information. A similar difference exists when you consider the vast difference in human cerebral cortex that is devoted to vision compared with sound (see figure above of left side of human brain). Note also, that there is a great deal of visual cortex that is folded along the midline of the brain and not visible in this picture.

Thinking in pictures provides the easiest way for us to think. It is also the easiest way to remember. Thus, when we use associations to help us remember, the associations are much more effective if they take the form of mental pictures.

The most common memory gimmicks employ making mental pictures and "pegs," as I mentioned in the opening chapter. Pegs are known items in a familiar environment, such as furniture in your room, or the dashboard in your car, or plants in your yard. A mental image of each item can serve as a peg on which to hang a mental picture of what you want to remember.

Several "peg systems" have been devised wherein sequential numbers are used as pegs tor on which to attach items to be remembered. The idea of mental pegs is attributed to Simonides, a Greek poet who lived around 500 B.C. Remember in those days, very little was written and knowledge was passed around by oral tradition. There was a high social premium placed on being able to remember well. So, it was not surprising that the ancients became expert at finding shortcuts and devices to help them memorize.

A common peg procedure is to use "peg lists," where a known list of items (pegs) provides associations with the thing you want to remember. For example, you know the left-to-right order of furniture in your bedroom: dresser, bed, lamp stand, a table and TV set, and a chest of drawers. Each of these can be used as a peg to make an association with something to be memorized. Suppose for example, you wish to remember a grocery lists of tomatoes, rice, steak, cereal, and green beans. You associate the first peg, the dresser, with tomatoes by picturing the dresser covered with tomatoes. The dresser is red, and some of the drawers are bursting open because they are too full of tomatoes. You associate the second peg, bed, with rice. Here you see the bed turned into a rice field, flooded with water. You might envision your bed as a water bed with rice plants growing out of it. Maybe you use "Uncle Ben's" rice, in which case you can image uncle Ben sleeping in the bed of rice plants. The third peg, lamp stand, is linked to steak by imagining that you are broiling the steak with the light from lamp. The juices run down onto the lamp stand and are messing up the rug. Next, the TV set is linked to cereal by imagining an ad for cereal. The announcer actually pours the box of cereal out through the picture tube onto your floor. Finally, you associate chest of drawers with green beans by imagining each drawer tied down with a bean stalk. The bean

71

stalk weaves through the handles and around the chest so hat you can't open any of the drawers."Jack" of "Jack and the Beanstalk" is a midget, and he is climbing up the bean stalk to get to your wallet, which you place on top of the dresser.

In a peg system, you must first memorize pegs. The number *one*, for example is not a peg, but it becomes one if you represent "one" as a "tree" (a tree has a single up and down appearance, as does the numeral for one). Similar associations can be used for creating a set of pegs. Thus a number peg system could go: one = tree, two = light switch (two settings of on/off, up/down, etc.), three = stool (three-legged), four = car (four wheels, four doors), five = glove (5 fingers in a glove), six = gun (six shooter, six cartridges), seven = dice (7 is craps), eight = skate (skating a figure 8), nine = cat (nine lives), ten = bowling ball (10 frames, 10 pins), and so on. Another peg system uses rhyming words. For example, one = run, two = zoo, three = tree, four = door, five = beehive, six = sticks, seven = heaven, eight = gate, nine = swine, ten = pen, and so on. Note that all these words are nouns. The reason is simple; pegs have to be tangible, something you can make into a concrete mental image. It is this image that you use to associate with what you are trying to remember. You can make up your own pegs as long as they follow some consistent rule and come to mind easily.

Another thing about using pegs is the idea of making mental pictures vivid and multi-sensory. For example, the number four peg (door) could be embellished to provide additional clues for the item to be remember. If the item being hung on the "door" peg is "make coleslaw" you can envision the white cabinet door with the silver handle where the cabbage grater is stored. You see yourself opening this door to get to the grater. Note also that action is involved in this memory scene. You are actually going through motions of doing things. All of this ancillary information about the door enlarges the range of cues that can be used during attempts at retrieving whatever was put on the door peg. (See this book's later chapter on "It's in There Somewhere. I Just Can't Find It").

You can use a peg system for remembering numbers, as in street addresses, phone numbers, and dates. You could use the number peg system mentioned above, but most memory experts prefer a separate system for numbers. The system most commonly used is based on assigning a consonant letter for each number and then making up easily visualized words by insert vowels among those consonants. The consonants for each digit are more or less self evident:

> 0 = z (or s, which are the first sounds for the word, "zero)
> 1 = t (One downstroke of a pen)
> 2 = n (Two downstrokes of a pen)
> 3 = m (Three downstrokes of a pen
> 4 = r (r is the last letter of the word "four")
> 5 = l (Hold up your left hand, with thumb extended - see an L)
> 6 = j (j is the mirror image of 6)
> 7 = k or c (Butting an upside down seven to an upright 7, and squashing it a little, produces a 7. C can sometimes sound like K. It's a stretch, but this is the best anyone has come up with)
> 8 = f (In cursive writing, an "f" has two loops)
> 9 = b or p (These are mirror images of 9)

The words you make up from these consonants can be a single word that includes all the consonants or several words that are sequentially linked. Now see the table for some examples of how this system can be applied to phone numbers:

| bank | 696-2180 | n, t, f, y | notify (image handing a note to teller to ask for withdrawal) |

73

daughter	822-6753	j, k, l, m	joke + lame (you tell a joke to your daughter and she laughs so hard she falls down and breaks her leg [becomes lame])
congressman	512-9281	b, n, f, t	benefit (you host a fund-raising benefit for your congressman)
tennis partner	844-4719	r, k, t, p	racket + pee (you make a bad shot in your doubles game and you get so mad that you throw down the racket and urinate on it)

Area codes often don't have to be memorized if you already live in the same area. But if so, you can use a separate word for the area code.

Whatever peg system you use, it will work best if you customize it to your own preferences.

Most of the things that are hard to learn, such as strings of numbers, nonsense syllables, or scrambled words, are hard to remember because they are hard to visualize and there is little to associate with the items. Remembering becomes difficult without context and related items to serve as building blocks for the memory. Memory works by attaching the new to the familiar, adding to an already learned set of associations.

Sometimes, using "sound-a-likes" handles this problem. A word or a person's name that cannot be imaged may be made easier to remember by associating it with something that sounds similar. Let me illustrate this technique by showing how to memorize the names of Presidents 11 through 20. "Polk" sounds like "poke," so you can envision a President poking someone in the eye. Now build up a chain of associations to reproduce the actual sequence of Presidents. Number 12 is "Taylor," which sounds like "tailor," so visualize a tailor at a sewing machine being poked in the eye. Next is "Fillmore," which sounds like "fill more." Now you can see our one-eyed "tailor" stuffing (filling) more and more stuff inside the suit he is sewing. He doesn't like the result so he "Pierce's" the suit with a knife to empty out the stuff. The suit still looks a mess so he gets "bucked off a cannon" (sounds like Buchanan) as he blows up the suit. The next President is Lincoln, which sounds like "links." So the tailor builds a chain-link fence out of all the pieces of the blown-up suit. Then he uses the fence to make an outhouse, "John" for "Johnson. Standing outside is a doorman to the outhouse who grants (Grant) permission to go in and ceremoniously ushers him in. The first person to go in is "Hayes" in the form of the sound-a-like bale of "hay." Next to go in is the cartoon character, "Garfield" who uses the hay as kitty litter. Of course this is ridiculous! It is also probably why you have just learned President's 11-20 - in one trial. Similar "short stories" of pictured sound-a-likes could be used for the first ten Presidents and Presidents 21-30. Notice also that another principle operates here: "chunking.": Items to memorize are grouped in small chunks.

Remembering people's names is also hard because the associations are not always obvious. It usually helps to identify some special facial feature, exaggerate it in your mind's eye and then find a way to associate the name (or its sound-a-like) to the facial feature. Remembering the names of some people is easy. If Mr. Bell, for example, has a large nose, you can imagine his face with a hug bell hanging down from between his eyes. Names such as "Carpenter, Miller, Carson, Gable, Hammer, Badger, Wolfe" have built-in images. For other names, you can take some liberties with your imagination. Mrs. Hubbard, for example, might be envisioned as "Old Mother" Hubbard. Mr. Rosenberg might be imagined as an iceberg with a rose in it. The book, *The Memory Book*, lists over 600 common surnames and suggests ways to construct visual images for them.[3] In addition to making associated pictures for names and faces, several other tips are helpful:

1. Make sure you register the name; ask for it to be repeated if necessary (this won't irritate people; they are flattered

that you care enough to get their name right).
2. Listen to the sounds of the name.
3. Make sure you know how the name is spelled.
4. Use the name right away, and use it several times in the conversation, each time visualizing the associations you have made between the name and facial features,
5. Exchange business cards when possible - you can use the card for review,
6. Repeat the person's name as you leave.
7. Rehearse the name and face soon after the meeting.

Anytime you meet a group of new people, set a goal for remembering three people well. Then, as this skill is acquired, raise the stakes to 5, then 7, then 10 people or more. You will discover that you become progressively better at this fundamental social skill.

Acronyms are a simple device for making associations. The letters in AARP, for example, are associated with the Association for the Advancement of Retired People. Words that are already familiar were used to create the title. The acronym thus is easy to remember, because the words they stand for are familiar. And the context of an association for retired people makes it pretty obvious what the RP stands for.

Check out these examples:

- U.S. Great Lakes – HOME [Huron, Ontario, Michigan, Erie, Superior]
- Treble clef in music – Every Good Boy Does Fine [EGBDF]
- First presidents - Washington And Jefferson Made Many A Joke [Washington, Adams, Jefferson, Madison, Monroe, Adams, and Jackson]
- Geologic time periods - Camels Often Sit Down Carefully. Perhaps Their Joints Creak. Persistently. Early Oiling Might Prevent Permanent Rheumatism. [Cambrian, Ordovician, Silurian, Devonian, Carboniferous, Permian, Triassic, Jurassic, Cretaceous, Paleocene, Eocene Oligocene, Miocene, Pliocene Pleistocene, and Recent]

In these examples, I hope you recognize how much easier these acronymns would be to memorize if you went beyond the word representation to add also visual imaging. For the Great Lakes, for example, picture your house (HOME) floating on a lake.

Clearly, acronyms might work even better if you make up your own, because ones that you make up will be more likely to involve the associations that you most readily call to mind.

Trying to learn things separately rather than collectively makes learning hard. It is analogous to trying to complete a jigsaw puzzle piece by piece without ever looking at the picture of the completed puzzle. If you work on small sections at a time, your learning of the puzzle solution is expedited by seeing the associations of the pieces to the content in the larger picture.

As you can see, there are many ways to make associations, but you should get the idea. Tony Buznan[4] gives a nice summary on how to make visualization effective:

- <u>Use as many senses as possible</u>. Images should be colorful, in three dimensions, and have sound, rhythm, and touch.
- <u>Create an organized sequence of images</u>. The ordering can be done on the basis or logic or by using numbered "peg systems" (see below).
- <u>Exaggerate</u>. Making images ridiculous or absurd makes them memorable.
- <u>Keep it simple</u>. The association needs to be direct and clear-cut.

These principles form the basis of a nifty little book on how to remember jokes by Philip Van Munching[5]. He first likes to organize jokes by categories: lawyer jokes, bar room jokes, sex jokes, topical jokes, classroom jokes, golf jokes, etc. Then for any given joke that he wants to remember, he identifies the key elements and turns them into linked mental images. Then he tells the joke to someone as soon as possible to help reinforce the mental pictures and the details of the joke.

Memorable Writing

Famous writings are memorable. One of the most memorable of all writings is President Lincoln's Gettysburg address. This address is not only great writing, but is also very memorable because of the way Lincoln chose his words. The address is a masterpiece of orderly flow of associations. Let us examine it again:

> *Four score and seven years ago, our fathers brought forth upon this continent a new nation, conceived in Liberty and dedicated to the proposition that all men are created equal.* [Note how past time is associated with our ancestors, and that was associated with their core belief about government.]
>
> *Now we are engaged in a great civil war, testing whether that nation or any nation so conceived and so dedicated can long endure. We are met on a great battlefield of that war. We have come to dedicate a portion of that field, as a final resting place for those who here gave together their lives that the nation might live. It is altogether fitting and proper that we should do this.* [Note how he associates the relevant past with the present. He associates the war with what the war means to the nation. The war is then associated with the battlefield, where they are honoring the dead for their sacrifice for the goals mentioned earlier]
>
> *But, in a larger sense, we cannot dedicate – we cannot consecrate – we cannot hallow – this ground. The brave men living and dead, who struggled here, have consecrated it far above our poor power to add or detract.* [Note the contrasting association between what the audience is unable to do with what was done by the soldiers who fought on this battlefield.]
>
> *The world will little note nor long remember what we say here, but it can never forget what they did here. It is for us, the living, rather to be dedicated here to the unfinished work which they who*

fought here have thus far so nobly advanced. It is rather for us to be here dedicated to the great task remaining before us – that from these honored dead we take increased devotion to that cause for which they gave the last full measure of devotion; that we here highly resolve that these dead shall not have died in vain; that this nation, under God, shall have a new birth of freedom; and that government of the people, by the people, for the people, shall not perish from the earth. [Note how he associated the just mentioned sacrifice of the dead with the obligations of the living. He associates the challenge to the living with the need to make sure the dead did not die in vain. To do this, he reminds them of their obligation, endorsed by God, to advance freedom, which he associates with the way a government should work in order to advance freedom. Finally, he associates the idea of freedom with the idea that it is fragile and not inevitable.]

Pavlov's Dogs

The initial ideas about learned associations stem from Pavlov's famous work with dogs. Pavlov discovered that some simple kinds of learning were automatic, like a reflex that develops under certain conditions. He called this learning "conditioned learning" and the responses that were indicative of such learning as "conditioned responses." Pavlov chose the one species to study that is the best for conditioned learning: dogs. A dog is a conditioned reflex machine. Most of what a dog does reflects conditioned reflexes or reflexes that come naturally ("unconditioned" reflex). You may think that your Fido is so smart, but the fact is that he has just accumulated an elaborate set of conditioned reflexes. They come easy to a dog. Here is an opportunity to reinforce what I said earlier in the book: namely, that learning a lot of information can make you appear smarter than perhaps you really are. In the case of dogs, pigs are actually much smarter.

Pavlov stumbled on his conditioned learning discovery. He was really trying to study digestion. He put cannulas in the stomachs of dogs in order to collect the stomach contents for study. Pavlov saw right away that gastric juices appeared quickly when a hungry dog saw or smelled food. This is an unlearned (unconditioned) response that occurs in all mammals, not just dogs. But because dogs are so easily conditioned, Pavlov also saw that stomach secretions appeared anytime a dog saw or heard something that the dog had learned to associate with food. For example, if Pavlov walked into the lab at feeding time, even if he had no food, the stomach juices were secreted. The dogs had clearly learned an association – that dinner time + Pavlov = food. Of course, Pavlov went on to test this formally by using light flashes and bells as conditioning stimuli. For example, he would present a light flash just before presenting a morsel of food. After many such trials, he showed that secretion of stomach juices started immediately upon seeing the light flash, *before* food was presented. The dog had developed a conditioned response to the light.

Pavlov also observed that the response in dogs that had learned this association could disappear if the conditioning stimulus (light flashes or bell sounds) were repeated without appearance of food. In this case, the dogs are said to have habituated to the conditioning stimuli. You can think of habituation as learning to ignore. The practical applications for human memory are that we remember associations where the conditioning stimuli are relevant, that is, paired with some meaningful event. Once the meaningful event stops appearing, we soon come to ignore the stimuli with which they were paired.

Habituation should not be confused with "extinction," which is equivalent to learning to forget. As with habituation, extinction can occur with conditioned responses in which the unconditioned stimulus stops occurring, but rather is an active forgetting or unlearning. One reason we know that extinction is active forgetting is that extinction of learned events is fragile, disrupted by stress, contextual clues, drugs, and other factors[6]. Extinction processes are not simple erasure of memory, because experiments show that extinction can be reversed by reinstating the cues.

The practical consequence is particularly evident in psychotherapy for phobias, traumatic stress disorders, and certain neuroses. The most exciting efforts in extinction research deal with drugs that act on the so-called NMDA receptor, a membrane-bound protein that responds to the neurotransmitter, glycine. Blocking of this receptor interferes with extinction. Thus, you might conclude that drugs that act to excite rather than block this receptor might promote extinction learning and thus be useful in psychotherapy. Earlier studies with cycloserine, which activates NMDA receptors, have shown that it facilitates extinction of conditioned fear responses in rats. Drug companies are pursing this approach to new drug development.

Another thing that is interesting about extinction is that this kind of learning is enhanced by "cramming," that is, massing the extinction trials in a short period of time.[7] All other kinds of learning are enhanced by spreading the learning out over time. Extinction does benefit from spreading the extinction trials out over time, but only if the trials occur in time blocks in which many repetitions of the extinction learning occur in each given block. In other words, it is the blocks that are spread out in time. This protocol is more effective than a single block of massed extinction trials; extinction is more complete and it lasts longer.

The most obvious practical application of conditioning learning is to try to teach humans to alter their visceral function. Functions such as heart rate, blood pressure, upset stomach, are notoriously hard to change through conscious will or learning. But they can be conditioned unconsciously through Pavlovian techniques. Neal Miller, at the Rockefeller Institute, was among the first to demonstrate with rats that such conditioning can be done[8]. He trained rats to raise or lower their heart rates, their blood pressures, their kidney functions, even the amount of blood flowing through their right or left ears. He did this with a different technique, which we now call operant conditioning. Essentially, the idea is to give an animal a reward anytime he accidentally does something the experimenter wants. After repeated reinforcement for "right" responses, the animal becomes changed according to the experimenter's wishes. This is the way circus animals are trained. Classically conditioned cues can be part of the procedure. For example, the animal has to know when the "game" has started. This might be done by taking the animal into a special pen which is the only place where the game occurs. The animal learns to make the association: pen + right response = reward.

At about the same time, David Shapiro and his team showed that humans were as smart as rats.[9] They taught male student volunteers to raise or lower their blood pressure. Their reward, anytime the pressure started to move in the desired direction, was to see a Playboy photograph of a nude female. The students had no idea what functions they were supposed to control. They were just told (obviously unnecessarily) to make the pictures appear as often as possible.

These findings have practical implications for psychosomatic diseases. Many medical professionals believe that abnormalities like high blood pressure, stomach ulcers, nervous tics, etc. are influenced by conditioned learning. For example, a child who gets a queasy stomach on days when an exam is to be given at school may have been conditioned to this response from the "reward" given by a mother who always let him skip school that day. Many hypertensive patients have an unusually high blood pressure in the doctor's office, which drops significantly when they go home and re-test there. Ulcers are caused by a bacterium, but conditioned nervous anxiety has a lot to do with setting up the conditions that allow the microbe to grow.

Television commercials and advertising in general are aimed at getting potential customers to make a Pavlovian association with the advertised product or service. Repetition is central. Have you ever noticed how often the same commercial runs? For example, I remember seeing the "double your pleasure" gum commercial with cutesy twins. The gum maker ran this same commercial for years, and it drove me - and probably you - crazy. But we remember.

A fundamental error made by many advertisers today is that the commercials are so clever, funny, or otherwise engaging that the customer does not make the association. What they remember is the clever shtick. If the product is not closely tied in, the association is never made. For a while Budweiser ran very funny TV commercials, but they surmounted the distraction problem by strategically placing labeled bottles of their beer at key points in the funny commercial. But many television advertising agencies get so carried away entertaining the viewer that the viewer forgets the product being advertised.

Associations Causing Maladaptive Behavior

Maladaptive behavior can also be conditioned. Let me tell you about an experiment performed by Ray Battalio, John Kagel, and several colleagues and I at Texas A&M[10]. This led to a series of classical papers in economics, because it was one of the first to use experimental animals to test economic theories. We treated rats as consumers that had purchasing power in the form of an allowance of lever presses that they could spend on one of two "treats." My contribution to the research was not in economic theory, but in helping them learn to teach rats to press a lever to get a drink reward and in determining what kind of drinks rats consider as treats (root beer and Tom Collins Mix). In the experiment, food and water were present at all times. Rats were given a daily quota of lever presses, which they could spend for either root beer or Tom Collins mix (without the gin). The price, in terms of lever presses needed to buy one slurp, was varied to test the prevailing consumer demand theory of economics.

The goal of the study was to determine the pricing conditions that would force a change in consumption patterns. Under baseline conditions where there was equal pricing of root beer and Tom Collins Mix, the rats spent their daily allowance of 300 presses about equally on each of the two drinks (solid line in the figure). You interpret the graph this way: The rats could drink any combination on or below the line. For example, assume the lines intersect the axis at 16 ml. The rat can spend all the allowance on either one, leaving no "money" for the other. Or the rat could drink 8 ml of root beer and 8 of Collins Mix or any combination that is on the budget line (4 and 12, 2 and 14, etc). If the allowance were raised to 400 bar presses, the rats could drink more of both drinks, again in the same ratios as baseline conditions (just think of moving the baseline up in parallel with the original). Under the baseline conditions, rats drank on average about 12 ml of root beer and 4 ml of Collins Mix each day, indicating that they naturally preferred root beer.

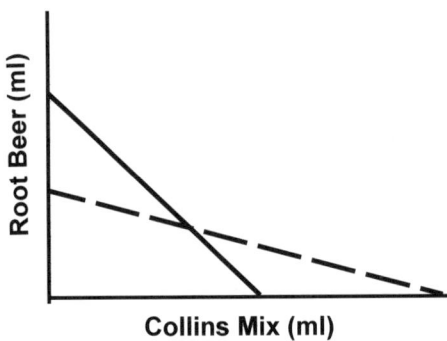

So-called consumer demand curve in which the consumption or purchase of two commodities is constrained by points along the lines in the plot. That is, you could consume any ratio of the two commodities, such as root beer and Collins Mix, as long as the ratio was a data point on the curve. For example, the solid line shows the case where if you consumed only root beer you could not consume any Collins Mix, and vice versa. The budget lines shown for choosing drinks by rats illustrate the consumption options when both commodities are priced the same (solid line) and when Collins Mix is made cheap (dashed line).

Existing economic consumer demand theory predicted that rats would generate similar results in the ratio of spending as the original baseline conditions if the experimenters doubled the price of root beer, halved the price of Collins Mix, and lowered the total daily allowance. What we saw was that this price structure caused rats to drink less root beer and more Collins Mix. When the price structure was returned to the original state, consumption went back to the normal preference for root beer.

When we doubled the price of Tom Collins Mix and halved the price of root beer, and adjusted the budget line so that the average total consumption would be the same as under baseline conditions, there was an extraordinary preference for root beer. So far, none of this may seem very surprising. Even rats learn to associate a price with a commodity and consume commodities in ratios that vary with the price structure. So what is the implication for humans? Maybe the way we spend our money depends on how economic constraints have conditioned us.

What was most surprising in the study were the results when we made basic necessities, food and water, rather than luxuries, as the commodities. Rats were kept hungry by keeping them at 80% of their normal weight. Rats lever pressed to get a fixed amount of food or water. Relative prices of food, for example, were changed by changing the number of food pellets delivered with each lever press. Severe disruption of eating occurred when food was suddenly made relatively much more expensive, even though the budget line was adjusted so that rats could purchase the baseline bundle of both commodities. The rats began to starve to death, even though they had enough allowance to eat more. In fact, the rats did not even spend all their daily food allowance. Spending patterns did not return to normal even when we returned to the baseline budget. This perverse behavior remains unexplained, but perhaps it has some relationship to some learned perverse behaviors in humans. In any case, such studies show the power of associative learning, which can be so powerful that it causes the learner to do irrational and maladaptive things.

How the Brain Does It

I have been talking mostly about primitive brain functions and compulsive behaviors involving neural systems that control the visceral functions. These systems are located mostly in the brainstem and spinal cord. But what about higher-level learning in the brain itself? How does the brain accomplish association? Because different stimuli are processed by different and often widely separated neurons, we suspect that these neurons form temporary networks to create the links among associations. Indeed, by recording the brain waves and measuring their degree of synchrony, many recent studies indicate that widely distributed neuronal populations become synchronized at specific oscillating frequencies when they process a complex stimulus or situation.

Recordings from individual neurons show that their firing rate responses to a stimulus decrease if the stimulus is continually repeated. Likewise, it is a common observation in brain imaging studies, which use blood flow or oxygen consumption as measures of neuronal activity, that as the brain acquires mastery over a task, fewer brain areas seem to participate and those that do show less activity. The common interpretation of such observations is that the brain has to work harder to learn something than it does to process things it already knows. No wonder people have always said that "learning is hard work."

One interesting wrinkle on this idea has come from experiments of Drs. Buchel, Coull, and Friston, in London.[11] They performed MRI imaging of brain activity in humans as they learned and recalled the association between 10 simple line drawings of real-world objects and 10 locations on a screen. As expected, activation in specific cortical areas decreased with time as learning progressed. In parallel with this adaptation, those parts of the brain normally involved in spatial and object processing seemed to develop more efficient connectivity. The time course of these learned changes was highly correlated with individual performance at any given point in time. Thus, it seems that part of the reason that the early stage of learning is hard work is because the brain has not had a chance to teach itself how to recruit and coordinate help among different neural circuits. It is as if the brain learns by organizing itself to parcel out components of a learning task to different areas and by becoming better able to orchestrate these areas to work together on the task.

Is there anything we can do to help the brain improve its self-organizing ability? Certainly, our minds can will our brain to accept the hard-work challenge of new learning. The brain isn't going to get any better by being a "couch potato." Anyone who has interrupted schooling and then gone back, as for example taking a few years off to work before going back to college, knows that the brain "gets out of shape" when it is not used. I have seen the phenomenon in my students after summer breaks. It takes a few weeks in the Fall for students to get their brains back in high gear. I experienced this first hand during veterinary school. It was obvious to me and my fellow students that our ability to memorize got better as the semester progressed. By the time we were sophomores, we could take on most any memorization chore (and our professors were happy to oblige).

You may recall in the opening chapter our discussion on the role of rich environments on brain development and ability to remember. A whole series of experiments revealed in general that raising rats in enriched environments made them more exploratory, more emotionally stable, and better at learning and remembering.[12] Many hundreds of scientists have taken up Rosenzweig's work and confirmed and extended it in the context of making memory associations. One study,[13] for example, was aimed at determining if environmental enrichment could enhance memory by increasing the ability to process contextual cues; that is, make better use of the associations of a learning situation. They compared rats, raised in rich or poor environments, for their ability to learn contextual cues when they became young adults. Their learning situation produced a freeze behavior, wherein a rat would become unwilling to move. A rat was placed in a conditioning chamber for a certain time and then given foot shock. Upon re-testing the next day, memory is indicated by how long the rat is afraid to move (he remembers the unpleasant experience and "doesn't know what to do," because there is nothing he can do to avoid the shock). The degree to which they remembered, as measured by the time of freezing, varied with their rearing condition (rich vs. poor) and with the time they spent in the conditioning chamber before the foot shock. See redrawing of the results below:

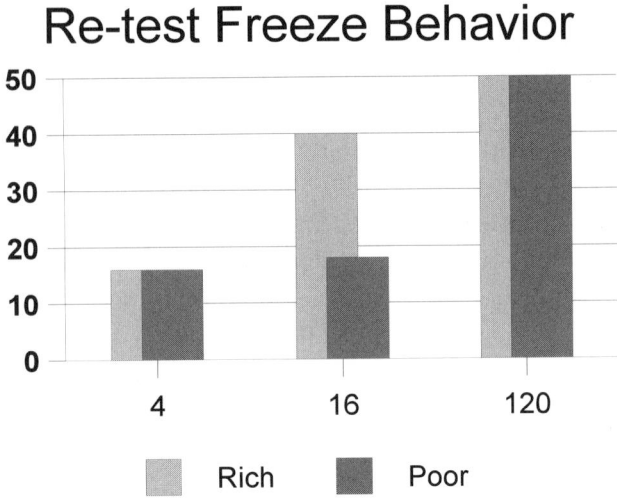

Percentage of total time without movement in the conditioning chamber during re-test. Note that a large difference was seen when rats were trained with 16 seconds to "think" about the situation before shock.

The meaning of this result takes a little explanation. In both groups, the time spent freezing during re-test (indicative of memory) was much greater when rats had 120 seconds immediately after learning to absorb the context of the situation than when less time was available. The chamber's context include black and white strips on the walls, a noisy fan, an overhead light, and of course the floor of metal rods used to deliver foot shock. The data clearly indicate that devoting time to the context of a situation enhances the ability to remember the primary learning event itself. The learning event (1 second of foot shock, the day before) and the context were the same in all situations. What changed was the length of time the rats had to make associations with the contextual cues and the primary learning event.

What do we make of the fact that the only situation that caused a difference between rich and poor was at the 16-second "thinking" stage. A four-second waiting period apparently was so short that neither group could register and make use of the contextual cues. Likewise, the 120-second waiting period was long enough that both groups got the maximum benefit of the cues. But at 16 seconds, the rich rats apparently had more ability to capture and use the contextual cues. We would be tempted to say they were "smarter." But that smartness only shows up under demanding circumstances. Given enough time, even the "dumb" rats get it. Of course, in this kind of learning situation, we are not talking about genuine intelligence, because no problem is being solved. But we are talking about the ability to remember and in particular about the ability to use environmental cues to facilitate memory.

There are all sorts of implications to experiments like this and the similar results in many other experiments. Society already accepts the premise that early childhood experiences create life-long benefits or handicaps depending on the "richness" of those experiences. This particular experiment helps us to explain one of the reasons that enriched upbringing may lead to greater success later in life. Project "Head Start" is the public policy initiative that grew out of research like this.

The brain is a self-programming biomachine. The more input the brain gets during early development the more able that brain is to sculpt an extensive library of circuits and associations among circuits to process information. In short, the brain during development is learning to learn, and the ultimate capacity is affected by the richness of those early learning experiences.

How does this relate to public education policy? We all know that school performance of young people entering U.S. schools has deteriorated, and the public schools are blamed. Could the problem be that the school environment in the early grades has actually handicapped adolescents? The "home schooling" movement is based partly on such a premise.

If home schooling always provided an enriched learning environment, then public schools are at risk of becoming extinct. But a home school environment is not enriching if socially isolated kids only get an hour or two of education (much of which is passive watching of television) from a mom who is an amateur teacher and who is easily consumed by her main job of being a mom and housekeeper.

Pigeon Holes in the Brain

Names of people and numbers are particularly hard to remember, because they are often arbitrary and there is nothing to associate them with. Memory retrieval typically requires some cuing, and cuing requires associations. "A rose by any other name" would still smell as sweet. You could just as well call it anything - the sweet smell can be a cue to help to remember the name. What about phone numbers? Is there any logical way to remember that one string of numbers is your phone number, while another is mine? A first step in remembering arbitrary facts is to find a way to classify the information according to a scheme that you already know.

People love to classify things. Our brains just feel more comfortable placing people, objects and events into categories. We group together items that share common properties. For example, we naturally group living things into people, animals, and plants. Then we create sub-groups: Caucasian, Oriental, Black, Hispanic, etc. ... or for animals, cats, dogs, cows, horses, etc. Apparently the brain finds this mode of operation an easy way to remember things. Categorization is an extension of association. The brain wants to associate like things together, so that when it comes time to remember, the associations are already in place and memory retrieval is facilitated.

A fundamental property of human thinking, and thus of memory, is the ability to categorize stimuli. Most categories are learned. Examples include animal vs. non-animal, live vs. dead, dog vs. cat, etc. By being able to place a new stimulus into the appropriate category, we facilitate learning a memory. Thus, it is easier to remember a picture of a cheetah if we reference its cat-like category.

Our capacity for categorization is especially valuable because we categorize on the basis of meaning, not just physical similarity. For example apple and billiard ball are put in different categories even though they are both round and physically similar. Likewise, apple and banana are put into the same food category even though they are physically dissimilar.

We classify round objects as balls, bananas as fruit, pies as dessert. This kind of classification goes on in all cultures and languages. Even our higher primate cousins do this, as experiments with teaching a crude language to chimps have amply demonstrated. Why is this propensity built into our nervous system? Some people think it has to do with language. Putting objects and ideas into categories makes it easy to name them. If the linguistic ability to assign labels is our more intrinsic capability, maybe young children find it easier to remember the names of things if they will assign them category labels. This phenomenon may be more than language. The author of *Peterson's Guide to Wild Birds* showed that bird species were easier to recognize and remember when he placed together pictures of birds that had similar features. Whatever the mechanism, it is certainly true that we learn the advantages of putting things in categories in the process of growing up. Learning to categorize is a skill that we get better at as we get older. This is central to "learning to learn ."

Numerous studies have shown that monkeys can learn to categorize stimuli as animal or non-animal, food or non-food, tree or non-tree, fish or non-fish, and by ordinal number. Presumably, these distinctions are made in parts of the brain cortex that process visual stimuli. Some recent experiments with monkeys reveal that category formation is a fundamental thinking process. To explore the neural basis, David Freedman[14] and colleagues at M.I.T. trained monkeys to categorize computer-generated visual stimuli as "cats" and "dogs." A morphing system was used systematically to vary stimulus shape to create various degrees of dog-cat hybrids in a way that precisely defined the category boundary. The monkeys looked at randomly presented images and indicated with a lever their "decision" as to whether it was more cat-like or dog-like. At the same time, the researchers recorded activity from neurons in a higher-order visual processing area, the lateral prefrontal cortex, by way of surgically implanted electrodes. Some neurons preferred cat pictures, as indicated by firing at a faster rate, while others preferred dog pictures. In terms of behavior, monkeys recognized dog-like cats correctly about 90% of the time and did as well with cat-like dogs. The neurons responded to morphed images according to their innate preference. That is, dog-preferring neurons responded at high firing rates to morphed dog-cat images as long as the morph was at least 60% dog. Cat-preferred neurons responded at high firing rates to morphed images that were predominately cat-like.

But one thing occurred to me that was not mentioned in the paper. Why didn't the monkeys consider at least some of the morphed images as a new category - much as humans would consider the part man-part horse characters of Greek legend as Centaurs. In the case of monkeys, does this reflect a limiting of their thinking ability or an efficient way to deal with ambiguity by a brain that has finite capabilities? Does it mean that monkeys, compared with humans, have a limited category sets?

This may say something about learning and memory in older humans. We have all observed that older people "get set in their ways." I call this phenomenon "hardening of the categories." I contend that such limited category sets impair learning, although it may at the same time facilitate recall of older, well established memories.

To learn and remember new things, we should work with our brains the way they are designed to work. We can actively promote categorization of things we are trying to learn. Maybe this is why so many students and professors instinctively create notes in which ideas and facts are typically categorized. It also facilitates memory to associate things within a category. For example, in memorizing a grocery list in the standard, rote memory way we would repeat the following objects over and over again:

apples	bananas	fish
beef	potatoes	broccoli
chicken	cola	oranges
green beans	ice cream	milk
pie	prunes	cake

To make this list easier to remember, first group them into like categories:

> <u>Main dishes</u>: meat, fish, chicken
> <u>Veggies</u>: green beans, potatoes, broccoli
> <u>Fruits</u>: apples, oranges, prunes
> <u>Drinks</u>: cola, coffee, milk
> <u>Desserts</u>: pie, ice cream, cake

Notice that you don't have to memorize the categories. You already know them. So now the information is organized so that instead of 15 unrelated things to remember, you only have 5 sets of related things. The next memory trick is to visualize the items, NOT think about the words.

So, for example, when we go to the meat counter, we might imagine seeing a fish swimming by, holding a rope around a cow's neck, pulling it along as they both are being chased by a chicken. Visualize the details: the chicken is pecking at the cow's hind feet. The cow is running away with a frightened look in her face. The fish is swimming with all its might trying to pull itself and the cow to safety from the chicken. For fruit, we can imagine a famous still-life painting of apples, bananas, and grapes. Or perhaps a more powerful association would be to imagine that we are harvesting grapes by throwing apples at them and scooping them up off the ground with a banana.

The whole scene is ridiculous, but that is the point. We remember associated things best when they are ridiculous. In case you have lingering doubt, you remember the images of Daffy Duck, Road Runner, and a host of cartoon characters simply because they are ridiculous.

So what is the practical application of these findings? It should follow logically that if we learn via categorization, then contriving ways to facilitate categorization will facilitate learning and memory.

Also, these findings could lead to insights about learning-style theory, which could be extended by including the idea of preferred ways of classifying things. How people differ in this regard is not

93

known, as far as I know, but I would bet there are differences that impact learning ability. This possibility could open a new field of educational research that is focused on "re-programming" people so that they categorize new events in the most effective ways.

Another aspect of grouping is the size of the group. Numerous studies have shown that people have a limit on the number of items that can be held in memory at one time. The typical phone number has seven digits (leaving out the area code). Do you know why? The reason is that many experiments have confirmed that seven (plus or minus 1) is a magic number. This is the typical limit that most people can hold in active memory. Even seven items tax the ability of most people when it comes to meaningless number strings. That is why a phone number is broken into two sets, the first three exchange numbers and the last four personal numbers. This solution with phone numbers is an example of "chunking," grouping items to lower the memory load.

Acronyms are another example of chunking, where one word is substituted for many words. So, a main principle of memory is that our "scratch pad" for temporary memories has limited capacity.

To extend the idea of categorization, I also want to emphasize the importance of organizing learning materials in rational ways. In particular, it is important to distinguish the information that you must memorize from the information that you can deduce. This helps you to use core principles and logic to arrive at answers and thereby reduces the amount of information you have to memorize.

My main axiom about memory is this: *Never memorize anything that you can figure out.* Let me give an example of such organization. Suppose you had to memorize the muscles of the upper arm, what those muscles do, and which bones they attach to and where the attachments are on the bones. First, think of the joints, not the muscles. Muscles serve to flex or extend joints. The joint of interest in our example is the elbow joint. Extension, which straightens the arm, is accomplished by the contraction of extensor muscles. These have to be on the back side of the arm, and must be anchored at one end on the upper arm bone (humerus). At the other end, the tendons of the muscles have to span the joint and anchor on the forearm bones (radius and ulna). Similar logic applies to muscles that flex the joint, only these obviously have to be located on the front of the arm.

So now you are left with having only to memorize the names of the flexor muscles and extensor muscles, plus perhaps some details about the specific areas on the bones to which they are attached. You start with biceps and triceps, which most people already know anyway, and they know that biceps are on the front of the arm and triceps on the back. The "bi" and "tri" parts of the words means that the have two and three points of origin. So the biceps has two points of origin on the scapula and the triceps have three heads, two of which arise on the arm bone or humerus and a third "long head" that arises up on the scapula. On the front of the arm, mostly covered by the biceps, are two other muscles which start with a "b," the brachialis and brachioradialis muscles. Both arise, as you would expect, on the humerus. The "radialis" muscle terminates on the radius, as the name implies, and the other muscle terminates on the other forearm bone, the ulna. So, if you are an anatomy student doing a dissection of the upper arm and you see a three-headed muscle on the back of the arm with three segments, it must be the triceps. The longest segment that runs all the way up to the scapula, must be the "long head" of the triceps. The head that lies on the medial side (next to the body) must be the medial head of the triceps. The head you see toward the outside of the body must be the lateral head of the triceps. On the front side of the arm, when see the two smaller muscles under the biceps, you know that the one that goes to the radius is the brachioradialis and the other one going to the ulna must be the brachialis. My point with this perhaps tedious explanation is that by thinking about and organizing your learning material, you can greatly reduced the amount of brute memory required.

A related issue is remembering where you put things. One formal study has established that people are most likely to forget where they stored important things when the items have been put in an unlikely place.[15] The reason for storing items in likely places is that it is easier to make associations. You always, for example, can easily associate your car keys in the side pocket of your purse, or your wallet in the top left drawer of the dresser, or your grocery list stuck on the refrigerator door. But as soon as your depart from these associations by putting such items in unlikely places, you lose your association handle. So why do people put things in unlikely places? First, they may be unorganized people. Getting organized simplifies living and memory too. Secondly, some people truly believe that putting things in unlikely places makes them more memorable. Wrong. Without good associations, memory becomes less likely.

Learning to Learn

The "rich rat" studies I reviewed suggest that early learning experiences actually help the brain develop an improved capacity to learn. And part of that capacity may result from a better ability to absorb contextual cues, to make associations among various cues.

Rich experiences during development also increase the likelihood of developing a more extensive repertoire of learning skills. One widely recognized problem among education professionals is that too many children are one-mode learners. There are visual learners, auditory learners, kinesthetic learners, for example. Unfortunately, in my view, the educational community puts the emphasis on adapting curriculum rather than adapting children. This reflects the typical educational mind set of teaching "stuff" to kids rather than teaching them how to learn. Today's approach is to structure curriculum in several ways, one way for visual learners, another for auditory learners, and so on. What we should devise are ways to increase the learning-skill repertoire of children, so that a visual learner, for example, is no longer handicapped by only being able to learn well in that one mode.

In any case, it is abundantly clear that it is possible to teach people how to learn to learn. Though we have very little theoretical understanding of what is involved, it is generally accepted that a primary purpose of formal education is that it teaches to some degree how to learn to learn.

The value of a college degree, in the eyes of many employers, is not so much the factual knowledge that goes with that degree, which is often irrelevant to the job requirements. What IS important to an employer is that the degree signifies that the degree holder has jumped enough learning hurdles that the person has learned something about how to learn, even if by accident or "osmosis." Even more so, the Ph.D. degree obtained in a rigorous Graduate School signifies that the holder has substantial learning and discovery skills. Many people have said that the Ph.D. experiences may raise IQ some 15 points or so. The change that I underwent, and my observation of others, convinces me of the general truth here, even though I know that IQ scores and the ability to learn are not related in any easily described way. So why don't employers fall all over themselves trying to hire Ph.D.s? First, Ph.D.s are more expensive. Second, they are often too narrowly trained. Third, they may not be good team players. But make no mistake; they usually are much better learners than anybody else.

A key idea about learning to learn is the idea of "learning sets," a theory of learning developed by a famous physiological psychologist, Harry Harlow. This theory posits that learning involves a repertoire of skills and tactics that a learner develops after becoming more experienced with a given class or type of learning. Typically, this learning set is acquired unconsciously, as a by-product of more experience.

Perhaps an example from an animal experiment[16] would clarify. Rats trained in a water maze learn the location of a submerged "safe platform" where they can sit without having to swim. Once trained in a water swimming task to learn the location of the safe platform, rats can learn a new place response much more quickly than it took them to learn the first time. Each new response can be learned within one or two trials, and retention lasts longer than it does if only one location is learned. Thus, they seem to acquire extra skills that can be generalized to other tasks from the experience of dealing with variations on the original task (that is, finding safe platforms in different locations).

What does this mean for us? It means that by learning related items of a similar type we progressively acquire ability to learn other items of this type. Many people, for example, who learn a foreign language find it easier to learn a second language, or even a third or

97

more languages if they are in the same group, as in "Romance languages." Learning how to set up equations to solve a math problem can make it easier to set up equations for other math problems. Learning how to play one song on a piano can make it easier to learn other songs.

Learners who first have difficulty with a given learning task should take heart. They will get better if they stay with it and don't get discouraged.

State-Dependent Learning

The rat experiment that we described earlier on freeze behavior showed that the ability to learn was affected by the surroundings and physiological condition of the rat at the time of learning. In this case, the state was the visual and tactile features of the conditioning chamber. It makes sense that you can retrieve information better when you are in the context that you learned it, but the mechanism of why it happens is harder to understand. In a study done by Duncan Godden and Alan Baddely (1975),[17] scuba divers listened to a list of words underwater and sitting on the beach. The divers recalled the most words when they were retested in the same place as they learned them. Visual stimuli in this case must serve as a unconscious retrieval cues. Since memories are a web of associations, the learned words are strongly associated with specific visual scenes. The two reinforce each other. This visual priming could also help explain déjà-vu, where various cues in a place trigger memories of similar cues, making you believe you have been there before.

The visual scene acts as a primer for retrieval. Priming is discussed elsewhere in this book, especially in the chapter on retrieval ("It's In There Somewhere. I Just Can't Find It."). Priming stimuli actually become part of the learning process. The words in the study above were not memorized in isolation but in a context wherein remembering any one part of the situation or scene helped to recall the rest. Such observations have caused some scientists to think of memory as a hologram, where all the information about a picture is contained in any one part of it. Few scientists believe that the brain works like a hologram, but almost all accept that items stored in memory are not stored in isolation but in context with other associations.

Peter Russel, author of "The Brain Book"[18] explains the memory storage mechanism in his own way: "Memory is not like a container that gradually fills up; it is more like a tree growing hooks onto which memories are hung." Memories on the same branch link to each other.

My experiences as a teacher provide a practical example of state-dependent learning. When I give an examination, student recall is much more likely if the same cues are present when recall is attempted as were present during first learning. For example, if I give an examination to students in the same classroom in which the instruction had been given earlier, their scores will be higher than if we go out on a beautiful day to a picnic area to take the exam.

Drug addiction provides another example of state-dependent learning in that learning consists of an inextricably linked constellation of cues and associations. When addicts take drugs, they not only reinforce their memories of the pleasurable effect of the drugs but also they have an associated memory of the place and conditions when the drugs were taken. Drug addicts in rehabilitation programs are warned to stay out of their old environment, and to avoid as much as practical the things in their past. Going back to the same friends, same neighborhood, same shops and hangouts will greatly increase the odds that the addict will go back on drugs. Renewing friendship with an old addict friend will make you remember drugs and rekindle the desire for drugs.

Let me give another example. There are far more smokers and former smokers than there are addicts of illicit drugs. Most former cigarette smokers will tell you that the hardest part of quitting smoking is having to get through each morning's coffee or, for some, a drink in a bar, without being overwhelmed with the desire to smoke.

Remembering What You Read

This business of thinking about images instead of words is a basic requirement of good reading skills. Poor readers read too slowly and focus on the words themselves. That is a main reason they can't remember what they read. Countless times I have heard college students say, "I read that chapter three times, and I still can't answer your questions." When I ask thought-provoking questions about the material, they often can't answer the questions because they can't remember the meaning of what they read. Even with straightforward simple memorization questions, they often can't remember, because their focus on the words themselves kept them from associating what their eyes saw with their own pre-existing knowledge and thus facilitating remembering. In short, to remember what you read, you have to think about what the words mean.

I recommend the following sequence of steps for remembering what you read:

1. Skim the material, noting the headings and their inter-relationships. Get the grand scheme of things.

2. Read with a purpose. Know what you are looking for. Slow down and think hard about the parts that have information you are looking for. Skim-read everything else.

3. Read in short segments (a few paragraphs to a few pages), all the while thinking about and paraphrasing the meaning of what is written.

4. Think about the content in each segment in terms of what you already know and don't know. Ask yourself questions about the content. "Why did the author say that? Do I understand what is meant? What is the evidence? Do I agree with ideas or conclusions? Why or why not? What is the practical application?" Apply the ideas to other situations and contexts. Generate ideas about the content.

5. Use a highlighter to mark a FEW key points to act as the basis

for mental pictures and reminder cues. Add key words and drawings in the margins if you don't find useful clues to highlight.

6. Make a mental picture of the key ideas, using if possible a picture of the section heading as a peg for hanging other pictures of the content in that section.

7. Proceed to the next section and follow the steps above.

To rehearse what you are memorizing, see how many of the mental pictures you can reconstruct. Use headings and highlighted words if needed to help you reinforce the mental pictures. Rehearse the mental pictures every day or so for the first few days after reading.

Mental pictures are not the only way to facilitate memory for what you read. I understand that actors use another approach for memorizing their lines for a play, movie, or TV show.[19] Actors "get into the part" and study the meaning of the script in depth, which seems to produce memory automatically for them. When the same script is memorized with mental images, it appears that the text is being looked at from the outside, as something to be memorized. Actors, on the other hand, appear to be looking at the same text from the inside, as something to be experienced. The actors probe the deep meaning of the text, which inevitably involves attending to the exact words. For example, they seem to explore why their character would use a given set of words to express a particular thought. This is still a process of association, except that actors are associating words with real meaning and context as opposed to contrived visual image meaning and context.

Remembering What You Hear

Seminars and workshops are often given in seminar format where lecturing is the basic means of transmitting information. Many teachers, especially college professors, teach by lecturing. In my view, this is not a good way for many students to learn, but since that is the environment in which they are thrust, they must learn how to learn under those conditions.

Students are told to take notes during the lecture. But in my experience, they get little good advice on how to take notes. Note taking is the standard process whereby information is transferred from the teacher's notes to the student's notes (sometimes without passing through the minds of either). The problem is that students are too busy writing notes and not busy enough thinking about what the teacher says and means. Good teachers hand out their notes before class so that students can pay attention to the lecture and get engaged with the content rather than with pencil and paper. Better teachers hand out "skeleton notes," that give the student freedom to couch ideas in familiar terms and to leave out things they already know or can figure out. This approach really pays off when it comes time to study for exams.

When I was a student, I always had the goal of remembering as much as I could about each lecture right then and there (so I wouldn't have to use so much of my fun time studying). As long as I was surrendering my time to be in class, why waste it by being an inefficient listener?

Note taking should be minimal. Follow the principles given for "Remembering What You Read." The idea is to think about what is being said, asking yourself or the teacher questions, expressing the ideas in your own terms, making mental images, and so on. So what do you do in case you miss some key information while doing all this thinking? If the teacher permits, tape record the lecture and play it back later to update and refine your notes and to refine and rehearse your mental pictures. Use a tape recorder with variable speed playback, so you can slow down for difficult parts and speed up through parts that are not particularly useful.

* * * * *

Association is the basis for memory. Rote memory is the worst way to remember anything. Remembering is expedited by associating what you want to remember with something you already know. Such associations work best if they are visual images, inasmuch as our brains devote far more neurons to vision than to any other sensation. Advertising executives are well aware of how important it is for the public to make associations to their products, and visual images are at the heart of effective advertising.

Associations are also effective in learning bad habits and maladaptive behavior. We can be conditioned, like Pavlov's dogs, to pair certain stimuli with visceral responses. Sometimes this leads to such psychosomatic health problems as high blood pressure and ulcers.

Our public schools need to teach students how to make associations, which are the key to learning what schools are trying to teach. Schools, unfortunately, are preoccupied with teaching students *what* to learn without teaching them *how* to learn.

Most of life's learning experiences involve remembering what you read or hear. The trick is in organizing the way you read or listen to facilitate the making of memorable associations.

Key Ideas:

1. Study in small segments (10-15 minutes). Then immediately apply the information.

2. Use mental pictures to represent what you are trying to remember. Don't memorize words. Memorize pictures that represent the words.

3. For lists, a "peg" system will help in making mental picture associations.

4. Mental images should be: a) based on multiple senses, b) organized in a logical sequence or hung on pegs, c) exaggerated and absurd, and d) simple and concrete.

5. Other association devices include "sound-a-like" acronymns.

6. Memorable writing: create order, associate ideas, and link ideas with words that can be imaged in smooth transitions.

7. Psychosomatic disease (high blood pressure, ulcers, digestive disorders, etc.) often develop as conditioned reflexes that arise from external contingencies that reinforce the abnormal bodily function.

8. Conditioned learning is reinforced and made permanent by repetition of the contingencies that produced it.

9. Strong associations and conditioning contingencies of the wrong sort can make people do irrational, maladaptive, and perverse things.

10. New learning is hard work for the brain. Make your brain put out the effort to make associations and mental pictures.

11. A brain "gets out of shape" by reduced use. Keep your brain exercised, particularly by practice with making mental pictures and associations.

12. Context of new information creates associations that make remembering easier. Take the time to let the context "soak in."

13. Learning experiences during early childhood can produce life-long changes in mental capability.

14. Classify, categorize, and group items to be remembered. Remembering one thing in a category makes it easier to remember another in the same category.

15. Group items to be memorized in numbers of seven or less. That is the typical limit that most people can hold in their "scratch pad" or working memory.

16. Never memorize things you can figure out. Organize learning material accordingly.

17. Learning skills can reinforce each other. Learning related items can create generic sets of learning skills that can transfer to multiple related situations.

18. Recall works best when it is performed in the same environment in which learning occurred. Contextual cues that were present during learning aid the recall, even when you are not consciously aware of the cues.

19. To remember what you read: a) skim read to find the points you need to memorize, b) read with a purpose, c) focus on ideas, not words, d) associate the ideas with what your already know, e) read in short segments - then think about and paraphrase what you read, f) ask questions about what you read, at the time of reading, g) challenge statements that seem wrong or incomplete, h) generate new ideas, I) mark-up text with highlighting of a FEW key thoughts - write in the margins where helpful, j) make a mental picture to capture the ideas that you need to memorize, k) rehearse your mental pictures several times while they are still in your working memory, l) rehearse your pictures a few times a day for the next several days.

20. To remember what you hear: a) use proper note-taking techniques, b) spend more time thinking about what is said than writing notes - use a tape recorder if possible, c) make your goal to memorize as much as you can at the time, so that you won't have to spend much time on it later - be an *efficient* listener, and d) apply the principles used for being an effective reader.

Sources:

1. Books that teach memory gimmicks include: Hersey, W. D. 1990. *Blueprints for Memory*, American Management Association; N.Y., N.Y.; Burg, Bob. 1992. *The Memory System,* National Press Publications, Shawnee Mission, KS; Lorayne, H. 1998. *How to Develop a Super Power Memory*, Lifetime Books, Inc. Hollywood, Florida.; Lucas, J.2001. *Learning How to Learn,* Lucas Educational Systems, Dallas, Tx.

2. Rigney, J. W., and Lutz, K. A. 1976. Effect of graphic analogies of concepts in chemistry on learning and attitudes. J. Ed. Psychology 68: 305-311.

3. Lorayne, Harry, and Lucas, Jerry. 1974. The Memory Book. Dorset Press, News York.

4. Buzan, T. 1984. Make the Most of Your Mind. Simon & Schuster, New York, N.Y.

5. Van Munching, Philip. 1997. How To Remember Jokes. Workman Publishing, New York.

6. Barad, M. G. 2003. Introduction: extinction as learning. From Symposium: Learning to Feel Safe: Extinction of Conditioned Fear. Society of Neuroscience Annual Meeting, New Orleans.

7. Barad, M. G. 2003.Extinction differs from other learning. From Symposium: Learning to Feel Safe: Extinction of Conditioned Fear. Society of Neuroscience Annual Meeting, New Orleans.

8. Miller, Neal. 1968. Learning of visceral and glandular responses. Science. 163: 434-445.

9. Shapiro, D., Turksy, B., Gershon, E., and Stern, M. 1969. Effects of feedback and reinforcement on the control of human systolic blood pressure. Science. 163: 588 -589.

10. Kagel, J. H., Battalio, R. C., Rachlin, H., Green, L., Basmann, R. L., and Klemm, W. R. 1975. Experimental studies of consumer demand

behavior using laboratory animals. Economic Inquiry. 13: 22-38.

11. Buchel, C., Coull, J. T., and Friston, K. J. 1999. The predictive value of changes in effective connectivity for human learning. Science, 283: 1538-1541

12. Rosenzweig, M. R. 1977. Research on memory - and memories of research, p. 221-240. In Discovery Processes in Modern Biology, edited by W. R. Klemm. Krieger Publishing Co. Huntington, N.Y.

13. Woodcock, E. A., and Richardson, R. 2000. Effects of environmental enrichment on rate of contextual processing and disciminative ability in adult rats. Neurobiology of Learning and Memory. 73: 1-10.

14. Freedman, David J., Riesenhuber, Maximilian, Poggio,T. and Miller, Earl K. 2001. Categorical Representation of Visual stimuli in the primate prefrontal cortex. Science. 291:312-315.

15. Winograd, E., and Soloway, R. M. 1986. On forgetting the locations of things stored in special places. J. Exp. Psychol.: General. 115: 366-372.

16. Whishaw, I. Q. 1985. Formation of a place learning-set by the rat: a new paradigm for neurobehavioral studies. Physiol. Behav. 35: 139-143.

17. Godden D. & Baddeley A. D. 1975. Context-dependent memory in two natural environments: On land and under water. British Journal of Psychology. 66: 325-331.

18. Peter Russell. 1991. The Brain Book. Dutton, New York, N.Y.

19. Noice, H., and Noice, T. 2000. Two approaches to learning a theatrical script, p. 444-455. In Memory Observed, edited by Ulric Neisser and Ira Hyman, Jr. Worth Publishers, New York, N.Y.

Catch It While You Can.

Making Learning Last

Dial M for Memory

The Short and Long of It

Permanent Memories Have Changed You

Birds of a Feather

Recent Memory Can Vanish
   Into the Ether

Working Memory and Intelligence

Improving Working Memory

Brain Areas Working Together

Changes in the Brain During
   Consolidation

Where Is Memory?

Practice, Practice, Practice

I remember your name perfectly but I just can't think of your face.
— W. A Spooner

Dial M for Memory

You look up the phone number of a store. Before you finish dialing, you realize that you forgot the last few digits. Back to the phone book. At my age, I have learned to keep the phonebook open to the right page until I connect with the party I am calling.

This everyday experience teaches that there are least two kinds of memories, those that are short term, seemingly to be written on an erasable mental scratch pad, and those that are more lasting. These temporary memories can be a blessing, in that they keep our minds free of being stuffed with useless junk that we would not use very often anyway. But obviously, temporary memories are a curse if you need to have the information memorized permanently. For these cases, the trick is to get temporary memories converted into permanent ones. Scientists call this process *consolidation*.

Both declarative and procedural memories can be short term or long-lasting. Clinicians who assess memory in patients with different sorts of mental dysfunction like to evaluate short-term memory, because it is usually the kind that is most vulnerable to brain dysfunction. A typical short-term memory test is to recall a string of digits that are presented to you in random and ungrouped order, such as 4,6,3,2,5,0,1. The longer the strings you can recall, the better your short term memory. A widely used short-term memory test is the Wechsler Digit Span Test.

Another way to think about memory time span is the amount of information you can temporarily hold and work with in memory. This defines "working memory." A good example is a recently introduced Digit Ordering Test,[1] in which the patient not only has to remember the string of digits but also has to reorder them, in either ascending or descending order.

The Short and Long of It

The focus of this chapter is on how to get those short-term memories consolidated into long-term form. An experiment that I conducted over 30 years ago[2] illustrates some key points about consolidation. This experiment actually was designed to test the hypothesis that sex hormones could facilitate the consolidation of short-term memory into more permanent form.

The experiment was conducted as follows. A rat was put on an elevated platform that safely protected it from an electrified grid floor. The rat initially did not know that stepping off the platform would result in footshock, and so the rat always stepped off the first time, because rats are insecure in the middle of wide-open spaces. They want the comfort of hiding near walls. The untrained rat stepped off the platform within one or two seconds and tries to run to the walls. However, the footshock, which lasted for 5 seconds before I picked up the rat and moved it to the safety of its home cage, was a learning experience teaching the rat to inhibit the natural tendency to leave the safe platform. When I came back the next day to re-test such rats, some rats refused to leave the platform. Other rats would eventually step off, but they took a long time to leave the platform, as if they partially remembered something unpleasant but weren't quite sure what it was. They had learned, in one trial, that stepping on the floor was dangerous and unpleasant.

When I measured the time delay before leaving the safe platform, there was no statistically significant difference between females in estrus, females not in estrus, females with ovaries removed as adults, males, and males that were castrated as adults. So, in all these groups, learning seemed to be about the same. Now the task was to find a way to study the memory consolidation process. One approach is to introduce a major stimulus that might disrupt memory formation before the process had been completed. Electroconvulsive shock (ECS) was, and is, the accepted way to do that, because it is quick, intense, apparently harmless, and had been shown in humans to abolish (prevent) memories of events that occurred just prior to the ECS.

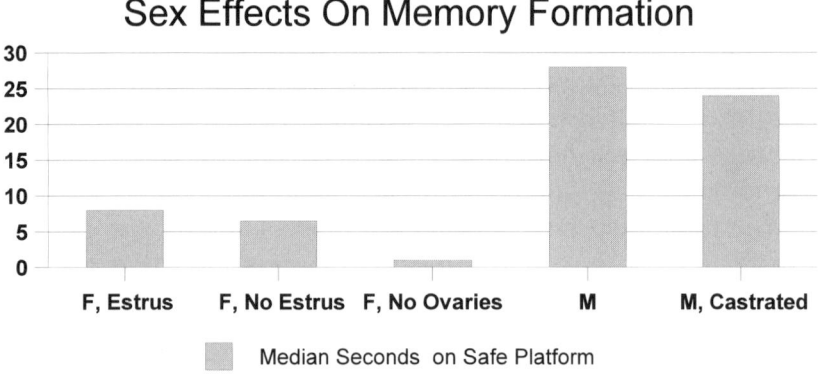

Sex hormones affect retention of a one-trial learning event. Memory formation was disrupted by giving electroconvulsive shock shortly after the learning experience. Time, in seconds, spent on the "safe" platform was the measure of remembering. Females were more prone to forget and step off the platform, especially those females that were in the stage of the estrous cycle when female hormone levels were low.

So when I tested other rats in these same categories of females in estrus, females not in estrus, etc. by giving them ECS immediately after their one-trial learning experience, there was an interesting difference in performance during the re-test on the next day. They all forgot what they had learned, except for the males, either castrated or intact. The males had step-off latency scores that were very similar to those in the groups that did not get any ECS. Notice that there was more disruption of consolidation in castrated females than in intact females, whether or not they were in estrus. This suggests that female hormone also contributes to the ability to consolidate.

You might think of other ways to interpret these results. For example, suppose males are less fearful and have less drive to run and hide near the walls. You know - a macho thing. Certainly, the male hormone has such effects, and this might account for why intact males did better than intact females. But, why then do castrated males that lack the hormone do nearly as well as intact males? Also, how would you explain my observation of the control groups (not shown in chart) that intact males and intact females performed equally when there was no ECS used to disrupt memory consolidation.

I did do a later study in which the walls were close to the safe platform[3]. In fact the walls were close enough that if the rat stood on its hind legs it could rest the forelegs against the wall. So under these conditions, a macho effect is not likely to explain why females in diestrus left the platform. The results (see below) made it clear that memory consolidation was much more vulnerable to ECS when females were in the stage of their cycle when estrogen levels were low.

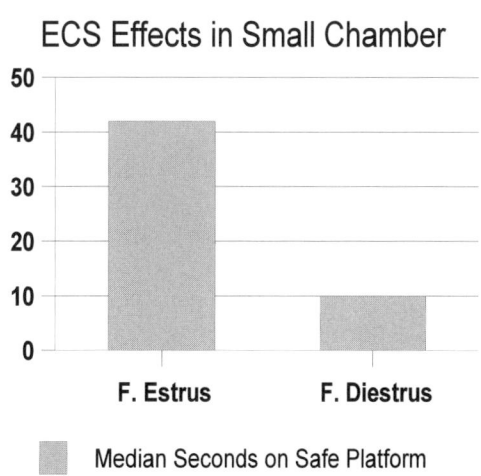

Effect of female estrous cycle on memory consolidation. Time spent on safe platform during re-testing was much greater in estrous females.

Moreover, these rats were over-trained by giving them back-to-back learning trials until they demonstrated that they understood. So, when they were re-tested on the next day, it was very likely that any failure was a failure of memory, not of learning. Another test showed that in a large chamber with only one learning trial, both groups remembered less well, but again, females performed better when in the stage of their cycle with high estrogen levels.

Does the lack of effect of adult castration in males mean that male hormone plays no role? Of course not, because we clearly showed that adult males remembered better than adult females. Perhaps the ability of castrated males to consolidate memories reflects a developmental effect, a permanent change in mental capability resulting from growing up in the presence of male hormone.

This question prompted another experiment that tested the hypothesis that presence of male hormone during maturation was important. Consolidation was compared between adult males that had been castrated as weanlings and adults that were castrated as adults. The results clearly showed that growing up with male hormone helps consolidation, even though the hormone is not present at the time of learning and testing. This is consistent with the reports of other investigators who showed that other behaviors are permanently influenced by whether or not male hormone is present during development periods.

Many other workers had shown that the interval between learning and the time of ECS was important. ECS does NOT disrupt consolidation if you wait long enough after learning, say one hour. I tested this in the adults that had been castrated as weanlings, because their performance was so poor. I saw a clear gradient, ranging from where no rat in the group that got ECS immediately after learning could remember the next day to the case where 40% of the rats could remember if the ECS were delayed for an hour after the learning experience. Such data produced what is called a retrograde amnesia curve.

Studies with this kind of design have been used by many investigators in other contexts, both before and after my experiments. One of the important discoveries that others made was that the interval between learning and ECS (or other disruptive event) was crucial. If ECS is given within seconds after the learning events, memory consolidation generally fails to occur. But if ECS is delayed, say for an hour or so, the disruption of memory consolidation is no longer evident.

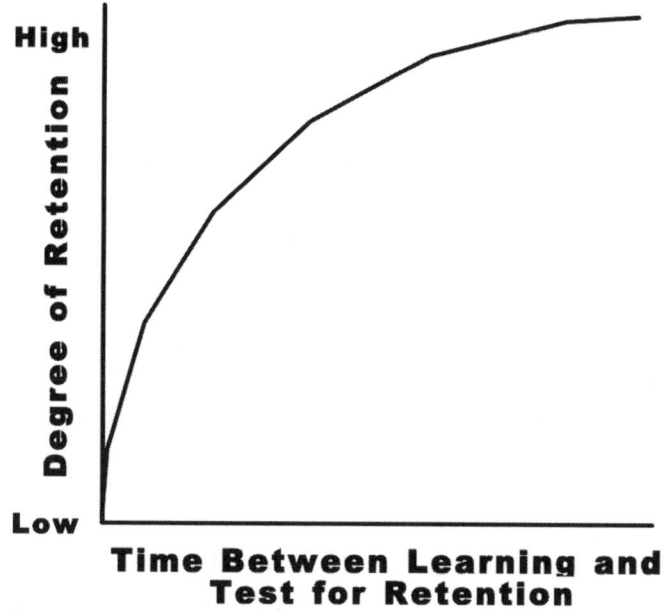

Typical retrograde amnesia curve. If a memory-disrupting event occurs within the first few minutes after learning, the memory may not consolidate into permanent form. The memory remains vulnerable to disrupting influences for many minutes or hours.

In those days, ECS was all the rage among researchers, because it was quick, controllable, and apparently not damaging. However, I did a study that revealed that performance could be affected by ECS even if it were given *before* the learning trial and even if given as long after learning as 8 hours. Other people at that time were also showing unexpected effects of ECS. So, ECS is not used much any more to study memory consolidation. Also, humans have become more favored as subjects, because they are much more adept at a variety of one-trial learning situations.

Permanent Memories Have Changed You

When memories consolidate, there must be some physical change in the brain to record them. Like changing the magnetic film on a VCR during a TV show recording, there must be some way to store the images and thoughts of our memories. In the case of the brain, this storage most likely occurs in the junctions between neurons, the synapses. Indeed, many years ago, Russian scientists had used electron microscopy to compare synaptic "anatomy" in normal test animals with animals that had been over-trained in a certain task. The synapses that were in the sensory pathways for that learning task showed greater density and thickening. At the time, other scientists seemed to think that this observation was too facile, too convenient for satisfying theory. Yet, a few years later it became increasingly clear that synapses were made more robust when new memories had been created.

A most common experimental tool for studying such changes is to monitor electrical responsiveness in the part of the hippocampus that gets direct input from the cerebral cortex. If an experimenter implants stimulating electrodes in the cortex and recording electrodes in the hippocampus, the electrical response of the hippocampus to stimulation becomes evident.

If you then stimulate intensely, with a long train of high-frequency stimulation (called tetanic), the hippocampus becomes hyper-sensitive. It responds to a later single-pulse stimulation much greater than it did before the tetanic stimulation priming. So, in this sense, we can say that the synapses have "learned" from the tetanic stimulation. The synapses have been facilitated or potentiated. But what is most interesting is that the potentiation can last for days after the learning experience. It is a form of long-term memory. This long-term post-tetanic potentiation protocol serves as an experimental model for consolidation of short-term memory into longer-term form.

The physical representation of the longer-term memory is being examined these days to learn more about the biochemical representation. For example, Irina Antonova and colleagues at several research institutions in New York, have identified some of the biochemical changes that occur in cultured hippocampal neurons.[4] The research team included recent Novel Prize winner, Eric Kandel. They produced long-term potentiation in cultured hippocampal neurons by exposing them to the natural excitatory neurotransmitter, glutamate. Such stimulation increased the number of postsynaptic glutamate receptors. In addition, a presynaptic protein, synaptophysin also increased. Thus, two coordinated biochemical responses serve to support the newly formed memory: one in the presynaptic neuron and the other in the receptors of the postsynaptic neuron. We can expect that similar biochemical changes occur in other neuronal junctions that use transmitters other than glutamate.

What this kind of evidence indicates is that memories have a physical/biochemical support system. The memory representation must lie in facilitated transmission in certain pathways that are associated with the learning.

There is also a larger implication here. What we experience and think about and believe is actually changing our brain. As memories for these experiences, thoughts, and belief systems consolidate, they are actually re-wiring the brain, facilitating certain synaptic pathways at the expense of others. These changes are creating the new person that we are becoming in response to our experiences, thoughts, and belief systems. The social implications cannot be overstated.

Birds of a Feather

Most everyone knows that a baby duck will attach itself to the first thing it sees after hatching. Usually, this is the mother duck, which of course is the biologically adaptive response. This phenomenon was widely studied by Konrad Lorenz in the 1930s. This work and other related studies of animal behavior won Lorenz the Nobel Prize. Lorenz showed that this *imprinting* behavior, as he called it, appeared to be a case of one-trial learning. Memory of the initial imprinting stimulus appeared to be immediate and irreversible.

However, things are not quite that clear cut, as seen in experiments by Howard Hoffman and Peter DePaulo at Bryn Mawr College[5]. They created a simple testing environment in the laboratory. A large box was divided into two compartments, separated by a mesh wire screen. The baby duck was placed in one compartment and the stimulus (a moving toy train engine with a block of foam rubber on it, was placed in the other. The train compartment could be made dark or illuminated. The baby duck's responses were monitored by its distress cries, which could be filtered electronically with ease, because the cry has a narrow frequency range of 3,000 - 4,000 cycles per second. The initial approach was to expose the baby duck to the sight of the illuminated engine moving back and forth for six 20-minute sessions during the first 48 hours after hatching. This lighted engine was to serve as an imprinting stimulus. Then after a three-day interval the ducklings were tested in another session in which the imprinting stimulus was repeatedly presented and withdrawn. Each time the stimulus was withdrawn (the light in the train compartment was turned off), the ducklings emitted distress cries. No distress cries occurred when the stimulus could be seen. The distress cries began after a few seconds from when the stimulus was withdrawn, continued persistently until the stimulus was again presented, and the cessation of cries was immediate (less than 1 second). Later, other experiments showed that it was the *movement* of the imprinting stimulus that caused imprinting. If the train stood still, no imprinting occurred.

In other experiments, turning off the light on the same moving train elicited distress cries in ducklings that had not been imprinted to it. In one experiment, ducklings were imprinted as a group and then tested with repeated presentation and withdrawal of the stimulus, either as individually or in the company of a second duckling. When subjects were paired, few distress calls occurred during stimulus withdrawal. This indicates social overtones to the imprinting stimulus, even though the stimulus is inanimate. To the duckling, the stimulus seems alive.

The imprinting stimulus was also capable of being a conditioning stimulus, much like the shaping of behavior used by animal trainers. In Hoffman's lab they showed that the presentation of the imprinting stimulus could be used to strengthen and maintain a pole-pecking response. The experiment was conducted as follows: a balsa-wood pole connected to a pressure-sensitive switch was placed in the duckling's compartment. In ducklings that had been imprinted to the moving train, the train was made visible each time the duckling accidentally approached the pole. Then, only motions that resembled a peck were reinforced with presentation of the imprinting stimulus. Finally, presentations were given only when the duckling actually pecked the pole. After training was complete, ducklings would peck at the pole for hours on end as long as the imprinting stimulus were present.

Presentation of the imprinting stimulus could even reinforce distress crying. In these experiments imprinted ducklings were given a 15-second presentation of the train stimulus after each episode of crying during train withdrawal. Birds reinforced this way learned to increase their distress calling in order to get the "relief" of seeing the imprinting stimulus.

Hoffman and his group tested the corollary question: will withdrawal of the imprinting stimulus reduce the likelihood of response? The answer is yes. Under these conditions, withdrawal of the imprinting stimulus was seen by the duckling as punishment for whatever it was doing at the time. The duckling stopped behaviors that were associated with punishing withdrawal of the imprinting stimulus.

All of the experiments confirmed that the memory of the imprinting experience was lasting.

But imprinting appears not to be a typical learned response, as Lorenz and everybody else had thought. Hoffman and colleagues conducted a study in which fertilized duck eggs were housed in a box that prevented any visual stimulation when the duckling hatched. Just as the first pecks on the shell were occurring, the egg was transfered by remote cables and pully to the test chamber. Thus, newborn hatchlings could be tested under conditions where the first thing they saw was either the imprinting stimulus or just the test apparatus. Those ducklings that saw only the apparatus made distress calls as soon as they came out of the egg. Those that hatched to see the imprinting stimulus never made distress calls, unless the stimulus was removed. The imprinting is innate. It requires no learning. But there is memory, even if there is no learning. Ducklings that are imprinted and then denied the imprinting stimulus for 5 days will show the imprinting behavior when the stimulus is re-instated.

However, there is a role for learning and memory. As we saw above, the test stimulus can be used to teach ducklings to behave in certain ways. Also, if ducklings do not get any imprinting stimulus for the first five days, then presentation of the moving train frightens them and they emit distress calls when they see it. What this says is that fear interferes with learning. We will have much more to say about that in the chapter dealing with emotions and memory.

Fear can be overcome, and Hoffman and colleagues reasoned that they could re-instate the susceptibility to imprinting in older ducklings if they could just remove the fear. They did this by letting ducklings live in the test chamber with the imprinting stimulus on all the time. The ducklings gradually learned that there were no negative consequences to this stimulus, and thus fear went away. Eventually, they got imprinted to the stimulus. Thus, once they learned that the stimulus was safe, they became imprinted.

The extent to which this might apply to human learning is not known. Something like imprinting has been demonstrated in baby monkeys. And anyone who has ever brought a new puppy into the house sees that a special bond develops between the pup and one member of the family.

Consider the possibility that very young children can learn not to be afraid of certain stimuli if they receive that stimulus early enough in life under conditions that create no reason for fear. Also realize that humans can do so much more with memory because we have the power to reinforce memories by elaborating them with conscious thought and words. Whatever is happening in the tiny brains of ducklings is certainly happening below the level of consciousness and may well be operating subconsciously under similar conditions in humans.

A baby human brain is vastly more complex that that of a duckling. Nonetheless, the bond that forms between mother and infant may approximate the duckling response. Maternity wards in hospitals have standard routines designed to enhance mother-baby bonding.

Among these is breast feeding. Multiple stimuli can reinforce bonding: the suckling movements, the taste and smell of mother milk, the taste and smell of secretions from nipple glands, and the physical caressing of the baby. Mammary nursing is fundamental to being a mammal.

Finally, initial bonding (read imprinting) can have lasting effects on the ability to form new social attachments. Hoffman and co-workers showed that ducklings that had been imprinted could also be imprinted to other stimuli. In fact, the initial imprinting *facilitated* the development of an attachment to a second stimulus. We have to wonder how much social pathology among humans is due to inadequate mother-infant bonding. There is such a thing as "learning to learn," and the relation of human bonding behavior to later-life sociability may be an example.

Recent Memory Can Vanish Into the Ether

Over 100 years ago, two experimenters, Müller and Pilzecker[6], conducted human experiments that showed that distractions can prevent consolidation of new learning. This observation has been amply replicated in hundreds of subsequent studies. Today, many memory researchers think in terms of what they call the "Interference Theory of Learning." This theory focuses on what happens immediately after learning that might interfere with consolidation. Many things can interfere with consolidation. The oldest known effect, reported two decades before the Müller and Pilzecker experiments, is that of head trauma. Stimulant chemicals, taken immediately after learning, can enhance consolidation, whereas depressant drugs, such as alcohol, have the opposite effect. The positive effect of stimulant drugs can be duplicated by voluntary arousal and focused attention.

You don't have to be knocked in the head to interfere with learning. Any distraction that is interposed between a learning event and when consolidation occurs can interfere with the consolidation. Observations of retrograde amnesia suggest that processes underlying new memories initially persist in a labile state and consolidate over time into more permanent form. This "consolidation hypothesis" dominates memory research today.[7]

Educators, who of all people should know better, have designed school systems where classes are scheduled one class period right after another, which almost guarantees that students will have difficulty remembering what was presented in a given class. As soon as one class is over, all the students rush into the hall to socialize and get their minds off of what happened in class. Then they rush into another class where they are exposed to a whole new set of learning experiences. What they really need is 5-10 minutes of quiet time to reflect on - and consolidate - the learning that just took place.

Humans differ little in the way their memory works. People with a low IQ and people with high IQs have similar requirements for new memories to consolidate. Moreover, spaced repetition (rehearsal) is required. For example, when we learn a foreign word, most of us require a repetition on that same day and on each of the next several days in order to get useful command of the word. How much rehearsal and how close the spacing needs to be depends on other variables that we discuss throughout the book, such as the motivation to remember, the emotional impact of the event, whether or not the event was imaged in the mind's eye, and what happens immediately after the learning event.

Forgetting is normal. Everyone's forgetfulness can be quantified by graphing the percentage retention from a memorizing session as a function of time. We can roughly describe forgetting as a loss of learned material that progresses rapidly with time. How much memory of a given learning event occurs, if there is no rehearsal, varies inversely with the strength of the learning experience. Memory of weak learning experiences decays more rapidly than that of strong learning experiences.

The first significant study in this area was carried out by Hermann Ebbinghaus and published in 1885 and eventually translated into English as *Memory. A Contribution to Experimental Psychology*. Ebbinghaus studied the memorization of short strings of nonsense syllables, such as "NGA" and "BZE". By repeatedly testing himself at various times and recording the results, he was the first to describe the shape of the forgetting curve. He saw that forgetting is most pronounced when the items have no meaning, as in nonsense syllables. That is a major reason that foreign languages are so hard to learn. At first the letters in words of a foreign language might as well be nonsense syllables. Later, as rules of the language become clear and a vocabulary develops the syllables make more sense and are easier to remember.

What happens immediately after learning largely determines whether memory gets consolidated into permanent form. The temporary memory has to be kept alive in order to facilitate consolidation. A revealing experiment[8] on spatial learning in rats suggests a general principle that might be useful for us. In this study rats showed an unusually long persistence of accurate spatial working memory over delays of several hours. One explanation is that the working memory was kept intact and viable by response strategies and the use of olfactory cues in addition to visual cues. We humans don't have a sense of smell as good as that of rats, but that is not the point. The basic principle seems to be to use multiple senses during and immediately after learning. Also, the rats were "thinking" about task-relevant response strategies immediately after the training trial. This constitutes a powerful form of rehearsal that we can surely emulate.

Drugs can selectively block either short-term memory or long-term memory. Interference of short-term memory can occur when the drug imposes a physiological or mental state that prevents consolidation. Interference with long-term memory may follow because of the poor consolidation, and there may also be more direct effects on the biochemical and structural changes required in the nervous system for long-term memory.

Slow consolidation provides time for the influence of emotions. Intensely emotional experiences are well remembered, as are stressful situations. The hormones released during stress (adrenalin, corticosterone, and certain pituitary hormones) have memory-promoting effects of their own.

Some interesting research has been published about consolidation of motor memories, as in situations where you might want to learn a given motor skill such as playing the piano or learning how to ride a bicycle. We all know that practice makes perfect. What we may not have realized is that you can undo or interfere with learning motor skills if you try to learn too many conflicting skills at once. One reason that learning to ride a bicycle is so difficult is that you can't do it in small steps. Your motor control systems have to learn a whole repertoire of muscle-set contractions all at the same time.

These influences appear specific for motor learning, as opposed to declarative learning. Reza Shadmelu and Thomas Brashers-Krug at Johns Hopkins University[9] have shown that subjects who learn one internal map of a motor action will lose that memory if they attempt to learn a second internal motor map too soon (within about 4 hours). For the learning process of a second motor skill to interfere, it had to require a conflicting set of movements toward a target. Thus, to learn a second conflicting motor skill, you must allow plenty of time for the first skill to be consolidated. You might think that the first map has to be unlearned in order to accommodate the second, and that allowing time for the first map to consolidate would make it more, not less, difficult to learn the second map. This is a paradox that the Hopkins group examined in a follow-up study. They found that by allowing a longer interval to consolidate the first map, learning of the second map became easier because it was unbiased by the processes that were sustaining the consolidation of the first map. It is as if the brain were starting fresh with learning the second motor map.

Working Memory and Intelligence

What we call intelligence may depend in part on working memory. People usually think that smartness involves quick mental processing and insightfulness, figuring out things that people of ordinary intellect cannot do. But think about it. To figure things out, you have to hold information in your working memory as you go along. A chess master, for example, would not be a master without the ability to remember the anticipated consequences of a long series of moves. In one test of this idea,[10] Patricia Carpenter and Meredyth Daneman at Carnegie Mellon University in Pittsburg compared college-student SAT scores with their short-term working memory ability. They had 41 college students read or listen to a set of unrelated sentences, requiring them to remember the last word of each sentence. The number of words remembered correlated nicely with SAT scores. Actually some 77 studies of this general kind have been done, and a meta-analysis of the 6,179 students involved showed a high correlation of working memory with intelligence.

In another study[11] the ability to solve puzzles correlated with working memory. Patricia Carpenter and her colleagues gave a puzzle task to 34 students. These so-called Raven's problems required students to figure out and remember rules that governed a series of geometric images. The problems that most students missed were the ones that had the greatest number of rules to remember.

It is a little hard to sort out the causal-consequential relationships here. Are you smart because you have a good working memory, or do you have a good working memory because you are smart? Intuitively, we are inclined to believe the former, because being smart requires certain mental tools that include working memory. Certainly, improving one's working memory has many practical advantages. Becoming smarter would be a nice fringe benefit.

Improving Working Memory

Why don't schools try to teach children to improve working memory? Would drills and contests create lasting improvements in working memory capacity? Surely this is as important as spelling bees (which notably are drilling students in long-term memory).

A main reason for failure of schools to develop working memory skills is that, to my knowledge, there are no established procedures. It would be easy to make up learning exercises that might not only work but also have educational value in their own right: chess strategies, lists of words in a foreign language, or strings of notes in a song.

Another reason we don't try to improve working memory is that many studies indicate an innate limitation of working memory capacity. As I mentioned earlier, most people can hold in their working memory only about seven serially ordered items.[12] This limit may even be a biological constant. Rats (and humans) running a radial maze and trying to keep track of which arms they have already entered seem to have the same limit on working memory capacity.[13]

Nobody knows why there is such a limit or what, if anything, can be done to extend that limit. Is the limit the product of evolutionary selection forces? What conceivable advantage would there be to having such a limit?

Can we extend the limit? My own experience indicates that practicing working-term memory tasks does improve at least the ease with which one can remember seven items. Grouping numbers, as in chunking credit card numbers in groups of four, makes it possible to extend the limit somewhat. Finally, converting items into mental pictures that are serially linked in story-like fashion can extend the limit considerably.

Brain Areas Working Together to Form Memories

The first clues about which brain areas are important in consolidation came from clinical studies in humans with brain lesions. A classic case is that of H.M., a man who had both temporal lobes of the cortex surgically removed. The major structure removed is known as the hippocampus. After the surgery, which was performed to stop out-of-control epilepsy that originated in the medial temporal lobe, H.M. could no longer learn anything new. Every new learning experience had to be repeated, and it was never learned. Things he had learned before the surgery were remembered. Thus, scientists came to suspect that the hippocampus is necessary for memory consolidation, which has been amply confirmed in subsequent animal experiments and human clinical observations.

It is now abundantly established that the medial temporal lobes of the cortex are crucial for converting short-term, working memory into more permanent form. This part of the cortex, as the name implies, lies at the temple area of the head, with the key memory areas folded under the outer cortex so that they lie adjacent to the brain stem. A diagram of their relationships is shown below:

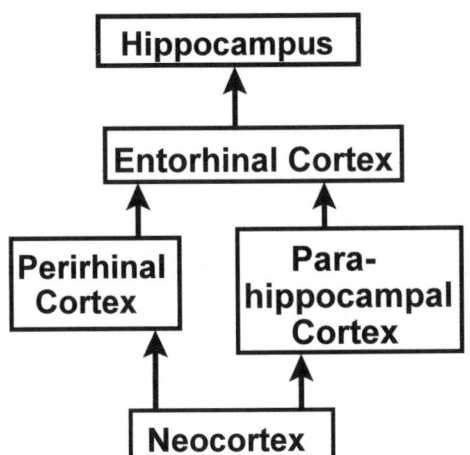

Diagram of the brain structures that process information generated in the cerebral cortex and create a memory that can persist beyond a few minutes.

These structures act as a feed-forward information filter, taking information that is processed in the main parts of the cortex (neocortex) and routing it through a series of structures, the most important for memory being the hippocampus. How the hippocampus supports memory consolidation is not known, but we do know from patients such as H.M. and numerous animal studies that memory consolidation depends on these pathways.

Although there is no known connection, the hippocampus and related medial temporal lobe structures are prone to be sources of epilepsy. Indeed, our first clues of the role of these areas in memory consolidation came from observing consolidation defects when the epilepsy was so bad that these parts of the brain had to be removed surgically.

This system of structures is not necessary for preservation of long-term memories, once they already exist. In other words, the playback

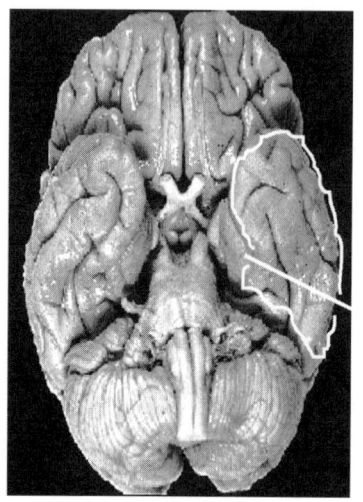

Ventral view of the human brain showing some of the medial (near the center) temporal lobe structures involved in memory consolidation. The structure outlined is the temporal lobe. The white line points to the area known as the parahippocampal gyrus. The other memory structures and the hippocampus itself are folded underneath the temporal lobe where they are not visible from this view.

of long-term memories does not require the medial temporal lobe structures. Patients like H.M. have perfectly normal memory for events in their past. It is forming *new* memories that is the problem. Without a functional medial temporal lobe system, patients like H.M. never learn how to learn. Their impairment for creating new memories is permanent.

I should mention that learning events that are procedural or implicit do not require the medial temporal lobe for consolidation. For example, in teaching a "Tower of London" game to H.M., experimenters observed that he never learned the rules, which had to be repeated each time a new game started. But his skill at the game continually improved. In other words, there were implicit aspects of the game that he was learning, despite his inability to consolidate the explicit instructions.

An intriguing study comparing the explicit and implicit processes was recently published by Robert Clark and Larry Squire[14] at U.C. San Diego. I introduced this study in the chapter on attention, in the context of paying attention to cues and their time relationships. Here, the context is consolidation and the difference in explicit and implicit learning. Clark and Squire used a variation of Pavlov's famous conditioning technique, but they used humans and used eye blinking as the conditioned response. Let me review here how it works: if you blow air into the eye, the eyelids blink. This is an unlearned (unconditioned) response. But if you precede the air puff with some other stimulus, such as a tone, after many such pairings, the eyelid will blink as soon as the tone is heard - before the air puff. Blinking to the tone is a learned (conditioned) response.

Clark and Squire compared this kind of learning in normal subjects and in amnesic patients who had bilateral damage to their medial temporal lobes. Some of their tests involved what is called simple delayed conditioning. It is called that because the unconditioned stimulus (US - air puff) is delayed from the onset of the conditioned stimulus (CS - tone). The delay ranged from 0.7 to 1.25 seconds. The investigators also compared the learning under conditions where the CS is on only for a brief time, followed by a long interval before presenting the air puff. Here, the interval between CS and US ranged from 0.5 to 1 sec. This latter test design is called "trace conditioning," but I don't know why. Maybe it is because only a trace of the conditioning stimulus is present.

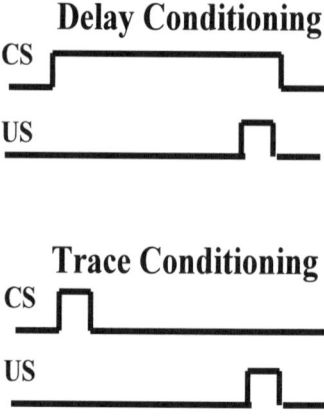

Two kinds of conditioned learning designs. In the delay design, the unconditioned stimulus (US) is delayed after the onset of the conditioning stimulus (CS). In trace conditioning, the CS is not on all the time; only a "trace" of it occurs before the US.

Anyway, the design made a big difference in the results. Normal subjects acquired both tasks readily. It might surprise you to know that the brain-damaged amnesics acquired delayed conditioning as quickly as normal subjects, although they never acquired trace conditioning. Previous studies in animals, where the hippocampus was surgically removed, had also shown that delayed conditioning occurs normally in such brain-damaged animals. The interpretation is that delayed conditioning is some kind of procedural, implicit learning that, like other learning of this type, does not require an intact hippocampus.

It also suggests that trace conditioning has some kind of explicit aspect to it. That is, subjects must somehow be able to keep track of the CS-US time relationship and build up a memory for that across many trials (30 minute sessions were used in this study). In fact, when subjects were queried after the experiments, only the ones in the normal group who were consciously aware that there was a delay between CS and US were the ones who acquired the learning. None of the amnesics had such awareness, and none of them acquired trace conditioning. The interval between CS and US creates a less obvious association between the two stimuli and may thus make it more difficult to acquire the learning. In terms of brain structures, the conjoint activity of the hippocampus and the cortex (where sensory input is registered) may be the critical element that confers explicit knowledge.

So, is there any practical application here? Nobody has looked into this, but I draw several conclusions. First, learning may occur best and most readily under explicit conditions. That is, you will remember better if you can make it a point to be consciously aware of the relationships and associations among things to be remembered. Another possibility is that learning associations might work best if you can keep the new information going in your mind continuously in association with what you already know. It is not so much the intensity of the US that matters, but rather the temporal relationship of it to the CS. For example, suppose you wanted to condition lower blood pressure. First, you have to identify a short stimulus that lowers blood pressure, acting as a US. Such a stimulus might be looking at a restful picture (a beach, or mountains, or forest). Then, you pick another stimulus to serve as CS, preferably one that occurs frequently during the day. It might be looking at your pencil. The idea is to build up a conditioning relationship between looking at your pencil and looking at your favorite restful scene. Eventually, you would hope to lower blood pressure by looking at the pencil, which you have to do many times a day anyway. If this would work at all, the experiments mentioned above indicate that it would work best if your training trials used the delayed conditioning design. You would want to look at the pencil continuously and then look at the restful scene, preferably both in the same field of view.

Changes in the Brain During Consolidation

We should ask how does the brain retain information that has been learned. For short-term, working memory the answer seems intuitive. The same brain circuits and neuronal firing patterns that create the thought or the learning are the ones that are playing back the memory. But what about when sleep (or anesthesia) ensues, and those circuits and neuronal firing patterns are gone? How do we get the memory played back then? There must be some lasting changing in those circuits that enables a later reactivation of the firing patterns that constituted the learned event in the first place.

Consolidation often takes several hours, and the memory is vulnerable throughout this period. Why does it work so slowly? The answer probably lies in the fact that permanent memories have to have some permanent change in the molecular machinery of nerve cells, particularly at the synapses where neurons communicate with each other. Biochemical change takes a while. However, some very intense learning experiences can be consolidated almost immediately. Maybe in such cases, the neural response patterns persist through events or situations that would otherwise prevent consolidation.

To understand human memory consolidation, scientists realized that the place to begin a search for the engram was the hippocampus. Because the hippocampus seems essential for the initial deposit of consolidated memory, we could assume that at least part of the brain change associated with memory was associated with the hippocampus and its associated connections. However, such a system is very complex, and Eric Kandel[15] was among the first to realize that perhaps the basic mechanisms of memory formation ought to be sought in a simpler system. He chose to study learning in the giant marine snail, *Aplysia*. There were only about 20,000 neurons, compared to the many billions of neurons in humans. And *Aplysia* had simple behaviors, such as a gill withdrawal reflex in response to touching its siphon. This is an innate defense reaction that protects the delicate gills by withdrawing them into the protective shell anytime something potentially dangerous touches the siphon (which normally draws in water and food particles). This reflex could be conditioned, *a la* Pavlovian methods of pairing another stimulus with the touching of gills or siphon. For example, Kandel's team noted that if they delivered a noxious stimulus to the tail just before they touched the siphon, the withdrawal reflex became magnified. Thus, the animal learns to be hypersensitive. In humans, this would be akin to a conditioned fear response.

Under control conditions, only the siphon touch was used, and the

Catch It While You Can

duration of the response stayed about the same no matter when testing was done. If this reflex were preceded by four single shocks to the tail on the learning day (day 0), then on the next day touching the siphon caused a response that was about double the expected size. That is, *Aplysia* seemed to have learned and remembered the conditioned response. However, the size of this response fell off by the fourth day after initial learning. If more intense tail pinch were delivered, such as four trains of electrical pulses per day for four days, the response to siphon touch was greatly magnified on the first day and remained magnified as long as 7 days later.

Some sample results from their experiments illustrate the point.

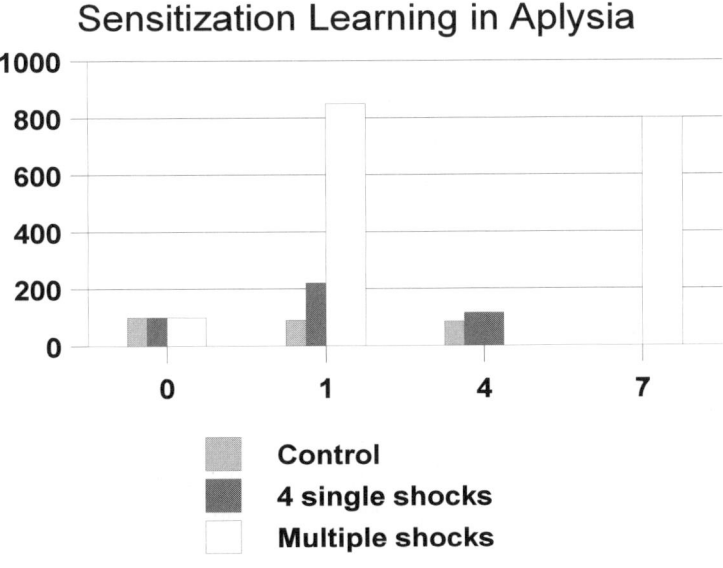

Approximate data obtained in Kandel's experiments where a noxious tail pinch was associated with touching the siphon. Amount of learning, shown on vertical axis, increases greatly in the mollusc when it has been sensitized by multiple stimuli.

Kandel and his colleagues over the years have shown the molecular basis for this memory representation. The neurotransmitter in the circuits involved is serotonin, and the sensitization memory can be produced by injecting serotonin onto the appropriate nerve cells. The serotonin activates proteins in the presynaptic neurons, and these proteins strengthen the synaptic connections because they enhance the release of serotonin. So, exposure of a synapse to serotonin induces certain genes to make the proteins that activate transmitter release.

Of course with other kinds of learning, other circuitry, and other species, other transmitters are likely to be involved. But the principle of synaptic strengthening by way of long-lasting change in the molecular mechanisms that release the transmitter seems established and may well apply generally. In fact the work done so far in mammals on the cells in the hippocampus, which uses different neurotransmitters, supports the idea that the molecular and cellular strategies used by *Aplysia* are conserved in mammals and apply to higher kinds of learning.

So, the upshot of all this is that intense and/or repeated learning experience can be made long-lasting because the synapses are actually changed chemically. In other words, "practice makes perfect."

Where Is Memory?

The studies thus far described suggest that memory is represented by changed (enhanced) synaptic capability. In simple systems, such as *Aplysia*, it is possible to know where those synapses are; that is, what parts of the circuitry "contain" the memory. But in higher animals it is not possible to identify with any great precision where the memory is.

The classic experiments of Karl Lashley provided the original basis for the idea that memory is distributed. He over-trained rats to run

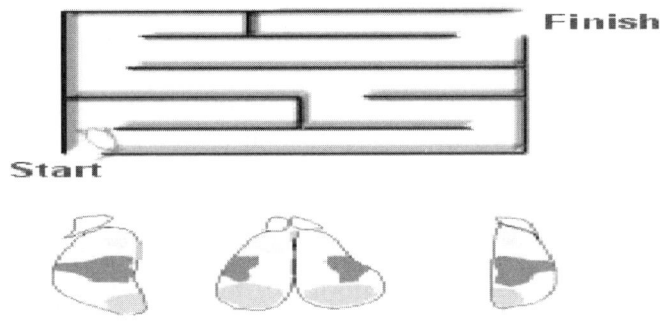

Diagram of the Karl Lashley experiments that attempted to locate where in the brain memory was located.

a maze and then, under anesthesia, removed different parts of their cortex. Some rats had the front part removed, others the back, still others the right or left side, and others with various combinations involving several locations. Then after they recovered from the surgery,

Lashley re-tested the rats in the same maze. Whether or not there was any decline in memory performance depended not on where the lesions had been made but on the total extent of lesioning. In other words, memory loss depended on the total amount of cortex that was removed, not on where the lesions were made.

A 1971 study of monkeys[16] tested the question of where short-term memories of an object were stored before consolidation. The study was conducted by Joaquin Fuster and Garrett Alexander at UCLA. Monkeys with recording electrodes in the prefrontal cortex were shown two identical objects, one on the right and one on the left. One of the pictures was "baited" with a piece of apple. The images were then hidden for up to 60 seconds. Monkeys could reach for the apple if they remembered which one had been baited. Neuronal activity increased in one circular zone in the prefrontal cortex while monkeys were waiting between presentations, presumably reflecting the coding for which picture had the bait. Similar results were obtained in the early 1970s by Kisou Kubota and Hiroaki Niki at Kyoto University in Japan. Prefrontal activity increased in their monkeys while they performed a slightly different recall task.

These pioneering experiments were not appreciated widely until 1989 when Patricia Goldman-Rakic[17], Shintaro Shunahashi, and Charles Bruce at Yale University reproduced the early study, except that they controlled for the possibility that the frontal neurons were active simply because the eyes were staring at the baited target. This was accomplished by training monkeys to maintain eye fixation on the center of a TV screen and to note the location of flashed targets by their peripheral vision. After a several-second delay, monkeys revealed their working memory by moving the eyes to the spot where the target had been flashed. During the delay interval, when eyes were fixated on the central spot, the same set of prefrontal neurons that had been identified by the UCLA and Kyota teams became activated. Moreover, different cells became activated, depending on the spatial location of the image flash.

In the last two decades, a wide variety of studies have shown that working memory requires the interaction of multiple areas of the brain, in particular multiple areas in the cerebral cortex. If any one area is more important than others, it would have to be the prefrontal cortex, the anterior-most part lying just behind the forehead that has long been known as a center for higher mental functions. Some of the distributed processing arises out of the differing sources of information that the brain receives. Visual information, for example, might be routed through a visual buffer, auditory information through an auditory buffer, and so on. Some neuroscientists think that the prefrontal cortex acts to orchestrate working memory processes in other parts of the brain.

Obviously, prefrontal neurons have to get visual information from the visual cortex. There is ample evidence to show that functional connections do exist. Working memory fails for such visually based tasks if the prefrontal cortex is destroyed. The role normally played by prefrontal cortex is not clear. It may be acting as an executive agent for working memory or more likely an integrating coordinator of activity with circuits distributed in the prefrontal cortex, visual cortex, and perhaps elsewhere, depending on the contextual meaning of the stimulus.

In the mid 1990s non-invasive imaging techniques became available that allowed tests of these issues in humans. Using the so-called PET scan (positron emission tomography), Susan Courtney and colleagues at the National Institute of Mental Health found evidence for more complex divisions of labor in humans.[18] They observed that working memories for facial features and locations are processed in separate regions of the prefrontal cortex and also in separate sensory areas. Also during this period, John Jonides and colleagues of the University of Michigan found PET scan evidence for different locations of spatial and verbal working memory[19]. Remembering the spatial location of three dots, for example, was associated with increased brain activity over the prefrontal cortex and a few other areas on the right side of the brain. But the task of recalling four alphabetic characters was associated with activity mostly on the left side, including the speech centers which are also on the left side. So, we see now that different brain areas participate in working memory depending on whether it involves an object, and object's location in space, or its linguistic significance. At least part of the prefrontal cortex always seems to be involved.

How activated the prefrontal area is seems to depend on how much information has to be held in working memory. Maybe part of its job is to hold the remembered information on-line while it is being coordinated via the other cortical connections and to sustain the information long enough for the formation of permanent memory.

Practice, Practice, Practice

We all know that practice (rehearsal) helps memory. Rehearsal promotes consolidation and blocks out disruptive thoughts and stimuli during the critical memory consolidation period.

Experiments in animals have shown that during learning, neural responses decrease as the learning experience is repeated. This repetition suppression could reflect a progressive optimization of memory formation process. That is, the neurons don't have to work so hard, because they are making progress in encoding the information to be remembered.

Repetition suppression during rehearsal has been recently demonstrated in brain imaging studies.[20] The investigators used functional magnetic imaging (fMRI), which is like regular MRI except that the scans and computations proceed much more rapidly. Two hypotheses were tested: 1) that repeated stimulus presentation during learning will lead to progressively reduced responsiveness of neural tissue, and 2) that at the same time connectivity in certain cortical systems would increase.

The learning task consisted of recalling the association between 10 simple line drawings of real-world objects and their locations on a screen. The stimulus had two attributes, stimulus location and identity, which are known from other studies to be processed in different regions of the cortex. The connectivity between these two cortical areas was assessed by so-called "path analysis," which evaluated correlations of activity among the various cortical regions.

The fMRI pictures showed that as subjects learned the association between a drawing and its location on the screen, initial levels of activation became progressively smaller in several cortical regions in the ventral and dorsal visual pathway. One way to interpret this is that as learning occurs, the brain areas involved don't have to work so hard, because they are working together, sharing the work load and decreasing the extent of brain tissue that has to be engaged in the task. The point seems to be that rehearsal enables the brain to work more efficiently at creating long-term memories.

One of the main reasons that practice is necessary is that when a memory is recalled, the trace may have to re-consolidate, during which time it can be susceptible to disruption. Whether or not disruption occurs depends on how robust the original learning was and of course on what other events may happen during the rehearsal. Experiments by Mark Eisenberg and colleagues involving conditioned taste aversion in rats and aversive conditioning in fish show that the stability of retrieved memory depends on the behavior controlled by that memory.[21] This study was focused on extinction, that is, the disappearance of a learned behavior after removing the associations that enabled the original learning. For example, fish become conditioned to swim away when they see a light flash because they have been trained by a mild electric shock after the light flash. Then, if the mild shock is eliminated, the fish soon stop responding to the light. The aversive behavior is extinguished. For many decades scientists thought this was just simple passive forgetting or unlearning. Now, it appears that extinction is an active process. The Eisenberg group and others have shown that extinction can be disrupted by such treatments as injection of protein synthesis inhibitors or anesthesia given immediately after retrieval. In other words, extinction requires a fully functional brain. The brain learns to forget.

One big surprise in their study was the observation that the vulnerability of extinction processes was inversely related to the intensity of original training. That is, when original learning is robust, the extinction is more readily blocked by brain disruptors such as protein synthesis inhibitors or anesthesia. What is the practical implication? Well, we don't know, because this finding is new and follow-up has not yet occurred. But such a phenomenon might explain the well-known observation that cramming for an quiz may work for that test, but leaves the student with little useful memory months later for the final exam. Cramming is an intense learning experience, and the extinction processes that ensue after the test could be very vulnerable to the inevitable distractions, new learning, emotional upheavals, and other events that occur immediately after recall for the test. The corollary of this idea is that slow and steady preparation for a quiz, spread out over days, may be more likely to lead to memory that does not extinguish and are available for recall at final exam time.

* * * * *

Memory of a learned event begins as temporary storage. While still in this "scratch pad" storage form, the memory is very susceptible to erasure by such influences as distractions, drugs, or new learning experiences. Consolidating the learned experiences into more permanent form is influenced by many things. Physiological influences include age (the very young and the very old have more problems with consolidation), sex hormones, stress hormones (see later chapter), drugs, sleep (see later chapter), other demands placed on the working memory, such as assorted new stimuli and other new learning experiences. As memory consolidates, it makes lasting changes in connections among neurons. Thus, what you experience and learn becomes a part of who you are.

Key Ideas

1. Consolidation of memories is both time- and event-dependent. It takes a certain amount of *uninterrupted* time after a learning event to consolidate memory of it. The intensity of a learning event influences the ease with which it can be remembered.

2. For optimal consolidation, don't let anything distract or interfere with your thoughts about the learning material. The longer you can delay the distraction, the better.

3. Learning changes the anatomy and biochemistry of the pathways involved. In other words, learning changes the brain and thus who you are. Take care with what you let your brain learn. "Garbage in, garbage out."

4. Rehearse what is to be learned, especially soon after being presented with the information.

5. Post-menopausal women, and women who have had an ovario-hysterectomy, should take estrogen replacement therapy to have normal memory consolidation function. [Of course there are more compelling *medical* reasons to take hormonal replacement therapy].

6. Pre-pubertal children may not form new memories as well as conventional wisdom has led us to believe. Educational systems should take that into account. What is easy for the teacher to remember may not be so easy for children to

remember. The middle school years, when hormones begin to surge, are the very years when children can discover a learning capacity they did not know they had (assuming that the *other* effects of sex hormones do not obscure this revelation).

7. Fear interferes with learning, even one-trial and imprinting-like learning.

8. Life-long changes can result from certain imprinting-like effects in humans, such as mother-infant bonding.

9. Consolidation of memories requires spaced repetition (rehearsal). Rehearsing is most effective when multiple senses are used to reinforce each other.

10. Forgetting is most pronounced for items that have little value or meaning.

11. Motor memories consolidate best if you only try to learn in small stages, one thing at a time.

12. Working memory correlates highly with intelligence. We don't know if improving working memory can cause intelligence to increase, but it is a possibility.

13. Information to be memorized is best remembered if that information is important. If it does not seem very important, and you still need to remember it anyway, contrive reasons and emotions to assign importance to the information.

14. Consolidation occurs best under explicit conditions, where you are consciously aware of what you are trying to remember and its associated cues.

15. During rehearsal of newly acquired learning, distracting influences can interfere with the re-consolidating processes that occur during rehearsal.

16. Intense learning is much more likely to be remembered long-term if the learning is spread out, rather than crammed into short study periods.

Sources:

1. Werheid, K., *et al.* 2002. The adaptive digit ordering test. Clinical application, reliability, and validity of a verbal working memory test. Arch. Clin. Neuropsychol. 17: 547-565.

2. Klemm, W. R. 1969. ECS effects on one-trial avoidance behavior in intact and gonadectomized male rats. Communications in Behavioral Biology. 4: 55-58

3. Klemm, W. R. 1969. ECS and estrous cycle interactions in one-trial avoidance behavior of rats. Communications in Behavioral Biology. 4: 59-65

4. Antonova, I. *et al.* Rapid increase in clusters of presynaptilc proteins at onset of long-lasting potentiation. Science. 294:1547-1550.

5. Hoffman, H. S., and DePaulo, P. 1977. Behavioral control by an imprinting stimulus. American Scientist. 65; 58-66.

6. Müller, G. E., and Pilzecker, A. 1900. Z. Psychol. 1: 1.

7. McGaugh, J. L. 2000. Memory- a century of consolidation. Science. 14: 248-251.

8. Maki, W. S., *et al.* 1984. Spatial memory over long retention intervals: nonmemorial factors are not necessary for accurate performance on the radial-arm maze by rats. Behav. Neural Biol. 41: 1-6.

9. Shadmelu, R., and Brashers-Krug, T. 1997. Functional stages in the formation of human long-term motor memory. J. Neuroscience. 17: 409-419.

10. Wickelgren, I. 2001. Getting a grasp on working memory. Science. 275: 1580-1582.

11. Carpenter, P. A., Just, M. A., and Shell, P. 1990. What one intelligence test measures: a theoretical account of the processing in the Raven Progressive Matrices Test. Psychol. Rev. 97: 404-431.

12. Miller, G. A. 1956. The magical number seven, plus or minus two. Some limits on our capacity for processing information. Psychol. Rev. 63: 81-97.

13. Glassman, R. B., Leniek, K. M., and Haegerich, T. M. 1998. Human working memory is 7 ± 2 in a radial maze with distracting interruption: possible implication for neural mechanisms of declarative and implicit long-term memory. Brain Res. Bull. 47: 249-256.

14. Clark, R. E., and Squire, L. R. 1998. Classical conditioning and brain systems: the role of awareness. Science 280: 77-81.

15. Essay adapted from the author's Nobel Prize address. Kandel, E. R. 2001. The molecular biology of memory storage: a dialogue between genes and synapses. Science. 294: 1030-1038.

16. Fuster, J. M. 1995. Memory in the cerebral cortex: an empirical approach to neural networks in the human and nonhuman primate. M.I.T. Press, Cambridge, Mass.

17. Goldman-Rakic, P. S. 1996. Regional and cellular fractionationn of working memory. Proc. Nat. Acad. Sci. 93: 13473.

18. Courtney, S. M., Ungerleider, L. G., Keil, K., and Haxby, J. V. 1997. Transient and sustained activity in a distributed neural system for human working memory. Nature. 386: 559-560.

19. Jonides, J. et al. 1996. Verbal and spatial working memory in humans. The Psychology of Learning and Motivation. 35: 43.

20. Büchel, C. Coull, J. T., Friston, K. J. 1999. The predictive value of changes in effective connecting for human learning. Science. 283 1538-1541.

21. Eisenberg, M., Kobilo, T., Berman, D. E., and Dudai, Y. 2003. Stability of retrieved memory: inverse correlation with trace dominance. Science. 301: 1102-1104.

Catch It While You Can

We Get Emotional About Our Memories - and It Creates Business for Psychiatrists

- If You Want To, You Will
- Freudian Slip
- Speaking of Sex
- Nervous Nellie Never Remembers Well
- Taking Anxiety Too Far: Stress
- Violence Damages Your Memory Too
- Feeling Bad & Remembering Poorly
- Exercise Lifts Our Spirits and Our Memory
- Happy Memories Lead to Comfort Foods ...and More
- Our Gut Reaction Is To Remember
- Drug Abuse

The extent to which emotional upsets can interfere with mental life is no news to teachers. Students who are anxious, angry, or depressed don't learn; people who are caught in these states do not take in information efficiently or deal with it well.

- Daniel Goleman,
Emotional Intelligence

We Get Emotional About Our Memories

Emotions and memory go together. They are even processed in the same parts of the brain. Feelings can promote or interfere with memory. If feelings interfere with memory, changing your feelings will be rewarded with better memory.

I could begin this chapter by illustrating with stories from my childhood, but I don't remember that much about my childhood. What I do remember are the events that were associated with profound emotions, such as: the two fist fights I won; watching the gamecocks that I helped my dad raise peck each other in cock fights; steering my dad's car as I sat on his lap driving from Naples to Miami through the Everglades; embarrassing myself while learning to ride my new bike by driving it into the nearest telephone pole; trying to become "teacher's pet" of a teacher I had a crush on, and so on. I may have repressed a lot of other memories that were too unpleasant, perhaps for example, the fights I *lost*.

Well, the point is that emotion often has profound effects on memory, making it more likely that the event will be remembered, but perhaps distorted or repressed.

If You Want To, You Will

Sales people are usually pretty good at remembering names. Is that because people who are good at remembering names decide to become salespeople? More likely, I think, sales people remember names well because they NEED to. It is part of their job, their bread and butter. To most of us, the most important words in the English language are our own names. We therefore appreciate and react positively to near strangers who remember our name.

So, if you are motivated to learn, you are much more likely to succeed, whether that learning involves people's names, foreign languages, mathematic equations, or whatever. But where does motivation come from?

At the brain level, motivation comes from basic drive states of seeking pleasure and avoiding pain or distress. I remember talking to the famous James Olds when he visited my lab. Dr. Olds had made his discoveries at the U. of Michigan and had recently moved to Cal Tech. He was on a speaking tour for Sigma Xi, The Scientific Research Society, and I was lucky enough to get him to spend a little time in my lab after his talk. I asked him how he got the original idea that caused him to test for the existence of a "pleasure center" in the brain. The answer is not to be found in his published papers, because it seems so unscientific.

He confided that he was stimulating rats through electrodes implanted in the brain to study another phenomenon. I forget now what it was, but it had nothing to do with emotions. Anyway, one day he had a rat that when it was stimulated "seemed to like it." The rat would stop whatever he was doing and look around as if trying to figure out where the stimulation came from. Then Olds would stimulate some more and soon saw that the rat started going to the area of the open field where he remembered getting the stimulation. It was if he had learned an association between the stimulation and the place where he got it. Because he kept seeking out that place, Olds correctly assumed that the stimulation was deemed desirable, motivating the rat to seek stimulation.

Because other rats had not shown this behavior, Olds assumed that the electrode was accidentally placed in an unintended brain area. Placing electrodes in a rat's brain is done under anesthesia, when the rat's head is held in a metal frame, and micromanipulators determine the anterior-posterior plane, midline-lateral plane, and the depth to which the electrode needs to be lowered. The error can be as much as one millimeter or more in each plane. Thus, it is not surprising that in a brain as small as that of a rat, that electrodes sometimes end up in the wrong place. Olds was anxious to know where this misplaced electrode was. He sacrificed the rat and examined the brain histologically, revealing that the electrode was in the lateral part of the hypothalamus. The hypothalamus is located at the base of the brain, just above the pituitary gland.

The more formal test for a possible "pleasure center" was soon pursued. Olds now rigged rats with electrodes deliberately placed in the lateral hypothalamus and trained them to press levers. But instead of pressing levers to get a food reward, each lever press brought the rats a mild electrical stimulation through the implanted electrode. Rats were highly motivated to learn this association and worked like demons to keep stimulating their brain. Some rats would work themselves to exhaustion.

As a control test, Olds repeated these experiments in other rats with electrodes in other locations. No such positive stimulus-seeking was seen. In fact, other investigators using similar methods found an aversion area in the brainstem, in which stimulation was apparently unpleasant. Rats not only refused to work for such stimulation, they could also be trained to lever press to avoid such stimulation.

So, how do we relate this to memory? The experiments tell us that there are brain systems that cause us to seek pleasure or avoid displeasure (by the way, these electrical stimulation experiments have been replicated in conscious humans). The seeking and avoiding drives create motivation. Motivation influences how much effort we expend to learn and remember.

One group of researchers has formally tested this idea.[1] They tested the role of motivation on working memory. Volunteers performed working memory tasks of different levels of complexity. The tasks were randomly associated with different degrees of reward. The researchers wanted to see if brain imaging measurements would show if motivation affected the selective activation of brain areas. The simple working memory tasks activated the well-known working memory areas in the dorsolateral prefrontal cortex. When tasks were made more difficult, lateral frontal areas also became active. When high rewards were associated with the tasks, the working memory areas were activated more intensely, and new areas, such as the cingulate cortex, were recruited into activity. At the same time, some other areas became *less* activated, in direct correlation with increased task difficulty and high reward. The scientists could only speculate on the reason for these changes. The idea they advanced is that high reward shuts down certain cortical areas that otherwise were limiting optimal performance by restricting the amount of cortex that could participate in working memory tasks. Recall our earlier point that memory is distributed in many parts of the brain. Motivation seems to facilitate recruiting of the key memory-processing brain areas into performing the task.

Reward is also important for memory in a way that is more direct than merely making us more motivated. Animal studies show that rewarding the desired memory recall actually strengthens the relationship between stimulus and learned response. Thus, I assume that human learning can be enhanced by rewarding correct recall. This may be one reason why good students tend to remain good students. They have learned to provide themselves with intrinsic rewards for good performance. Poor students often do not find learning rewarding in and of itself.

Freudian Slip

Sigmund Freud made a living and became famous by showing that repressed memories, buried deep within the subconscious, can cause emotional disorders. We all carry within us our little child, whose memories, conscious and repressed and often distorted, feed our emotions even into old age. These memories influence our belief systems and ways of thinking. What Freud missed, however, was how important emotions are to learning and memory.

Teachers have long understood that emotions have profound effects on children's ability to learn. But the entire educational system needs to be re-engineered to capitalize on this intuitive understanding. One educational fad today is the self-esteem movement. While self-esteem is important for learning, it is a limited facet of the range of emotions that affect learning Teachers at all levels know from experience that motivation is the most important requirement for learning. Unfortunately, too many children never get enough positive reinforcement as they go through learning processes. "I can't do this" and "I'm not good at this" are common statements that turned-off students make. They don't learn, because they don't even try. They don't try, because they have come to expect failure. Such thoughts arise out of disturbed emotions involving confusion, frustration, and lack of confidence. In my view, we will never successfully reform public school education until we have helped students to overcome the obstacles created by bad attitudes and emotions. Educational reform efforts have emphasized conveying a great deal of information and facts and put more emphasis on glitzy presentations via television and computers. But little has been accomplished in improving the learning process. When teachers present material to the class, it is usually in a polished, "spoon feeding" form that omits the natural steps of making mistakes (feeling confused), recovering from them (overcoming frustration), objectively assessing what went wrong (not becoming dispirited), and starting over again. Thus, students are not given the chance to experience and learn healthy emotional responses to learning that come from victory over confusion, frustration, and loss of spirit and enthusiasm. Learning naturally involves failure and a host of associated emotional responses. Effective learners have core emotional competencies that assist learning. One underused use of computers is to use them as learning "companions" that stimulate the child's motivation for learning with questions or feedback and by detecting and responding to the child's emotional reactions, such as signs of frustration and boredom or pleasure. A companion is not a tutor that knows all the answers, but a friend who helps learning to occur. Kids are motivated by learning success to seek the positive reinforcement of more learning success.

So the point is that teachers need to put more emphasis on teaching students how to cultivate their emotions in ways that nurture learning. These positive emotions include a sense of awe, wonder, excitement, hopefulness, personal satisfaction and confidence. What passes for educational reform these days is doomed to failure until we find ways to change the attitudes and emotions of students.

A close association between emotions and memories should not be surprising. Both are regulated by the same parts of the brain, collectively called the limbic system. The brain areas comprising this system are intimately interconnected. One part, the hippocampus, is needed to consolidate memories for new learning. Another part, the amygdala, is especially involved in emotions. Another part, the hypothalamus, controls our viscera and is involved whenever emotions are "read out" into the viscera in such forms as sweaty palms, dilated pupils, ulcers, and high blood pressure.

Speaking of Sex

It is hard to speak of Freud without speaking of sex. Freud had little to say about sex and memory, other than repression of memories involving sex. What we want to stress here is that sexual hormones do influence memory.

Common experience teaches us that sex hormones can influence memory. The confusion in menopausal women comes to mind; taking estrogen pills quickly restores such women back to the normal memory function. Lack of estrogen also has an indirect effect on memories by causing depression. Rebecca Rupp reviews some of the research in her book, *Committed to Memory*[2]. One study of post-menopausal women, showed an impaired recall 30 minutes after short prose selections. When they were put on estrogen replacement therapy, they did markedly better. Another study showed that estrogen takers performed slightly better on memorizing names and word lists. Why estrogen works is probably related to the fact that it stimulates growth of neuronal junctions by promoting the release of the protein called nerve growth factor. But estrogen has a more direct neurochemical effect. Many neurons in the brain have receptors for estrogen. When such receptors are bound by estrogen, it affects the ability of these neurons to release their neurotransmitters and function in the normal way.

Somewhere in their 40s or 50s women go through menopause. They (and their husbands) know that this time often messes up the brain. The women feel mentally fuzzy, perhaps irritable, can't concentrate, and memory becomes unreliable. The sudden drop in estrogen is the cause. Gradually the brain adjusts to this new hormonal environment, and if hormone replacement therapy is provided, the brain and its memory recover quickly.

A similar phenomenon occurs in older men. In a study of healthy older men,[3] 25 men were given 100 mg injections of testosterone for six weeks. The men showed improvements in spatial memory (recalling a walking route and recalling building blocks in a pattern they saw earlier) and in verbal memory (recalling stories). Maybe hairy knuckles and male pattern baldness signal men who have above-average memory.

Unfortunately, both estrogen and testosterone have serious side effects (including promoting cancer). People with normal sex hormone levels should not take sex hormone medication.

Nervous Nellie Never Remembers Well

We all know people who claim they are not good test takers, because they get so anxious that they can't remember things that they really know. There may be an element of face-saving here, but it is true that too much anxiety can interfere with memory. Worse yet, this is a learned behavior that gets reinforced every time it occurs.[4] In other words, our emotions can be conditioned, much as Pavlov's dogs. Such conditioning can be created for a variety of emotions: anxiety, stress, depression. The good news is that repeated association of rewarding events helps us to learn positive emotions, such as self-esteem or happiness.

Anxiety is a form of fear. Fear is fundamental to human existence. Our primitive ancestors could not have survived the rigors of a hostile world without a healthy daily dose of fear - and they had to remember and learn from fearful experiences. It is therefore no accident that the evolution of animal and human brains linked together the functions of fear and memory in the same neural structures, in particular the hippocampus and the amygdala and the structures with which they connect. As mentioned in many places in this book, the hippocampus has a central role in converting temporary memories into permanent ones. The amygdala is a pair of grape-size clusters of neurons buried deep under the temporal cortex that lies adjacent to our temples. Impaired amygdala function, independent of hippocampal damage, can also impair memory. But the amygdala's most important role is to subconsciously process fear and to make fearful things more memorable. The amygdala also perpetuates, unfortunately, irrational fears and phobias. Fear can be profound and debilitating. All sensory inputs pass through the amgydala. For instance, odor inputs go directly to the amygdala and nowhere else. No doubt that is why odors are so inextricably linked with emotional reactions.

Although anxiety is reduced by tranquilizers and certain other drugs, we have pointed out in this book's chapter on attention that such drugs promote amnesia, whether the drugs are taken just before or just after the learning event. One research group conducted a formal test of the hypothesis that at least low-level anxiety might be good for memory.[5] They performed their experiments on rats, which they had pre-selected into three test groups, based on the anxiety levels they showed in an anxiety test. The test of anxiety was to put them on an elevated maze, part of which had no walls. The most anxious rats avoided the open arms of the maze, where they probably feared falling off, and spent most of their time in the protected area with walls. Some rats were just the opposite and apparently loved the adventure of exploring out on the more dangerous maze arms that had no walls.

There were two learning tasks. One was a passive avoidance task where the rat had to remember not to leave a brightly lit chamber to enter a dark chamber where a foot shock would be delivered. Normally, rats prefer darkness, but not when it is associated with foot shock. The other learning task was a two-way avoidance task in which the rat had to leave whatever side of the chamber it was in whenever a warning sounded. Failure to leave right away would result in foot shock. What the experimenters observed when they re-tested the rats after the learning experience for their ability to remember is shown below.

A similar, though less pronounced, effect was seen in the two-way avoidance task, where anxious rats remembered better than non-anxious ones.

After they finished the behavioral studies, the investigators sacrificed the rats and examined their brains for possible differences in proteins that bind benzodiazepine anti-anxiety drugs. In the hippocampus (but not the amygdala), the anxious rats had more binding proteins than did non-anxious rats. Other investigators had reported that these binding proteins adapt in response to stressful situations. Apparently, anxious rats produce more binding proteins because they are more stressed than more mellow, non-anxious rats.

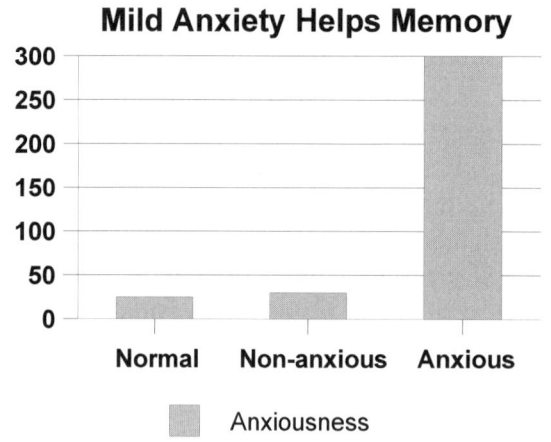

Time (in seconds) that rats stayed in the safe side of the chamber in a passive avoidance memory task. Note that the best memory was seen in rats that had been pre-selected for their anxiousness.

Interpreting these results is not entirely straightforward. First, anxious rats would have been most likely to be stressed in this learning situation. Stress induces the release of cortisone-like compounds from the adrenal gland, and the temporary release of these steroids could be the direct cause of the improved memory. The increased stress in anxious rats is manifested by their making more binding receptors for their endogenous "tranquilizer," an as yet undiscovered natural chemical that is mimicked by benzodiazepine tranquilizers. Adrenal hormones can make rats more attentive, which would magnify the registration of the learning cues.

The other interpretation problem is that only one level of anxiety and stress condition was involved. Clearly, memory performance could be made worse by too much anxiety and stress. Then there is the question of how transferrable this finding is to humans. Anecdotally, humans do seem to perform better when under a level of stress with which they can cope.

The enhanced memory of moderately stressed, hyperalert humans, may result largely from the release of adrenalin that occurs in such states. Many experiments have shown that post-training injection of adrenalin enhances memory in a variety of learning tasks, both positive and negative. Likewise, single post-training injections of other stress-related hormones, such as ACTH, vasopressin, and cortisone, can improve memory.[6]

Chronic stress is another matter. Continual release of adrenal stress hormones has been shown to kill neurons, particularly neurons in the key memory center of the hippocampus. These hormones, called corticosteroids, include such commonly used drugs as cortisone and hydrocortisone. They are taken orally or by injection for severe allergies and a variety of other conditions.

One study[7] used test conditions similar to clinical dosage regimens to answer the question, "Do these steroids interfere with memory?" They compared the effects of a single dose versus repeated doses in adult humans. Placebo-controlled treatment with the steroid was given at 2300 hr for four consecutive days (0.5, 1, 1, 1 mg, respectively). Plasma sampling (0800 and 1600 hr) and memory testing (1600 hr) were performed on study days 0 (baseline), 1, and 4, and 7 days after treatment. Memory testing consisted of a paragraph recall task. In the steroid-treatment group, recall became impaired by the 7th post-treatment day, whereas in the placebo group, recall progressively improved due to the practice effect.

Early childhood stress is well known to cause multiple changes in intellectual capability and in responsiveness to stress that last into adulthood. This is not the place to go into all that literature, but it should come as no surprise that early childhood experiences might influence memory. One recent experiment[8] on neonatal rats is particularly interesting because it relates to some things we have said about habituation (learning to unlearn) and about false memory, as I discuss in the chapter "Memories That Lie." In this experiment, young adult rats were habituated to social exposure. That is, a pair of rats, unknown to each other, were placed in a fresh neutral cage in four 5 minute sessions spread out over two days. Sniffing each other was the index of learning to recognize each other. When a rat became socially habituated, it stopped sniffing the other rat. Normal rats developed a habituation that typically lasted less than two hours. To make sure that they were not socially or olfactorily fatigued, such habituated rats were then exposed to yet another unfamiliar rat, whereupon vigorous sniffing ensued.

One group of rats was given mild novel stimulation every day when they were neonatal pups. During the first three weeks of their life, they were gently placed in a novel cage with fresh bedding for 3 minutes per day. Control rats were physically handled to the same extent, but were not placed in a novel cage. The social recognition testing did not begin until the rats became young adults.

When tested for social recognition, the control rats developed habituation, which lasted for about 2 hours or less. The rats that had been stimulated as pups also developed habituation, but theirs lasted for at least 24 hours. Habituation is an active learning process of learning to unlearn. Here we see that handled rats do this better than normal controls. They remembered the rat partner to which they had been exposed much longer than control rats. There is also a relationship to stress. The rats handled as pups apparently learned to accommodate to stimuli that otherwise might be stressful. As adults, the handled rats had significantly reduced levels of their stress hormone (which in rats is coriticosterone). Thus, this kind of early exposure to mild stress actually helped rats cope with stress as adults and helped them to remember under conditions that would have otherwise stressful and memory impairing.

The implications for humans seem clear. Newborn babies should receive novel stimuli under non-threatening conditions. The effects may last a lifetime. People have suspected this possibility for a long time, which is why people hang mobiles and other visual stimuli over cribs. Now there is some solid science supporting the idea. But maybe it would be better to take the baby to the stimuli rather than the stimuli to the baby. That is, move the baby out of the crib into a new place several times a day after birth.

Violence Damages Your Memory Too

The TV producers are shooting themselves in the foot by putting so much violence in the programs. It turns out that violence makes it more difficult for viewers to remember the commercials![9]

Psychologist Brad J. Bushman of Iowa State University found after conducting three experiments that watching violent television programs can impair a person's ability to remember what is being advertised during the commercials. The first experiment tested 200 students (100 male and 100 female) for their ability to recall the brand names of items from two commercials that advertised for Krazy Glue and Wisk laundry detergent after watching a violent or nonviolent film clip. Both types of film clips did not differ in pre-test measures of self-reported arousal (exciting, arousing and/or boring) and measures of physiological arousal (blood pressure and heart rate). Those who watched the violent clips recalled fewer brand names and commercial message details than did those who watched the nonviolent clips.

The second experiment tested another 200 students (100 men and 100 women) on brand recall, commercial message details and visual recognition of the brand marketed in the commercial. Dr. Bushman explained the study this way: "These students were also given a distractor task where they had to recall other glue and detergent brands immediately after watching a violent or nonviolent video. The results match those of the first experiment. Those watching the violent videotape performed more poorly on recalling the brands, remembering the commercial messages and visually recognizing the brands from the slides."

"Finally, in the third experiment, 320 students (160 men and 160 women) reported their moods after watching four videotapes to determine whether anger obstructed their ability to remember the content of the commercials," said Dr. Bushman. After viewing either violent or nonviolent videotapes, the students completed a mood form that assessed their anger and positive emotions (alertness, determination and enthusiasm).

I can't say for certain why watching violence impairs memory. But we should not be surprised either. Participating vicariously in violence stirs strong emotions, such as anger and fear. Emotions are governed by the same part of the brain, the limbic system, as is the formation of declarative memories. The message to advertisers is to pay attention to the potential emotional impact of the shows that they sponsor.

Taking Anxiety Too Far - Stress

When anxiety becomes too intense and persistent, the level of stress becomes debilitating in many ways. There are many negative effects on the adrenal gland and its production of hormones that are designed to cope with stress. But beyond that, the brain is also affected. Everyone has probably had some kind of traumatic experience that caused hyyper-arousal and nervousness. The question arises about whether there are lasting effects. Is learned nervousness remembered, especially remembered at some unconscious level long after the conscious memory is lost? In some recent experiments in mice, aimed at simulating "post-traumatic stress syndrome," Hermona Soreq and colleagues in Israel report that even brief stress can affect the brain for many weeks thereafter[10]. The experimenters used forced swimming as a stressor; when you toss a mouse into a tub of water, it knows that it must swim or drown. Before introducing the swim test, they injected mice with chemicals that inhibited a major enzyme known as, acetylcholinesterase, that normally breaks down the acetylcholine. Comparison groups were injected with the stress hormone, cortisol. Within minutes after even a rather short period of swimming stress, the brain's electrical activity indicated hyperactivity. The hyperactivity lasted for weeks.

"Post traumatic stress disorder" (PTSD) is a well-known phenomenon of depression and anxiety triggered by horrific events such as rape or war. A definitive book has recently been written by Richard McNally, called *Remembering Trauma*,[11] that reviews the various studies of memory effects of PTSD. Many people think that memory of horrific events is driven underground, repressed, only to surface at some later time, such as during psychotherapy or a later stress event that provides sensory cues that remind one of the original stress. McNally asserts that most such claims of repressed memory are little more than psychiatric folklore that is not supported by empirical evidence. That is not to say the PTSD does not affect the ability to form new memories.

Too much stress is bad for you. The effects can be long lasting and cumulative, and even lead to the post-traumatic stress syndrome symptoms of high anxiety, nightmares, and flashbacks. But what has this got to do with memory? You might argue, along the lines I have already used, that alertness and even anxiety can promote the focus and concentration that would actually enhance memory. The problem is that excessive stress or the cortisol that is released by it, actually kills neurons. Worse yet, it kills neurons in the most important memory area of the brain, the hippocampus.

Feeling Bad and Remembering Badly

Remember the earlier example of how poorly many people remembered the details of the 9-11 terrorist attack on the World Trade Center? Notably, they remembered the disaster well - it is now indelibly stamped on everyone's memory. But the associated details were not remembered well.

A classic experiment has documented the principle that unpleasant events are themselves remembered well, but not their associated events[12]. In this study, young adults were first required to remember a paired list of 10 pairs. The first member of the pair was a string of nonsense syllables, each of which was paired with a real word (see List 1 in example below). Subjects were tested on this list until it was mastered. At this point, a second list of single words was presented (see List 2 below). These words were implicitly linked to the words in list one, but the implicit linking word was never presented. An example is shown below:

List 1	Implicit Linking Word	List 2
CEF - stem	flower	smell
DAX - memory	mind	brain
YOV - soldier	army	navy

Three of the words in List 2 were randomly selected to be paired with delivery of electric shock to the fingers of the subjects. Subjects had to learn which three out of the 10 words were associated with electric shock. Later, when re-tested with the List 1, memory was poor for those List 2 words that had originally been associated with finger shock. In other words, the unpleasant event itself (which List 2 words came with finger shock) was remembered very well, presumably because that was a much more intense and attention-getting experience. However, longer-term memory was disrupted for items that had been associated with the unpleasant event.

Sadness and depression also seem to interfere with memory. A team of researchers at the University of Michigan School of Nursing has reported a study that shows that difficulties with short-term memory and concentration can be signs of clinical depression. The chief investigators, Reg Williams and colleagues[13] had noticed that depressed patients often complained of poor memory and inability to concentrate. One patient could even predict her own bouts of depression when she started making errors in her checkbook. The research is based on a series of computer-based and written tests. The tests measured the ability to focus on a task at hand and short-term memory, the ability to recall an event that happened within two minutes.

The researchers studied 52 people over a 10-week period. There were 25 people in the group diagnosed with depression and 27 in a comparison group of people without depression. They took five written tests and six computerized tests that were given three times over the course of the study.

People in the depressed group performed more poorly on a task of balancing a checkbook. The depressed group was undergoing drug therapy and counseling at the time, and their scores on the checkbook balancing task reached the same level as controls at the end of therapy. So it would appear that being depressed affects your ability to think and remember.

In another study,[14] J. M. Strang and colleagues compared five measures of working memory ability in 26 patients diagnosed with "Gulf War Syndrome," 55 clinically depressed patients, and 40 healthy controls. Both the GWS and depressed patients had an equal degree of impairment on digit span ability and the ability to recite months of the year backwards. Depressed patients had even greater impairment than the other two groups in the other three measures of working memory.

Yet another study has confirmed the relationship between depression and poor memory.[15] This study was especially useful because it also examined the role of anxiety. In their test of memory performance in 3,999 Vietnam-era veterans, those with clinical diagnoses of depression (without anxiety) had impaired immediate recall of new information. However, long-term retention and recall were not impaired. Veterans whose neuropsychological tests showed them to have high levels of anxiety were impaired on all aspects of memory tested: immediate recall, total amount of information acquired, longer term retention, and retrieval. The memory impairment of veterans with depression was magnified if those veterans were also chronically anxious.

Depression creates a vicious cycle of poor memory, as numerous studies[16] have documented. Clinically depressed people have a bias for remembering negative events, especially those events that involved them. Thus, the depression is continually reinforced by remembering bad things. Non-depressed people generally have the opposite bias: they tend to remember positive events that involved themselves.

Exercise Lifts Our Spirits - and Helps Memory

Investigators from the Howard Hughes Medical Institute (HHMI) have found that voluntary running boosts the growth of new nerve cells and improves learning and memory in adult mice[17]. "Until recently it was thought that the growth of new neurons, or neurogenesis, did not occur in the adult mammalian brain," said Terrence Sejnowski, an HHMI investigator at The Salk Institute for Biological Studies. "But we now have evidence for it, and it appears that exercise helps this happen."

The investigators began their study by comparing the memory skills of a group of sedentary mice to those of a group of mice who exercised freely on a running wheel for one month. Mice in the exercise group logged an average daily distance of 4.87 kilometers, or 2.92 miles.

Both groups were trained to locate a submerged and camouflaged platform that was lying just below the surface in cloudy water. Mice dislike swimming and instinctively seek the platform as a refuge from the stressful activity. How quickly they swim to the platform is a measure of how well they had remembered where it was.

After six days of training each group of mice for the swimming task, the researchers began the study. The control group of sedentary mice took significantly longer to reach the safe platform than did the mice in the exercise group. After the experiment was over, the investigators sacrificed the mice to examine the brains. Exercised mice had about 2.5 times more nerve cells in the dentate gyrus, a section of the hippocampus. As I discussed several times before, the hippocampus is crucial for memory, and it has a special role in spatial memory, locating objects in space, as in this water-maze study.

The investigators also examined brain slices from the two groups of mice in order to measure a nerve-signaling process known as long-term potentiation, or LTP. In experiments like this, an input pathway into the hippocampus is repeatedly stimulated, simulating a learning experience. Then after an interval, test stimuli are delivered, and the response is seen to be larger than single stimuli could elicit before the "training" session. That is, the pathway is potentiated by the training and represents a cellular level of memory. In the Sejnowski study, the level of LTP was twice as large in the exercised mice as in the sedentary mice.

Something else that lifts our spirits is music. Music not only tames the savage beast, but may also grease the wheels that grind out memory. I think music may help you remember better. When I was in veterinary school at Auburn University, I thought that my studying was much more effective while listening to jazz music. The trick is not to think about the music or what the various instrumentalists and vocalists are doing - just let the music touch your emotions. Focus your thinking on the material to be memorized. Otherwise, music or anything else you do while memorizing will become a distraction and interfere with memory.

Of course, that is not a controlled experiment. But Francis Rauscher and colleagues at the University of California, Irvine, have done experiments in rats that led to the same conclusion.[18] Rats were exposed *in utero* plus 60 days post-partum to either complex music (Mozart Sonata), minimalist music (a Philip Glass composition), white noise or silence, and were then tested for five days, three trials per day, in a multiple T-maze. Rats exposed to the Mozart work completed the maze more rapidly and with fewer errors than the rats assigned to the other groups.

If there is any general music effect, it is most likely confined to complex music that can stimulate the brain and charge the creative and motivational dimensions of thought. Mozart's music is certainly complex, and so is that of the progressive jazz era in the 1950s and 60s.

Happy Memories Lead to Comfort Foods ... and More

Most of us like sweets and salty food. We also tend to eat foods that are associated with happy memories and avoid foods for which we have unpleasant memory associations. Remember how you hated broccoli when you mother tried to convince you it was good for you. It takes special will to give broccoli a second chance as an adult. A marketing professor at the University of Illinois, Brian Wansink, has studied how people come to identify certain foods as "comfort foods" and develop a preference for them.[19] Through interviews all across the country his team learned that nearly 40% of the foods that people defined as comfort foods were not selected because they "taste good." This group of foods included things such as soup, certain main dishes, and even certain vegetables. Such foods were commonly associated with happy childhood memories. All of us probably remember the warm comfort given by chicken soup on days when we had bad colds or when our stomachs were so upset that chicken soup was all that we could hold down. No wonder we develop a certain degree of affection for such foods. I remember as a 3-year old falling in love with Grandma's pies, which had as much to do with Grandma as it did the pies.

In Wansink's survey, the favorite comfort food was ice cream. But second and third choices differed between men and women. Women named chocolate and cookies as their second and third-favorite choices, while men selected soup and pizza or pasta. Age was also a factor. People 18 to 34 preferred ice cream and cookies, while people 34 to 54 preferred soup or pasta, and those older than 55 named soup and mashed potatoes.

These differences in food preferences were generally related to past memories and to personality identification. When asked to explain why a certain food was preferred, responses typically indicated some kind of comforting emotion: "My father loved green bean casserole" ... "My mom always gave me soup when I was not feeling well" ... "We kids always got ice cream after we won baseball games."

Sugar-containing foods can enhance memory. Paul Gold at the University of Virginia[20] performed a study where human volunteers listened to an audiotaped prose passage and then drank a glass of lemonade laced with either sugar or saccharine. Twenty four hours later, participants were asked to recall the prose that they had read the day before. The sugar drinkers came up with 54% more information than the substitute sugar controls. We don't know why this effect of real sugar occurred. Although brain cells burn only the sugar, glucose, for fuel, the blood sugar level is normally regulated so well that a spoonful of sugar is not going to cause a spike in blood sugar levels.

So what is the larger lesson here? Happy experiences promote memory of those experiences. Moreover, this memory enhancement happens in a life-changing way. What you learn in association with happy occasions can become so deeply ingrained that it becomes a core part of your very being. It may even affect your sense of identity and self esteem. Many teachers of young children have observed those rare life-changing events when something especially good happens to a child and a life-long change occurs. For me, one such example was the day in 10th grade chemistry when the teacher (my football coach) said in class: "Klemm, you explain this stuff to the class. I don't really understand it." From that day on, I knew I had the ability to be a scientist, even though I had never been interested in science before.

There is also this to realize: our psychological make-up influences what we remember. If we are happy and well-adjusted, we tend to remember the good things of the past. But if we are depressed or pessimistic, we tend to remember the bad things. Rebecca Rupp[21] describes an experiment on memories of elderly persons who were screened both before and after admission to nursing homes. After institutionalization, their memories turned sour. They now had more unpleasant memories involving pain, loss, loneliness, and death. As Rupp puts in, "The remembered past was a function of the experiences present."

One practical approach to learning is to get in a happy mood before trying to learn. Think and do things that make you happy, such as listening to your favorite music.

Our Gut Reaction Is To Remember

Visceral and glandular responses accompany emotions. For example, if we are excited, our heart rate and blood pressure rise. If we worry chronically, we may get an upset stomach and predispose our stomachs to ulcers.

The reason is explained by anatomy. Our viscera are ultimately controlled by the part of the brain known as the hypothalamus. The hypothalamus is bi-directionally connected with several other brain areas: the amygdala, which controls aggression and anxiety, brainstem areas that control muscle tone, and the hippocampus, which is a key nodal point for consolidating memories. These areas, and a few others with which they connect, are collectively called the "limbic system." All of these areas can operate as an emotional control system that is somewhat independent of the cerebral cortex and conscious awareness.

The issue arises as to whether our visceral and glandular systems can learn. For example, it is possible that people with high blood pressure have that high blood pressure because their body has learned to respond to chronic stress in that way.

These visceral and glandular responses are controlled by a subdivision of the nervous system that lies largely outside the brain, mostly in the chest and abdominal cavities: the so-called autonomic nervous system. This system has traditionally been regarded as rather stupid, and unable to learn.

This attitude persists in spite of the classical studies by Pavlov, who showed that dogs can learn to salivate at the sight of a food cue, under conditions when presentation of food follows some kind of cue that signals the imminent presence of food. Pavlovian conditioning is also called classical conditioning and is considered the most primitive sort of learning. You can even condition flatworms, which after many pairings of a light flash and electrical shock, learn to contract their bodies in response to light.

Visceral learning effects underlie psychosomatic disease, such as high blood pressure, heart palpitations, ulcers, tension headaches, facial tics, and some forms of backache. Consider the possibility that psychosomatic diseases emerge as a result of implicitly learned bodily responses to stressful events, events that are sufficiently distressing emotionally to make the bodily response persist, as in the case of the hyper-arousal of the swim-stressed mice just mentioned.

If stress is repeated, the persistence of bodily responses may become cumulative, with the implicit memory being sufficiently "rehearsed" to become a well-entrenched long-term memory. Such a possibility seems especially likely if stressful episodes are repeated during childhood. Consider high blood pressure, for example. Most physicians assume that the high blood pressure seen in many older people is due to their genes or diet. But a genetic link is far from being certain, and many people with high blood pressure do not have plugged arteries. No experiments that I know of have tested the possibility that high blood pressure in adults could arise from or be aggravated by a long-term implicit memory response to childhood stress.

This brief excursion into psychosomatic disease allows me to make the point that these diseases often target a specific organ. Some people respond to stress with high blood pressure, others with ulcers, and so on. It is as if visceral learning is a form of implicit memory that consolidates into a "long-term memory" by way of conditioning of nerves to a specific organ. The repeated stress constitutes a reinforced "memory rehearsal" in that particular neural pathway and its target organ.

One way to help "unlearn" such visceral memories is to use biofeedback training. Such training is usually a form of conditioned learning where the body is taught to lower blood pressure, slow the heart rate, or change other visceral responses. No one seems to have considered the possibility of extinction to stressors, teaching people's bodies to "learn to forget." For instance, if high blood pressure developed because of repeated stresses in childhood, are there ways to train *adults* to habituate to stressors by presenting the stress to adults in ways that are no longer threats to a reasoning adult?

Neal Miller, of Rockefeller University, was among the pioneers to challenge the dogma that the autonomic nervous system was too dumb for higher levels of learning.[22] A system of rewards or punishments (rewards work best) is used to reinforce certain behaviors. Miller and his colleagues showed that laboratory animals could learn certain visceral responses when rewards were given. In one early experiment, for example, they used water as a reward for thirsty dogs. Whenever the dogs showed a spontaneous burst of salivation, which was being continuously monitored, they were given a water reward. Note that this is opposite the normal bodily reaction of getting a dry mouth when one is thirsty. Such results could be due to some nonspecific effect. To control for this, they taught another group of dogs to learn the opposite response. That is the dogs got a water reward whenever they went for long stretches of time without salivating.

There was still the possibility that some unidentified skeletal muscle response was being learned, such as chewing movements or lack thereof that could influence salivation. The obvious solution would be to repeat the experiment in dogs that are paralyzed with curare. However, they found that curare induces continuous and copious salivation in the absence of any learning contingencies. The investigators realized the importance of controlling for skeletal muscle movements and sought another experimental design where curare could be used.

Because there are not many ways to reward an animal that is paralyzed by curare, they decided to use electrical stimulation of the lateral hypothalamus. Stimulation in this area is apparently rewarding, and the area has been called a "pleasure center." Neurosurgeons have stimulated this part of the brain in conscious humans (the brain does not feel pain), and the patients reported that it felt good.

What Miller's group decided to train was heart rate, which was easily measured. One group of rats received brain stimulation reward any time that they spontaneously showed a statistically reliable increase in heart rate. Control rats were rewarded anytime they showed a spontaneous decrease in heart rate. And the two groups of rats did change their heart rates in opposite directions. Training was made more efficient when the researchers used the technique that animal trainers use, so-called shaping behavior. This technique provides reward at first for only small and hence frequently occurring behaviors in the desired direction. As soon as these are learned, progressively larger changes become the criteria for reward. In this way, they produced within a single 90 minute training session, heart-rate learning changes averaging 20 percent in either direction, depending on which response was rewarded.

Other kinds of reinforcers also work. For example, "avoidance learning" was demonstrated in rats that were given a mild tail shock unless they learned to change their heart rates in a certain direction. A shock warning signal would be turned on. After it had been on for 10 seconds, the tail shock was given. The rat could turn off the tail shock by making the correct response of changing its heart rate in the required direction by the required amount. For one group of rats, the correct response was increased heart rate. Perhaps it is not surprising that they could learn this response, because heart rate normally does go up under stressful conditions. But another group of rats was successfully trained in the opposite direction. The imminent threat of stressful tail shock was accompanied by a learned decrease in rate. All of this occurred via a so-called dumb autonomic nervous system in relatively dumb animals (rats) that have no explicit way of knowing what the experimenter expects.

Miller and others went on to show that instrumental learning could occur in other organ systems, such as the intestine, stomach, and kidney.

Humans are certainly as smart as rats. Indeed, some scientists speculate that humans are so prone to psychosomatic disease because their viscera learn to respond in dysfunctional ways to events in the environment. For example, high blood pressure that persists may be due in part to an over-learned response to stress.

As we grow through childhood, much of our behavior is conditioned by our environment. This includes the behavior of our autonomic nervous system, the part that controls our viscera. For example, consider a child who fears to go to school because she is unprepared for a test that is scheduled that day. She may display the autonomic symptoms of a queasy stomach and skin pallor and faintness. Her mother, out of sympathy and concern, may tell the child she is sick and should stay at home. This is tantamount to rewarding the behavior. Thus, the child - and her viscera - are learning to respond to stressful situations with queasy stomach, skin pallor, etc. If these autonomic responses occur often enough and are rewarded each time, the child may well develop a genuine psychosomatic illness that lasts a lifetime. Only careful social research can determine to what extent psychosomatic disease is produced in this way, but the theoretical possibility seems quite real.

The good news is that our viscera can also learn to respond in appropriate ways. Therapy based on instrumental learning is well developed and accepted. So-called "biofeedback training" is characterized by teaching the autonomic nervous system to unlearn previous bad habits and to learn new, more healthful ones.

Visceral learning may account for differences among people and among cultures. For example, Herbert Barry III at the University of Pittsburg, showed that the amount of crying reported for children seems to be related to the way in which their society reacts to their tears. That is, if crying is rewarded by sympathy, then crying becomes more ingrained. That is no doubt the reason that boys do not cry as often or as easily as girls. Girls get comfort for crying; boys often get reprimanded by their fathers for not "being a man" or being tough. Herb Barry left this line of inquiry to go into psychopharmacology and became the editor of the premier journal in that field. I had the pleasure of working with him as a member of his Editorial Board for 5 years.

The most valuable lesson about visceral learning is that healthful responses can be learned. A whole psychological sub-industry of bio-feedback training has emerged . Companies that market biofeedback equipment include Future Health, Allied Products, Performance Edge, Motivational Hypnosis, Applied Biofeedback, Zaz, and many others.

We could also probably extend these ideas to consider many neuroses as learned responses. Here, I would consider the possibility that the flawed thinking that is the basis for neuroses may be learned. By repeating thinking errors, we could actually be *learning* to think in neurotic ways.

Drug Abuse

Drug abuse probably begins because the user has some kind of emotional problem or need that the drugs seem to alleviate. I teach a seminar in drug abuse, and I begin each semester with the rhetorical question, "What is the illness that drug abuse is supposed to cure?"

This is the kind of question we as a society ought to ask. Often nobody knows the answer, least of all the drug abuser. The important point is that the brain has mechanisms for dealing with sadness, despair, depression, low self-esteem, and other emotional problems. By taking drugs, we not only get psychologically and perhaps physically addicted, but we hijack our coping systems, taking them out of the loop of whereby we can learn to manage our emotions and sustain our mental health. Michael Gazzaniga, a famous neuroscientist, has written an entire book[23] explaining how the brain constructs our past and the emotions and memories that get packaged into that construct. The brain has this innate capacity to create and modify emotions, and secondarily our ability to learn and apply what we remember. Drug abuse takes this power away from us and our brain.

Memories of the good feelings from drugs help to sustain the addiction. Stanislav Vorel and colleagues at the Albert Einstein College of Medicine in New York recently reported experiments to confirm this conclusion.[24] Rats that had kicked a cocaine habit, when stimulated in a memory area of the brain (hippocampus), tried desperately to get another fix. But stimulation of the reward centers in the brain did not have this "relapse" effect.

The researchers first got rats hooked on cocaine by hitching them to intravenous catheters that delivered a drug dose every time they pressed one of two levers in their cage. Then, after they were hooked, the researchers weaned them off the drug by substituting saline for the cocaine. Within a week, rats stopped lever pressing altogether. Then, when researchers electrically stimulated the hippocampus via implanted electrodes, the rats furiously pressed the former cocaine lever for 5 minutes or more until it became clear that the drug was not there.

Drug rehabilitation centers have long known that addicts who seem to have kicked their habits in the sterile environments of a rehabilitation center frequently relapse when back on the streets. Too many memories are triggered in the old environment, memories that are associated with the reinforcing effects of the drugs taken in that environment. No wonder treatment of drug abuse is so difficult. You not only have to reverse the brain changes created by the drug itself, but you also have to erase or avoid the memory triggers that activate craving.

Marijuana. The New York Times ran a story not too long ago[25] about Dawn, a 12 year old who had started smoking marijuana, because her friends were doing it. She wanted to be "cool" and accepted by her friends. But after a while, Dawn realized that she was having trouble in school. "I'd learn something one day and the next day I'd have no idea what the teacher was talking about."

We should not be surprised that marijuana affects memory. The molecular receptors for it are found in the hippocampus, which is that part of the brain that is crucial for converting working memory into a stored form. By the way, the fact that there are receptors for marijuana in the brain suggests that these receptors exist normally to respond to an as yet unidentified neurosecretion in the brain that produces marijuana-like effects. This seems to be a generalizable principle. The brain has receptors for opiate and for benzodiazepine drugs, and neurosecretions have been identified that act on these receptors.

Alcohol. Even more widely recognized is the impairment of memory caused by alcohol. The "blackouts" that occur in alcoholics are well known. Alcoholics can have multiple episodes in their recent past for which they have no recollection.

Back in 1974, I and a graduate student name Russ Stevens, were among the first to show that alcohol does not have the same effect on all nerve cells. Some nerve cells, especially in the cortex, cerebellum, and hippocampus are more sensitive to alcohol than cells located elsewhere[26]. Two years later we confirmed and extended the initial observations.[27]

Even mild doses of alcohol can impair memory formation, if for no other reason that it dulls the senses and ability to focus attention. Recall our earlier chapter on the importance of attention. With electrodes chronically implanted in the brains of rabbits we could monitor the electrical discharges from neurons in different parts of the brain. We noted that the mild intoxicating doses that we used suppressed neuronal activity in some brain areas, excited other neurons (probably just released from inhibitory neurons that were suppressed), while others were unaffected. It all depended on which parts of the brain we monitored.

In recent years, I met at an alcohol research conference in Sweden a bright young Russian named Yura Alexandrov. He took up alcohol research where I left off, but based his research on an important new theme: the effect of alcohol on nerve cells should depend on the neurons "behavioral specialization."[28] That is, the normal function of a neuron in behavior provides the key indicator for whether the neuron is especially vulnerable for alcohol. So, in his recordings of nerve cell electrical discharges (he also used rabbits), he also kept track of the normal behavioral function of the neurons. Because my work had shown that many of the vulnerable neurons were in the hippocampus and limbic system structures that are involved in memory, Yura recorded activity from limbic system neurons and noted that they generally existed into two categories: those associated with movements ("M neurons"), and those associated with new learning ("L neurons"). These L neurons changed their firing as the rabbit learned a task, which in this case was to approach a feeder, reach for a floor pedal, and press the pedal to get a food reward. There was also a third class of neurons whose firings were unaffected by anything in the test environment ("U neurons").

Then, when Yura's team gave a moderately intoxicating dose of alcohol to the rabbits, they saw that the neurons that were depressed were specifically the L neurons. They then postulated that L neurons might also be selectively susceptible during chronic administration of alcohol. For eight months they gave rabbits free-choice access to water, and water containing 10% alcohol. Laboratory animals do acquire alcohol-consuming behavior, although they do not like the taste. You have to start them with lower percentages of alcohol and gradually work up to the highest level that they will tolerate (which is about 10%). After rabbits had become partially tolerant to alcohol, they were then given a single challenge dose. The neuronal recordings indicated a "loss" of L neurons. They were harder to find, and the ratio of L neurons to M neurons decline by more than half. Where did the L neurons go? Had they died? Maybe they were still there but had lost their task association. Part of the answer lies in the challenge injections of alcohol. The chronically treated rabbits responded to a single challenge dose of alcohol with increased relative numbers of L neurons and the ratio of L to M neurons became normal. So, alcohol actually could have restored the normal learning function. Perhaps this is akin to human situations where an alcoholic writer writes better when he has a few alcoholic drinks. Formal studies have confirmed this in humans.

In any case, this is a form of "state-dependent" learning, which I explained in the chapter "Memories Hang Out With the Right Crowd." The idea is that you remember best when you are in the same physiological, emotional, or physical state that you were when the learning experiences were taking place.

Some recent studies from the Duke University Medical Center have indicated that alcohol disturbances of memory are more profound in both young animals and young people.[29] In an animal study, a single dose of alcohol, which was not enough to sedate rats or affect their ability to swim, caused the rats to fail at learning how to swim to a safe-island platform in a water-filled maze. The blood level of alcohol was about .08 percent, which is now the new legal safe-driving limit for humans. So even though motor function may be adequate, memory function is impaired.

Just one drink, which typically has no noticeable effect on adults, can impair learning and memory in young humans. The researchers claim that the ban on under-age drinking, which historically is based on political or religious reasons, has a sound basis in science. Young people are damaged more than adults by alcohol. The Duke scientist, Scott Swartzwelder, and his team have published two recent studies that led them to conclude that "even occasional and moderate drinking could impair a young person's memory systems much more than an adult's." In their studies, memory loss lasted throughout the time people were under the influence of alcohol and none of the information presented during that time was ever memorized. Another thing they noticed: young subjects developed tolerance more quickly than adults. Thus, there is an incentive to drink more to get the same high. This might explain the rapid rise in binge drinking among teenage humans.

In a study of humans aged 21 to 30, alcohol decreased the ability of everyone to recognize words from a list that had been read to them 20 minutes earlier, but the errors were significantly correlated with age: the younger the subject, the greater the errors. Age 25 seemed about the cutoff: those younger did worse, those older did better. The study's author made the following logical inference about these results: "If alcohol's effects varied that much within such a narrow age range, then there's a compelling reason to believe its effects are even stronger in adolescents and children."

Methamphetamine ("Speed"). Despite arousing the brain, this drug actually impairs memory. Worse yet, the loss in memory capability seems to be permanent. Even after months of abstinence, these memory impairments have been recently documented in a study by Linda Chang and colleagues at the Brookhaven National Laboratory[30]. They used two short-term memory tasks, a sequential reaction-time test and a single digit recognition task. A group of 20 recently abstinent methamphetamine abusers, who on average had been abstinent for 8 months, formed the test group and 20 nonusers formed the control group. Each control group member was selected to match one of the members in the abuser group in terms of gender and age. Memory performance was impaired in the abuser group by 21.5% in the sequential reaction time tests and by 30% in the single digit test.

* * * * *

Memories are like knee-jerk reflexes. When someone insults us, it can trigger a flash of anger. A joke makes us laugh. An act of kindness can elicit our appreciation or love. But emotions are also learned, triggered by memories of past events that we perhaps no longer consciously recall. Childhood emotional experiences can create memories that we no longer remember consciously but which nonetheless serve as implicit emotional memories in adulthood.

Emotions and memories of emotions affect our ability to memorize new experiences. Memory ability is impaired by stress, anxiety, fear, or depression. Memory ability is facilitated by exercise, healthy lifestyles, and good emotions, such as confidence, contentment, and happiness. Emotions and memory are inextricably inked. Psychoactive drugs are emotional crutches that not only hijack our natural emotional coping mechanisms but also impair our ability to remember.

Key Ideas

1. If your feelings interfere with memory (and your life), you *can* change your feelings.

2. To remember well you have to be motivated. If motivation does not come from others or the learning contingencies, you *can* motivate yourself.

3. A major reason that schools seem to be failing is that they have to teach students who have bad emotions and attitudes.

4. Kids are motivated by learning success to seek the positive reinforcement of more learning success.

5. Pat yourself on the back for good memory performance. Rewards strengthen the relationship between learning events and their recall.

6. We all carry within us our little child, whose memories, conscious, repressed, and often distorted, can cause emotional dysfunction.

7. A deficiency of sex hormones can impair memory.

8. A little anxiety may be a good thing for memory. Anxiety makes you more attentive and sensitive to learning cues. Too much anxiety or chronic stress are likely to be counterproductive.

9. Sedatives and tranquilizers, though they may relieve anxiety, will usually impair memory.

10. Don't take psychoactive drugs. They impair memory. "Just say no."

11. Violence or even witnessing violence on TV impairs memory for the events at the time. This probably affects eye-witness recollections of crime and has experimentally been shown to impair memory of commercials on violent TV shows. The ultimate cause of poor memory may be the anger or fear aroused in those who witness violence.

12. Unpleasant or shocking events may be remembered well, but not the associated events.

13. Sadness and depression impair memory ability. Depressed people have a bias for remembering unpleasant events. Thus, the depression is continuously reinforced.

14. Happy people have the opposite bias. They are more likely to remember happy or positive memories.

15. Aerobic exercise seems to improve memory, because it may increase the growth of new neurons and connections among neurons.

16. Music, at least complex instrumental music, may help memory.

17. We develop emotional preferences and bias toward those things for which we have happy or comforting memories.

18. Happy experiences promote memory of those experiences. The corollary is that it is hard to learn things that you don't enjoy. Attitude counts. You can change your attitude about things you have to learn.

19. Do not reward or reinforce maladaptive behavior. The behavior may well become a permanent learned response.

20. Psychosomatic disease, such as ulcers or high blood pressure, can be induced by stressful memories. Counter-conditioning using biofeedback can be effective treatment.

21. Many neuroses may result from repeatedly thinking in flawed ways, thus learning to think in flawed ways.

22. Drug abuse is learned behavior. Taking psychoactive drugs hijacks our natural coping systems and cripples their ability to learn how to manage our emotions and sustain mental health.

23. Drug abuse has a state-dependent learning component wherein craving is triggered by memory cues coming from the environment and social/emotional context.

24. Alcohol-induced memory impairment is more pronounced in young people than in adults. The impairment has been observed even in a narrow age range (21-30 years) of young adults.

Sources:

1. Pochon, J. B., et al.. 2002 The neural system that bridges reward and cognition in humans: an fMRI study. Proc. Natl. Acad. Sci. U.S.A. 99: 5669-5674.

2. Rupp, Rebecca. 1998. Committed to Memory. Crown Publishers, New York, N.Y.

3. Cherrier, M. M. et al. 2001. Testosterone supplementation improves spatial and verbal memory in healthy older men. Neurology. 57: 80-88.

4. Eichenbaum, Howard. 2002. The Cognitive Neuroscience of Memory. Oxford University Press, Oxford, U.K.

5. Ribeiro, R. L. et al. 1999. The "anxiety state" and its relation with rat models of memory and habituation. Neurobiology of Learning and Memory. 72: 78-94.

6. McGaugh, J. L. 1995. Emotional activation, neuromodulatory systems, and memory, p. 255-273. In Memory Distortion, edited by Daniel Schacter. Harvard University Press, Cambrdige, Mass.

7. Newcomer, J. W., Craft, S., Hershey, T., Askins, K., and Bardgett, M. E. 1994. Glucocorticoid-induced impairment in declarative memory performance in adult humans. J. Neuroscience. 14: 2047-2053.

8. Tang, A. C., Reeb, B. C., Romeo, R. D., and McEwen, B. S. 2003. Modification of social memory, hypothalamic-pituitary-adrenal axis, and brain asymmetry by neonatal novelty exposure. J. Neuroscience. 23: 8254-8260.

9. (http://www.sciencemag.org/cgi/content/short/291/5509/1684). TV violence American Psychological Association as the original source. See also:
http://www.sciencedaily.com/releases/1998/12/981202074804.htm

10. Meshorer, E., Erb, C., Gazit, R., Pavlovsky, L., Kaufer, D., Friedman, A., Glick, D., Ben-Arie, N., and Soreq, H. 2002. Alternative splicing and neuritic mRNA translocation under long-term neuronal hypersensitivity. Science 295: 508-512.

11. McNally, Richard J. 2003. Remembering Trauma. Belknap Press. Cambridge, Mass. 423 pages.

12. Glucksberg, S., and King, L. J. 1967. Motivated forgetting mediated by implicit verbal chaining: a laboratory analog of repression. Science. 158: 517-519.

13. Williams, R. A., Hagerty, B.M., Cimprich, B., Therrien, B., Bay, E., and Oe, H. 2000. Changes in directed attention and short-term memory in depression. J. Psychiatr. Res. 34: 227-238.

14. Strang, J. M., Donnelly, K. Z., Grohman, K., and Kleiner, J. 2001. Attention and working memory in Gulf War Syndrome and depression. Arch. Clin. Neuropsych. 16: 799.

15. Kizilbash, A. H., Vanderploeg, R. D., and Curtiss, G. 2002. The effects of depression and anxiety on memory performance. Arch. Clin. Neuropsych. 17: 57-68.

16. Mineka, S., and Nugent, K. 1995. Mood-congruent memory biases in anxiety and depression, p. 173-193. In Memory Distortion, edited by Daniel L. Schacter. Harvard University Press, Cambridge, Mass.

17. Sejnowski, T., Gage, F., and va Praag, H. 1999. Proc. National Academy of Science. Nov. 9

18. Rauscher, F. H., Robinson, K. D., and Jens, J. J. 1998. Improved maze learning through early music exposure in rats. Neurol. Res. 20: 427-432.

19. The original news release can be found at http://www.admin.uiuc.edu/NB/00.09/comfortfoodtip.html Based on a news release from the University of Illinois.

20. Gold, Paul. 1987. Sweet Memories. American Scientist. 73: 151-155.

21. Rupp, Rebecca. 1998. Committed to Memory. Crown Publishers, New York, N.Y. P. 223.

22. Miller, N. E. 1969. Learning of visceral and glandular responses. Science. 163: 434-445.

23. Gazzaniga, Michael S. 1998. The Mind's Past. University of California Press, Berkeley.

24. Vogel, S. R., Liu, X., Hayes, R. J., Spector, J. A., and Gardner, E. L. 2001. Relapse to cocaine-seeking after hippocampus theta burst stimulation. Science. 292: 1175-1178.

25. Carroll, Linda. 2002. The New York times. Jan. 29, Pg. F6

26. Klemm, W. R. And Stevens, R. E. 1974. Alcohol effects on EEG and multiple-unit activity in various brain regions of rats. Bran Res. 70: 361-368.

27. Klemm, W. R., Mallari, C. G., Dreyfus, L. R., Fiske, J. C., Forney, E., nad Mikeska, J. A. 1976. Ethanol-induced regional and dose-response differences in multiple-unit activity in rabbits. Psychopharmacology. 49: 235-244.

28. Alexandrov, Y. I., Grinchenko, Y. V., Matz, V. N., et al. 2000. Neuronal subserving of behavior before and after chronic ethanol treatment. Alcohol. 22: 97-106.

29. News release from Duke University Medical Center. See ttp://www.sciencedaily.com/releases/1998/03/980317065941.htm

30. Chang, L. Et al. 2002. Perfusion MRI and computerized test abnormalities in abstinent methamphetamine users. Psychiatry Research Neuroimaging. 114: 65-79.

We Get Emotional About Our Memories

It's In There Somewhere

- Buried in the Unconscious
- Accessing the Hard Drive
- Getting Your Memory Into RAM
- Priming the Recall Pump
- The Sound of Blocked Retrieval
- The Key is In the Cue
- Non-Memory Effects on Recall
- Crutches

I Just Can't Find it

Memory is often not so much lost as hard to find
— *Steven Rose*

What a maddening thing a memory can be, dodging away from you when you're trying desperately to snag it, descending around you like a collapsing tent when you most want to forget it.
— *Los Angeles Times*

It's In There Somewhere

Forgetting is not a defect, it is a normal function. Forgetting serves to filter out information that exceeds our needs or that is no longer needed. Sometimes, forgetting serves the very useful purpose of moving on in life, leaving painful memories behind. However, many of these memories may still exist, lying dormant until the right set of cues uncovers them.

We have all heard of people with near-death experiences. Typically, when they recover they claim that "their whole life flashed before them." They became overwhelmed with memories, many of which had been forgotten for years, even decades. Nobody knows what it is about near-death experience that unleashes all these buried memories, but clearly such memory exists - it just needs an assist in retrieval.

Have you ever heard the saying that the brain holds all the memories of everything you ever learned? The idea here is that the problem of memory is not that it deteriorates over time but that it can't be recalled. Few scientists believe this fable, but there is a large amount of truth in the notion that retrieval is a separate memory process that is obviously important to the recall process.

What is really irritating is to fail to recall something that you know you know. Everyone can cite personal experiences of not being able to recall something that you know you know. Students taking a quiz commonly complain that they know the answers to questions they missed, and in fact often recall the answers after they turn in the exam.

Picture this scene: you go to a fancy dinner party and spot this drop-dead gorgeous lady standing in the corner talking to a group of male admirers. You know her! She was one of the runners in the 10 K run last Spring. Now, here she is, high-heeled, long-legged, flat stomached, in a black velvet dress that looks as if it were glued in place. Her upswept hair-do exudes the elegance of caviar and champagne. And you can't remember her name. You are so excited, you are lucky to remember *your* name. You wanted to go over and say, "Hi, ..., remember me? We met when we ran in the 10 K at Andover last Spring." Without her name, you don't have nerve to break into her group. On the way home, after the party of course, it suddenly hits you - "Janice Hopkins! Where was that name when I needed it?"

Why was that so hard to remember? Actually you did remember it, you just could not recall it on demand. There are two reasons for failed recall here: 1) The context was different. She wasn't sweating and wearing baggy running clothes. 2) The second reason was stress and anxiety. You pressured yourself to recall. The subconscious mind that you have to call on to surface memories does not appreciate having demands made. Nor does it like to be pushed and rushed.

Recognition is a form of memory that is much easier to achieve than recall. Think of all the times you said, or heard others say, "I'd recognize it if I saw it." Multiple choice questions on student examinations are a good case in point. It is much harder for a student to generate an answer than to pick one from a list of choices where the correct answer is recognized once the student sees it. My many years of teaching have shown me that students will score some 10-40 points lower on the same exam when the questions are converted from multiple choice to short answer or fill-in-the-blank questions.

Recall requires digging up of the memory, and that often needs the assistance of cues that were associated with the memory at the time it was first registered. For example, when you meet a new person, remembering their name is facilitated if you make visual or verbal associations of the name with certain obvious characteristics of the person. If "John" is bald, you might think of a commode (john) with hair growing on the seat. Or if "Mary" is always smiling and laughing you might associate her name with being "merrie." Now the hairy commode seat and the merry girl serve as cues to help you dredge up the name.

Another example of cuing uses the technique of "acrostics." Here, a phrase is constructed in which the first letter of each word serves as a cue for the item to be remembered. Students of neuroanatomy learn the phrase, "On Old Olympus' Towering Tops A Famous Vocal German Viewed Some Hops." This stands for the names, in order, of the twelve cranial nerves: olfactory (I), optic (II), oculomotor (III), trochlear (IV), trigeminal (V), abducens (VI), facial (VII), vestibulocochlear (VIII), glossopharyngeal, vagus (X), spinal accessory (XI), and hypoglossal (XII).

You can also create an acronym, preferably a meaningful word, in which each letter represents what you want to remember. We discussed this retrieval device earlier in the chapter, "Memories Hang Out With The Right Crowd."

Buried in the Unconscious

Robert Baker has written a book, *Hidden Memories*,[1] that argues that many memories lie buried in our brain and are only brought to the surface under certain, often extreme, conditions. Much of the early evidence comes from the many studies of Freud, who used hypnosis to uncover buried memories of early childhood. Then there are also the modern studies of the neurosurgeon, Wilder Penfield, who evoked memories from neurosurgical patients by electrically stimulating certain parts of the cerebral cortex (note that neurosurgery is often done without anesthesia, because no pain sensors exist in brain itself and because the patient needs to be conscious to be certain that no unnecessary damage is done). These memories had been dormant for years or decades and were only "released" to conscious recall by the electrical stimulation. This is a good place to remember discussions in the first chapter of this book about the ability that everyone has to learn certain things implicitly, without conscious awareness.

Baker points out that "accurate records of many objects and events will enter our minds completely unaware and can show up in the form of intuition, likes and dislikes of which we are totally ignorant of their origin." He reminds us of procedural memories that have become unconscious and automatic. The corollary is that we know much more than we realize and that it may affect our behavior in unrecognized ways.

Baker extends his argument to claim that dreaming, hallucinations, and psychotic episodes are driven by hidden memories. What Baker does not do is acknowledge that these hidden memories are almost certainly distortions from the original memories (see the chapter on "Memories That Lie"). There is also the unacknowledged possibility that the brain can construct new memories "on the fly" by creative imagination. For example, you may dream of taking a trip to Mars in a spaceship. You certainly have no memory of you or anybody else doing that, but your brain knows enough about spaceships and Mars to create a detailed story line for your dream.

Baker also discusses the fact that we have memories that we do not recognize as belonging to us. Sometimes, for example, what we thought was an original idea or phrase, was actually a buried memory. The *déjà vu* phenomenon may also reflect a past memory of an actual event that we have forgotten.

Hypnotic recall of hidden memories may provide clues for memory retrieval. Many scientists now believe that hypnosis is not a distinct state of consciousness. Rather, it is viewed as role playing, where subjects voluntarily agree to become compliant and responsive to suggestion. How this loosens the bonds that tie up hidden memories is not known. Apparently, when we allow our mind to be more responsive to suggestion, we become supersensitive to retrieval cues. There is also the probability that misleading suggestions can dredge up memories that are falsely reconstructed during the retrieval.

While neuroscientists are currently arguing about "conscious" and "unconscious" mind, let us retain the traditional, common sense understanding as a matter of convenience. The classical problem of memory retrieval is that conscious and unconscious minds may not be working well with each other. As students or former students, we all remember those rare times when answers to questions do pop up in time to be used during an examination. Imagine the communication that might occur between conscious mind and unconscious brain when a problem in memory recall is overcome.

> *Conscious mind*, calling down to *subconscious mind*: "Hey partner, I see we are having a little trouble with this question. What's the hold-up down there?"
>
> *Sub-conscious mind*: "Yea, boss. I know I put that stuff in here somewhere, but I haven't found it yet. It is in here somewhere."

Conscious mind: "Don't worry. I know you have it on file. Take your time. I know you will find it. While you are rummaging around, feel free to interrupt whenever you come across the answer to the current question."

Note that effective recall requires the conscious and unconscious mind to work as equal partners. The sub-conscious balks at being pushed around. Also note that the importance of confidence (see the chapter on emotions). The subconscious mind is reassured when it is repeatedly told that it knows what it is doing and that it can be trusted to do its memory tasks.

Retrieval processes are among the least understood aspects of memory. In fact, one theoretician[2] argued that memory recall is not a retrieval process but rather one of reconstruction. The features and cues of the original experience are supposedly reconstructed during recall. While this view is not widely held, it does help explain several things. During a reconstruction process, the original event can be colored by subsequent experiences and rationalizations introduced under the spur of emotion. Details may be added or removed. Such a process would explain false memory.

Explicit memories have to be retrieved or reconstructed from the unconscious mind into consciousness. We don't know that much about the unconscious mind. Sigmund Freud showed us that the unconscious mind was important because of its huge storehouse of buried memories, although many neuroscientists disagree with the details of many of Freud's interpretations.

It is also possible that the unconscious mind uses its store of unexpressed memories to influence our attitudes, feelings, thinking, decisions, and behavior - both conscious and unconsciousness. The French philosopher Jean Paul Sartre persuaded many scholars to accept the notion that there is a seamless connection between consciousness and unconsciousness. Sartre also believed that we are our unconscious mind. Our individual essence and human responsibility do not stop at the edge of consciousness.

In the book, "Between the Lines,"[3] Robert Haskell's central premise is that the unconsciousness memories and thinking routinely get expressed as "subliteral" meanings in human communication. In other words, much of what we say not only has an obvious literal meaning, but also a less obvious, and sometimes very different, unconscious meaning. This idea applies to body language, of course, but Haskell extends it to encoded talk. The idea is related to such euphemisms as "political correctness," "double-speak," and of course, reading "between the lines."

Accessing the Hard Drive

Even casual computer users know the distinction between "memory" or RAM, the electronic workspace where current material is held for processing, and "storage," the hard drive, floppy disk, or CD on which that work is saved for future access. Of course, the brain does not work the way a computer does, but the analogy might still be useful to make the point that memory retrieval may be a "hard drive" access problem.

Naya and colleagues[4] found that the temporal cortexes of monkeys performing a visual pair-association task exhibited two distinct signals: a perceptual signal that propagated in the normal forward direction in the brain, and a backward-projecting signal that likely represented retrieval of object information from "storage" in long-term memory. A month later, deFockert and colleagues[5] shifted the focus to the brain's analog of RAM: working memory, in which the brain temporarily holds information used in reasoning and planning. The subjects performed a selective attention task in which they had to classify famous written names as pop stars or politicians while ignoring distractor faces that were superimposed on the names. The ability to resist distraction was tested under conditions wherein subjects had to hold in working memory a series of digits. If the digits were in the same order for each trial, the working memory load was considered low, compared with the greater load imposed when the digits to be held in working memory were in a different order on each trial. The high-load condition resulted in greater interference effects from the distractor faces. In other words, recall was disrupted when working memory had demands placed on it. This is a case where trying to do two things at the same time doesn't work well. The processing of memory about names and the corresponding career category needs working-memory space. Tying up working memory with difficult tasks makes it unavailable for memory processes that need that space. Another way to look at this is that working memory space is needed to process all the associations and cues related to a memory.

Getting Your Memory Into RAM

Recall depends enormously on how well the information was encoded in the first place. That is, information has to be encoded into RAM, so to speak, in order to be available for retrieval. It also obviously has to be encoded in your working memory to have a chance to be learned permanently.

Retrieval of already-learned information is a distinctly different process than encoding the information during learning. Even different parts of the brain are used.[6] A group of researchers at Stanford compared MRI images of brain oxygen consumption and showed that different parts of the medial temporal lobe were activated during encoding and during retrieval.

This difference can be illustrated in the graph below on MRI activation, in which the percentage of activated pixels (digitized points) in a MRI scan that were activated during retrieval and encoding tasks. It is clear that during encoding, much greater activation occurs in the parahippocampus, a cortical region adjacent to the hippocampus. Opposite effects are seen during retrieval, where the greater activity occurs in a nearby area known as the subiculum.

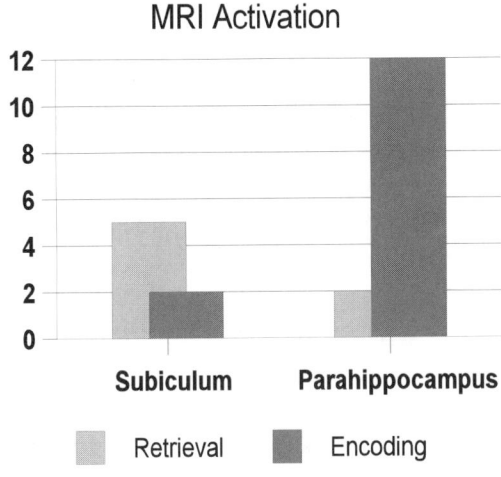

Degree of activation in two memory processing parts of the brain. During retrieval, activation in the subiculum is much greater than during encoding of the same memory. The opposite relationship occurs in the parahippocampus.

One aspect of getting memory items "into RAM" from the brain's hard storage is the serial position of each item. It is well known that when presented a list to memorize, people are most likely to remember the last few items presented. Obviously, you have to work harder to remember the earlier items in a list. As you might expect, if items to be learned have some logical sequence, and they are studied in that order, memorization will be more effective than if the items were presented in random order. The reason is that the logical relationships help build associations.

Priming the Recall Pump

When we recall an explicit memory, we are recalling something that we were consciously aware of when the memory was formed. This is not true, of course, for implicit memories, which can be both learned and recalled without conscious awareness.

Amnesic patients who have selective damage to the inner regions of the temporal lobes have difficulty in recognizing or recalling recently presented information that they were explicitly aware of when the information was first presented. But on implicit memory tests, these same patients perform normally. These and other observations indicate that awareness is a key element in the recall of explicit memories. In other words, if amnesic patients could make themselves aware of the circumstances surrounding the original learning, the association of the cues with the learning objects would increase the chances of recall.

This insight about recall has come from recent studies that we discussed elsewhere on the different results between a normal-delay eyeblink conditioning where the cue stimulus (tone) and the unlearned stimulus (air puff) overlap in time and in "trace" conditioning in which there is an interval between the cue tone and the air puff. Amnesic patients do not develop trace conditioning, but do condition to the same situation when the cue tone stays on while the air puff is delivered. There is something about the delay interval that amnesic patients can't handle.

New light on this enigma has emerged from a recent study by R. E. Clark and Larry Squire[7]. They found that the delay in trace conditioning could also produce a memory deficit in healthy volunteers when these subjects did not consciously realize the contingency between the cue tone and the air puff. Thus, we now see that amnesic patients fail at trace conditioning, because they cannot sustain an explicit awareness of the cue-air puff relationship.

This idea has been confirmed in word-stem completion tests of priming. Implicit learning benefits from priming. In typical priming tests, subjects are asked to complete fragmented words or identify a word or a picture after a brief exposure. Priming is evident when the subjects can complete or identify items that they recently saw or heard faster or more accurately than items for which there had been no prior exposure. Healthy volunteers exhibit priming of new associations in a word-stem completion test only when they are aware that they are producing words from a study list to which they were previously exposed.

Just to avoid confusion over what is implicit and explicit, we need to emphasize that it is the learning process that is implicit. Although words are explicit, the priming process is creating learning unbeknownst to the subject. But apparently the implicit learning process is augmented if the subject explicitly knows in general what is going on.

Research on priming can be done with either words or picture.[8] Experimental subjects are asked to name or to complete a fragmented word form. For instance, they may be expected to complete the word fragment, (ele.....) after having been primed by looking at pictures that included one of an elephant. With picture priming, subjects may be primed with brief glimpses of a set of pictures and then be asked to name them or to name pictures with missing elements that are gradually re-introduced.

Another approach is to use picture-fragment naming, using so-called ambiguous figures. Novices who have never seen these pictures before have trouble recognizing (remembering) the hidden image in the figure. A large segment of the general population has difficulty in extracting hidden images, while other people do it with ease. The operative mechanism seems to be the ability of the brain to respond to priming cues. The hidden images contain certain lines and shapes that serve as cues for retrieval of memory of the full image. The brain has remembered the image, or enough of the image elements that allow it to be constructed. Eventually the viewer will recall the hidden object, although for some subjects, a great deal of verbal prompting and help may be needed. Although at first experience, subjects may struggle with recognizing the hidden image, upon later testing the recall is usually instantaneous, signifying that they have memorized the linkage between the cues in the picture and the hidden image of the picture. Incidentally, I performed a brain-wave study in humans that revealed a correlation of specific frequencies over wide areas of cortex when hidden images were recalled into consciousness.[9] Thus, rather profound things are happening in the brain as it links priming cues to the recall of memories into conscious recognition. Another phenomenon that interested me was that each person has a default preference. For example, in the rabbit/Indian figure below, I see the rabbit readily and may have to struggle to see the Indian. Others can have the opposite response.

195

It's In There Somewhere

Example Stimuli

Man's face / naked lady

Indian face / Eskimo back

Young lady / old lady

Rabbit / Indian

Sample ambiguous figures that can be interpreted in two distinctly different ways. The titles for each picture indicate the two alternative images.

Patients who are amnesic for explicit memory may perform perfectly well on implicit tasks. This has been interpreted to indicate that there is a separate memory mechanism involved in implicit learning.

So what is the practical point? First, if there are two separate mechanisms for memory, you ought to try to get them to work together and reinforce each other. If you need to memorize something, it helps to have repeated exposures to the material and to realize during recall attempts that you have seen this material before. Maybe this only applies to implicit learning, such as learning to play the piano. A teacher hits a key (cue) and you hear the sound. The next time the teacher hits the key, you may recall that sound in your mind's ear better if you realize that you have been exposed to this pair of stimuli before. You know that you are supposed to know.

This priming effect may be a factor in the "total immersion" approach to learning a foreign language. Even though at first you do not remember all the foreign words swirling around in your head, having heard them before makes it easier to remember them as the need becomes more compelling.

One of the well-established things about priming is that pre-exposure to visual stimuli is sufficient to establish a subsequent preference, even when the previous exposure is subliminal. In other words, subliminal stimuli can be recalled in the form of a preference of which you are unaware. The mechanism for this effect has recently been elucidated by Rebecca Elliott and Raymond Dolan in London.[10] They used an MRI imaging technique with volunteer subjects who chose between a pair of abstract stimuli on the basis of whether they preferred the stimulus or remembered having seen the stimulus. They were tested under two conditions: one where one or the other stimulus had been previously presented subliminally and the other condition when both stimuli were novel. Judgments based on memory were associated with MRI activation of two specific regions of cortex, whereas preference judgments were associated with activation of two different zones of cortex. If a stimulus had been presented subliminally, the implicit memory of it was signaled by activation of yet another frontal cortex area.

Is there a practical application for this phenomenon of "mere exposure effect?" I am not aware of anyone studying the matter from this perspective. Perhaps if you wanted your kids to appreciate classical music, or jazz or whatever, you should expose them to it when they are young. It is well established that if kids are exposed to a home in which parents read and in which parents read to the kids, the children are more likely to grow up appreciating books.

Don't count on priming effects to be the same for all kinds of learning. There is evidence from patients with memory deficits that different brain systems support procedural learning and other forms of learning. W. C. Heindel and colleagues at the San Diego VA Medical Center[11] compared memory performance in three groups of patients: Alzheimers (AD), Huntington disease (HD), and Parkinson's disease (PD) (subdivided into patients with dementia and those without). Two implicit memory priming tasks were evaluated, one that engaged procedural (motor) memory and the other that engaged declarative (explicit) memory. HD patients were impaired on the motor learning priming but not on the verbal priming task. AD patients revealed the opposite relationship. The demented, but not the non-demented PD patients were impaired on both implicit priming tasks. In both HD and PD patients, the deficits on the motor learning task correlated with the severity of dementia but not with the level of movement dysfunction independent of memory. Thus, in normal people, it is possible that priming effects that work for motor memory might not work for verbal memory, and vice versa, because these two kinds of learning are mediated by different neural systems.

The Sound of Blocked Retrieval

Failure of retrieval under "tip-of-the-tongue" (TOT) conditions is thought to result because something is blocking retrieval. One leading theory is that words of similar meaning or sound "blocked" the path of the word you were looking for. Recent research by Lori E. James, Ph.D., and Deborah M. Burke, Ph.D., report evidence that TOT experiences have to do with weak connections among word sounds represented in memory.[12] The idea is that language retrieval depends on memory of both a word's meaning and its sound. Retrieval supposedly depends on the strength of connections within a network that includes conceptual and phonological levels.

So, James and Burke tested the theory that remembering sound is as important as meaning in being able to retrieve a word by asking 114 questions to 108 research participants. General-knowledge questions were used to evoke target words that are known to provoke a high rate of TOTs. For example, people were asked, "What word means to formally renounce a throne?" Target words-in this case, "abdicate," included proper names and other seldom-used words.

For some of the trials, participants heard ten priming words before the question. Half of the priming words shared at least one phonological feature of the target word. For example, when "abdicate" was the target word, "abstract" was used as one of the prime words. When participants pronounced words that sounded similar to the target word, more correct responses occurred and there were fewer TOT experiences.

This research may explain why, after a person is not able to remember a particular word, it suddenly comes to mind. These pop-ups may occur when you have recently heard a word that shares a similar phonology. That is, retrieval can improve when the recall task is accompanied by phonologically related words. The experimenters found this to be true for both older and younger study participants.

They also found that the TOT experiences are a function of weak connections among memory representations. The weak connections are strengthened by processing the phonology of a TOT target. But this enhancement of retrieval works best in younger subjects than in old.

So, as a practical matter, how can people keep their memory recall process from getting rusty? Use it, as Dr. James suggests. "People should keep using language, keep reading, keep doing crosswords. The more you use your language and encounter new words, the better your chances are going to be of maintaining those words, both in comprehension and in production, as you get older."

It's In There Somewhere

The Key Is In the Cue

"Oh yea, now I remember!" How many times have we done that after being given some reminder cue for a memory that we had but could not recall? The memory is there all along, but we need cues to bring them to the surface of consciousness. Why is a cue needed? First, recall that association is a key element in memory, and cues generally remind us of the original associations we used to create the memory.

Unlock Those Memories With Cues

All sorts of things can serve as cues for recall. One perhaps unexpected source of cuing is odor. Odors may have a priming effect. David Smith at Bishop's University in Canada, compared learning in subjects that smelled either jasmine or a perfume while learning long word lists.[13] They were re-tested some time later, and one or the other odor was present during the recall testing. Best results occurred when the odor during re-test was the same as the odor during learning. The effect of odor is one example of the so-called "state-dependent learning" that I have described in the chapter, "Memories Hang Out With the Right Crowd." Here we see how specific this effect is. It is not just having any odor present when trying to elicit recall of items learned in the presence of odor, but that the best results occur when the odor is the same in both conditions.

Recall may be blocked by some kind of interfering or competing phenomena due to similar or confusing cues. Interference may occur before the memory is formed (proactive) or afterwards (retroactive).[14] The original studies of proactive interference used a design in which three or four recall trials are given in rapid succession. Stimuli in each trial were similar (setting up the probability of interference). Each trial was separated by a distractor-filled interval. The material was hard to learn, but not if interference was reduced by using distinctive items on the last trial. A more real-world like demonstration was reported in a study in which subjects heard television news items while they viewed a videotape of the same events. Subjects heard three items during each trial and attempted to recall them after a 1-min delay. Four sets or trials of items were used. Control subjects received information on the same topic for all four trials. Subjects in the experimental group were treated the same except that on the last trial the items were on a different topic. In both groups, the percentage of correct responses declined over the first three trials, from about 85% correct on the first trial to 55% on the third trial. On the fourth trial, the percentage correct continued to decline (to 43%) in the controls, but increased sharply (to 74%) in the experimental group. The lesson seems to be that to remember well you must avoid interference at any time before, during, or shortly after a learning experience.

Retroactive interference occurs when new material, especially if it is similar to the material to be memorized, is introduced shortly after attempts to memorize. This is akin to interfering with consolidation, as I discussed earlier. But the interference with consolidation is magnified by similarities between the learned material and the post-learning distractors. Some interesting examples in studies of human infants have been reviewed.[15] These studies have shown, among other things, that infant memories are highly vulnerable to interfering information presented while the training memory is still active (that is, before consolidation), but are resistant to information after a reactivation treatment (after consolidation).

Recall interference can even occur with well-learned material. Most readers have experienced the following problem in a meeting or conversation: You have an "agenda item" that you plan to introduce. But you get so distracted by other pressing items in the conversation that you forget to bring up your agenda item. Sometimes the agenda item was the main reason for the meeting or conversation in the first place.

An experimental psychologist, Endel Tulving at Yale, has clarified the idea that memories can be enduring, even when we cannot recall them at given moments. Tulving's explanation is that we fail to recall because a critical cue is missing. I would add the possibility that some element of the current situation could actively interfere with the recall, as just mentioned. In any case, the cue-dependent forgetting idea holds that we remember an event if and only if a trace of the event is left behind and if something reminds us of it. Given that definition, it would be just as easy to name this cue-dependent remembering, even though Tulving called it "cue-dependent forgetting.".

Tulving[16] and others have performed simple, but elegant, experiments that illustrate the point. For example, adult humans were presented a list of words and then required to recall as many as possible. While each word in the list is known to the subject, the appearance in a given list is a unique learning experience.

One experiment involved presenting words in pairs of closely related words (bark - dog; for example). Subjects were told that the right-hand members of each pair were the target words that they would be tested on during a recall test. After seeing a list, subjects were given two successive tests: 1) left-hand members were presented as retrieval cues, as in bark - ... Not surprisingly, subjects did quite well, averaging 74% of the target words. But results of the second recall test were most interesting. Here, the target words were cued with an associated word that had NOT appeared anywhere in the list. Thus, subjects would be given cues such as grog (rhymes with ....). Generally such cues failed to trigger recall of the same words that appeared in the original list. These results suggest is that recall depends on highly specific cues, even when the memory trace itself has not been lost.

Another interesting experiment that Tulving and colleagues conducted was one in which subjects were shown 28 five-letter words, and their recall was tested with cues of two, three, four, or five of the initial letters of these words or with no cue letters. For example, the word grape on the list would be cued with gr ---, gra--, and grap-. In tests with no cues, subjects were asked to write, in any order, all the words that they remembered from the list. The results showed what could be expected: the more cue letters that were used, the higher the recall. With no cuing, subjects averaged only about 25% recall of words. But that performance rate was more than doubled with three-letter cuing. The information was there all the time. It just needed appropriate cuing.

Tulving cites another experiment of a contemporary in which subjects were presented a list of words and were required to recall the list with and without cues. The cue situations were varied so that cues were homonyms of target words, synonyms of target words, or cue words that were identical with target words. The results demonstrated a powerful impact of cuing. Similar results were obtained in other tests in which the words to be remembered were embedded in meaningful sentences.

One of Tulving's experiments tested the common idea of interference, which holds that memory is impaired by putting conflicting or distracting information between the time of learning and the recall test. In this test, subjects were presented lists of 24 words in each of 6 conceptual categories. For instance, one of the lists contained the words: hut, cottage, tent, hotel (category = housing type), Another list contained cliff, river, hill, volcano (CATEGORY = earth formations). Each list was shown three times, each time at the rate of one second per word. Then a non-cued recall test was given where subjects were to recall as many of the words as they could in a given category. Then the test was repeated with another category of words. After each category was presented and tested, subjects were asked to list all the words they had seen, without cuing. Immediately after this test, subjects were re-tested with cuing that consisted of giving them the names of the categories (housing types, earth formations, etc.). As you would expect, the amount of recall in the non-cued case declined precipitously with the

It's In There Somewhere

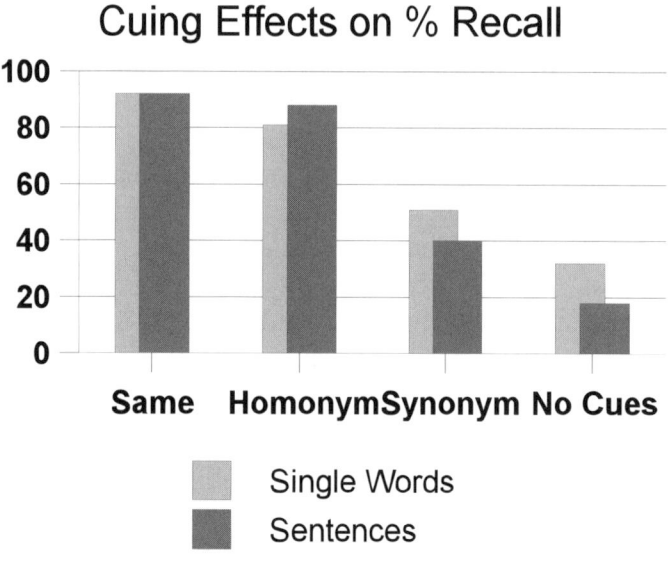

Results of experiments that tested cuing effects on a list of words to be memorized. Cues were either homonyms or synonyms of words in the original list to be memorized. Both single words and sentences were recalled more accurately when cues are presented.

number of lists that intervened between the first group of words and the last.

The next graph plots some of the data from one of Tulving's experiments that scored the average number of words recalled from a list of 24 words in three successive tests (original learning, non-cued recall, and cued recall). The graph shows the disruptive influence of presenting other lists learned between presentation of the original list and the non-cued recall test.

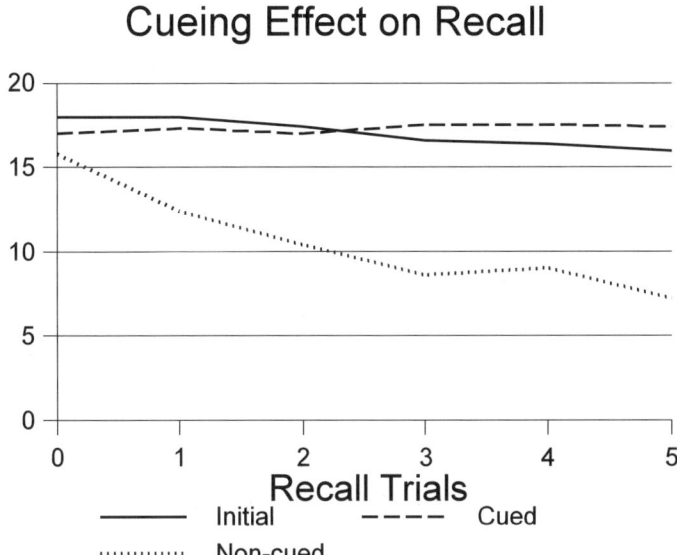

Note that the degrading effect on performance was not seen when the recall was cued. What this shows is that the memory was there all along. It just needed appropriate cues to trigger recall. This viewpoint does not preclude that some forgetting is due to deterioration of a memory trace. The important thing to remember is that we remember much more than we think we do and that appropriate cuing will disclose that.

I have explained before "state-dependent learning," which is the phenomenon that recall is more effective if it is performed under the same conditions that were present during the initial learning. These "states" influence memory because they are full of cues that include not only physical settings (room, climate, scenery, etc.) but even emotional mood. Gordon Bower at Stanford,[17] for example, showed that memory retrieval is mood dependent. Bower asked his subjects, college students, to keep week-long diaries of their emotions. In the laboratory, students were put through hypnotic and suggestion exercises that would increase the likelihood that they would achieve a good, happy mood, or a lousy, downer mood. After mood manipulation, students were tested on their ability to recall events from their diaries. Happy students remembered more of the pleasant incidents in their diary. Unhappy students remembered more of the sad and unpleasant incidents. Observations like these also illustrate why states of depression are so persistent - depression feeds upon unpleasant memories and thus intensifies the depression.

Extinction of a learned response is a useful model for evaluating contextual cues. In Pavlovian fear conditioning, for example, the fear can be extinguished if the conditioning stimuli are repeated but no longer paired with the aversive stimuli. For example, if a rat is trained to expect electric shock to its feet each time a light is flashed, that learned anxiety can be extinguished by eliminating the foot shock after each light flash. A recent study[18] has shown that this extinction is not simple habituation, but rather specific to the contextual cues present during the learning and extinction processes. The experimenters conditioned rats to fear two sound-conditioned stimuli, which they then extinguished in two different contexts. Rats exhibit fear by freeze behavior. When the freeze behavior was extinguished under a given context, re-testing showed that it tended to stay extinguished in the same context - but not when re-tested with the other sound conditioned stimulus.

There are important implications for treating conditioned fear and anxiety in humans. Although you can desensitize and extinguish learned anxiety reactions, the extinction may well be limited to one particular state or context. A different set of contextual cues may retrieve a buried learned anxiety or fear. This is a typical situation in "anxiety attacks," in which an overwhelming anxiety seems to "come out of the blue" with no rhyme or reason. Some cues in that context may have triggered the anxiety memory, which could no longer be suppressed because the context was not the same as the original situation in which the learned anxiety had been extinguished.

A leading explanation for forgetting, at least for extinction of conditioned reflexes, is that extinction is promoted by feedback from behavior during trials in which the conditioning stimulus is withdrawn. This was recently demonstrated in eye-blink conditioning of rabbits that learned an association between a tone and an air puff to the eye.[19] Extinction did not occur when during extinction trials the eye blink was prevented by blocking the nerve circuits that cause blinking. Thus, it seems that the behavior (blinking without the presence of the air puff in this case) in the early extinction trials creates a new learning situation (learning to unlearn) that promotes forgetting. This idea has not been tested for practical application, but the implications could be profound.

Non-Memory Effects on Recall

Especially in the chapter on emotions ("We Get Emotional About Our Memories"), I made the point that memory can fail because of stress or unpleasant emotions. The extent to which such failure can be assigned specifically to a failure of retrieval is not known, but it seems reasonable to suspect that recall failure can be a major factor. Retrieval may also be influenced by such other non-memory influences involving confidence, credibility of interviewers and witnesses, social compliance, conformance, and lack of sleep.

Crutches

When all else fails, you can always use memory crutches. I hate to even suggest it, because if you do all the things that this book shows are helpful for memory you should not need many crutches. Nonetheless, memory crutches do help organize your life and reduce the number of things you have to remember, perhaps giving you more mental energy and will to memorize the things that are really important. Examples of useful memory crutches include:

- Put important items back in the same place each time, such as bills, car keys, purse, wallet, the daily mail, etc.
- Use lists, on scrap paper or your PDA if you have one.
- Put sticky note reminders in key places.
- Keep a calendar (but remember to check it each day).
- Get organized. Have a place for everything and put everything in its place. Get a file cabinet (or two or whatever it takes) and label the files in the most meaningful ways.
- Have a tote bag or briefcase that always has in it what you need for the day.

* * * * *

This chapter reinforces the idea that we remember much more than we think we do. We have many buried memories. Recall depends on appropriate cues. Recall is influenced by such things as distracting information, either immediately before or after learning, cues that were present during learning, relevant cues presented after learning, the way information is grouped or categorized, and emotional mood.

Picture cues are the most effective. Recall the chapter "Memories Hang Out With The Right Crowd." A main reason that pictures are such powerful reminders that the many cues contained therein. Perhaps you remember a school teacher who presented information by drawing diagrams on the board. Remembering the structure of a diagram, which is relatively easy, makes it easier to remember the content.

Recall is promoted when you have confidence in your memory and trust it to work when you need it most.

Key Ideas:

1. Don't pressure or rush your sub-conscious mind to come up with whatever you are trying to remember. Think about something else for a while.

2. Be confident about your memory. Tell your subconscious mind that you trust it to remember and will be patient waiting for the answer.

3. Don't try to remember things when you are stressed or anxious. If you are in a stressful situation, calm yourself down before expecting best memory recall.

4. Merely exposing yourself to things you need to remember will make it easier to learn it permanently when you seriously try to memorize it.

5. Make up an acronym for things you want to recall. Then make a mental image of the acronym.

6. Buried memories may get reconstructed in the process of retrieval. Be aware that the retrieved memory may not be entirely correct.

7. Retrieval of memory is impaired if working memory is saturated. Space for working memory is needed to process in real time the associations and cues related to a memory.

8. Serial position of items in a list is recalled best if the items are arranged in some logical order that helps to build associations and cues.

9. Implicit memories can be learned and recalled without conscious awareness. Conscious awareness of the relationship of cues to memory items does make recall easier and more effective during early stages of learning. Examples include conversion of explicit to implicit learning in typing.

10. Priming facilitates memory, especially when you are consciously aware of priming taking place. Examples include skimming a book before reading it, re-learning a foreign language, and "total immersion" learning of a foreign language.

11. Sounds of words are important cues to recalling the word. Even different words that have similar sounds can help retrieve a word memory.

12. Distracting or irrelevant cues will interfere with recall. This interference effect can occur either immediately before a memory is formed or immediately afterwards.

13. Cues for recall generally are highly specific.

14. If items to be learned are classified by categories, then recalling the name of the category helps the recall of items within that category.

15. Emotions affect recall. Pressure, anxiety, or fear often interfere with recall. Positive, happy emotions promote recall.

16. Emotional depression feeds upon itself, because when you are depressed the memories most likely to be recalled (and reinforced) are the ones that make you depressed.

17. Learning to forget unwanted memories is also dependent on specific cues.

18. "Anxiety attacks" are usually triggered unconsciously by cues that are associated with buried unpleasant memories. Discovery of the cues and rational exploration of the buried memory and its associated emotions are central to therapy.

19. "Memory crutches," such as to-do lists, sticky notes, and habitual patterns of behavior, are O.K. to use only if they help organize the clutter in your lifestyle. But crutches should not be used to keep you from exercising your memory. Neither should they be used as a substitute for proving to yourself that you have a good memory.

Sources:

1. Baker, Robert A. 1996. Hidden Memories. Prometheus Books, Amherst, N.Y.

2. Bartlett, F. C. (1932). Remembering. Cambridge University Press, Cambridge Mass.

3. Haskell, Robert E. 1999. Between the Lines. Insight Books, New York. 349 pp.

4. Naya, Y., Yoshida, M., and Miyashita, Y. 2001. Backward spreading of memory-retrieval signal in the primate temporal cortex. 291 (5504): 661-664.

5. de Fockert, J. W., Rees, G., Frith, C. D., and Lavie, N. 2001. The role of working memory in visual selective attention. Science. 291 (5509): 1684-1685.

6. Gabrieli, J. D. E., et al. 1997. Separate neural bases of two fundamental memory processes in the human medial temporal lobe. Science. 276: 264-266.

7. Clark, R. E., and Squire, L. R. 1998. Classical conditioning and brain systems: the role of awareness. Science 280 (5360): 77-81.

8. Bowers, J. S., and Marsolek, C. J. 2003. Rethinking implicit memory. Oxford University Press, Oxford, England.

9. Klemm, W. R., and Li, T. H., and Hernandez, J. L. 2000. Coherent EEG indicators of cognitive binding during ambiguous figure tasks. Consciousness and Cognition. 9: 66-85.

10. Elliott, R., and Dolan, R. J. 1998. Neural response during preference and memory judgments for subliminally presented stimuli: a functional neuroimaging study. J. Neuroscience. 18 (12): 4697.

11. Heindel, W. C., Salmon, D. P., Shults, C. W., Walicke, P. A., and Butters, N. 1989. Neuropsychological evidence for multiple implicit memory systems: a comparison of Alzheimer's, Huntington's, and Parkinson's disease patients. J. Neuroscience. 9: 582-587.

12. Source: American Psychological Association as the original source. http://www.sciencedaily.com/releases/2000/11/001113071544.htm

13. Smith, D. G., Standing, L., and de Man, A. 1992. Verbal memory elicited by ambient odor. Percept. Motor Skills. 74 (2): 339-343.

14. Dempster, F. N. 1995. Interference and inhibition in cognition. An historical perspective, p. 3-26. In Interference and inhibition in cognition, edited by Frank N. Dempster and Charles J. Braided. Academic Press, New York.

15. Rovee-Collier, Carolyn, and Boller, Kimberly. 1995. Interference or facilitation in infant memory? p. 61-104. In Interference and Inhibition in Cognition. Edited by Frank N. Dempster and Charles J. Brainerd. Academic Press, New York.

16. Tulving, Endel. 1974. Cue-dependent forgetting. American Scientist. 62: 74-73

17. Bower, Gordon. 1981. Mood and memory. American Psychology. Feb., p. 129-148.

18. Hobin, J. A., Goosens, K. A., and Maren, S. 2003. Context-dependent neuronal activity in the lateral amygdala represents fear memories after extinction. J. Neuroscience. 23: 8410-8416.

19. Krupa, D. J., and Thompson, R. F. 2003. Inhibiting the expression of a classically conditioned behavior prevents its extinction. J. Neuroscience. 23: 10577-10584.

It's In There Somewhere

Memories That Lie

- Remembering What We Want to Remember
- History of False-Memory Research
- Nature of False Memory
- Memory Filters
- Adult Memories Of Childhood Are No Greater Than Chance
- Child Testimony
- How Does the Brain Get It Wrong?
- False Memory in Older Adults
- Stress Can Fool You
- Role of Education and Intelligence
- Pictures are Not Always Worth a Thousand Words

With some people, a clear conscience is nothing more than a poor memory.

******

The typical fisherman is long on optimism and short on memory.
– 14,000 Quips and Quotes, Crown Publishers

215

Everybody remembers the terrorist attack of September 11. Or at least they think they remember the event. Seventy six percent of the American public say they remember seeing the first plane hit the World Trade Towers. But there was no video of the first plane's crash into the building[1]. Not only did the people in the survey have this erroneous memory, but they were certain that they "saw what they saw." Psychologists from nine universities have studied this false memory of the Sept. 11 event. They found not only errors about the seeing the first plane, but also errors about the airlines involved and the number of planes involved. Some psychologists think that traumatic memories are more likely to be incorrectly constructed.

False remembering is perhaps best illustrated by the parlor game in which one person tells a complex story to another, and the second tells the story to a third person, and the story is then repeated from person to person. After the story has been transferred through seven or eight people, the story has often been so distorted that it bears little relationship to the original story. Of course, more than false memory is involved here. Many elements of the story may be mis-interpreted – we all tend to hear what we are predisposed to hear. But our predispositions are driven by our existing memories (which may themselves contain error), which we integrate with new information to form new memories.

Multiple reasons can explain such major failures of memory. One cause is that the listener was overwhelmed with more information than could be held in "working memory" that was used to pass the information on to the next person. The TV comedian Steve Allen used to have a skit on his *Tonight* show where some members of the cast burst onto the stage to enact a wild and seemingly violent scene. Shots were fired (blanks of course), clothes were torn, and so on. The whole scene lasted about a minute. Then, Allen would ask a few people from the audience to come to the stage and answer questions about the scene. Nobody seemed certain of anything. They could not remember who was shooting at whom, how many shots were fired, or what color clothes the cast was wearing. Emotional shock contributed to memory failure. People do tend to impose their own ideas into a story of sequence of events - a sort of "fill in the blanks" process.

Remembering What We Want to Remember

There are three kinds of falsehood: omission, commission, and misremembered. If any of the three types are deliberate, we call the falsehoods "lies." Michael Gazzaniga[2] gives us an overview of a common way to demonstrate how easy it is to unintentionally misremember. First, you present a person with pictures of a likely event. For example, you might show a series of pictures of a person doing normal things in getting ready for work or school in the morning: getting up, shaving, eating breakfast, brushing teeth, etc. Then wait a few hours and re-test the subjects with a new set of pictures, some of which were in the original set, some that are new but relevant, and some that are new and irrelevant. When most subjects are asked to identify which pictures they saw before, they make many mistakes. But the mistakes typically occur with previously unseen pictures that fit the story, that make sense. Most subjects are very good are detecting the unseen pictures that are irrelevant.

An important conclusion can be drawn from studies of picture memory in "split-brain" patients who have had the connections between the two hemispheres surgically severed in order to control severe epilepsy. In such patients, images can be projected selectively to either the right or left hemisphere. Both hemispheres did equally well in recognizing previously seen pictures and in rejecting ones not seen before. When related but unseen pictures were shown during recall, only the right hemisphere performed correctly. The left hemisphere made numerous mistakes, presumably because the language center that is contained there had constructed a schema that readily accommodated relevant but unseen pictures.

Another way to study false memory is to use a word lists in a similar way. That is, the training list might be such words as "bananas, pie, oranges, milk, bread, hamburger, and other foods. Then during a recall test, subjects would make errors with words for other foods that were not on the original list. Whether pictures or words, the mind drags information out from old stores and tries to place them in the new context. Maybe it is like telling a dog for the first time to fetch the newspaper and he brings you his old bone. When Gazzaniga and colleague, Michael Miller, performed brain scans during tests that revealed a person recounting false memories, both hemispheres became active during the recall test phase. But with word lists, the left hemisphere became more active when a false word was recounted. This indicates an active role for our language center in "making up" an answer.

Similar false memory studies by S. J. Ceci[3] revealed misattribution errors in preschool children. As many as 58% of those tested claimed that at least one false event had occurred in the original learning phase of the test, and 25% of the children made up false elaborations for most of the false events. For example, during the first week or two after exposure to the original story, a child might falsely claim that a certain even had occurred in the story. But by 10 weeks, the false elements had been embellished and taken on a life of their own.

We adults can't be smug about this. We all recognize similar memory errors in other adults whose memories change over time, as for example, when they tell jokes, childhood traumas, and personal victories (e.g. the size of the fish caught).

Where do such mistakes come from? .... During encoding? ... During retrieval? Both sources are possible, because the mind can theoretically reconstruct events and embellish under either circumstance.

False memories come in at least two varieties: "convenient" forgetting and erroneous remembering. Convenient forgetting is linked to this axiom:

We hear what we want to hear.
We see what we want to see.
We remember what we want to remember.

A good example of convenient forgetting comes from a study by Harry Bahrick and colleagues.[4] They asked college students to recall their high school grades and then checked the responses against the actual grade record. Of the grades recalled, 29% were wrong. Moreover, the mis-remembering was always shifted up, not down. That is, students remembered a better grade than they actually got. How convenient. Ego is at work here. We want to believe that we perform better than we actually do, and we remember our performance accordingly.

A related example comes from a study of parents when asked to recall their child-rearing practices.[5] The methods that they recall using in raising their kids were more likely to conform to expert opinion of what parents *should* do, not what they actually did.

Forgetting is not always convenient. We all have had sleepless nights where we tossed and turned, because we could not get a bad event that day off our mind. Most of us are tormented all our life by things that happened in our childhood that we would just as soon forget. In fact sometimes the harder you try to forget the harder it is to do so. Think of bad habits and how hard they are to forget.

The mind does sometimes purge unwanted memories, but we don't understand how the brain selects what to remember and what memories will be purged. All of us can find examples. For example, I don't remember the addresses of most of the places I have lived in the past, nor do I remember the phone numbers. Michael Anderson, a neuroscientist at the University of Oregon, has reported an experiment on purposeful forgetting[6]. His subjects were asked to memorize 50 word pairs. Then they were shown one word from each pair at a time, with instructions "NOT TO THINK" of the paired word. Later testing with these same word pairs, without the not-think instruction, revealed that recall was much poorer for the pairs where one of the pair words had been deliberately suppressed. Now the memory could not be recalled, even with cues or bribes to do so.

Active memory suppression could account for many lost memories of childhood, especially highly traumatic memories such as physical and sexual abuse. Sigmund Freud was among the first to

219

recognize that many childhood memories have been suppressed and lie buried in the subconscious. Some memories may be better off left buried, but therapists may not always know which memories need to be brought to the surface.

Then there is another class of memories that are expressed unconsciously, without any awareness that one is remembering. Examples include unconscious attitudes, emotions, body language, and behavior that are driven by past experiences for which we have no conscious, explicit recall. These are examples of implicit memory, which we considered in the chapter on "My Memory Is O.K."

Many researchers are investigating memories that are just plain wrong, even though the rememberer may strongly believe the events really happened. We think we remembered, but what we remembered was not what actually happened.

This problem crops up in courtrooms all the time. So-called "eye witness" testimony, which was once thought to be compelling evidence, is now known to be unreliable sometimes. Especially distressing are the cases of presumed child abuse, where a father, for example, is accused of child abuse by an adult child who suddenly "remembers" such abuse. The abuse may or may not have occurred, and scientific analysis is unable to determine whether such recovered memories are actually correct.[7]

Recalled perceptions may be distorted, mislabeled, or omitted when they occur under any kind of severe stress or trauma, which is a serious limitation of eyewitness testimony in judicial proceedings. Similar false recollections undermine personal relationships during times of conflict or stress.

Lawyers are well aware of the false memory phenomenon. One particularly illuminating case was a trial in Eau Claire, Wisconsin, where the family of a deceased woman sued the woman's therapists for making her believe falsely that her parents and her brother had physically and sexually abused her.[8] After a year or so of counseling treatment, the patient, then 20 years old, became convinced that her psychological problems stemmed from childhood abuse. Lawyers convinced the jury that false memory was at work here. The jury decided that it was the two therapists who had committed abuse and awarded $5 million in damages to the family.

We have known about the unreliability of eyewitness testimony for over 80 years, when first documented by Hugo Munsterberg.[9] Nonetheless, our judicial system continues to place more value on eyewitness testimony than on circumstantial evidence. Both can be unreliable indicators of guilt or innocence.

History of False-Memory Research

The history of false-memory research has been summarized by Daniel Schacter in his book *Memory Distortion*.[15] Modern research on false memory is said to have originated in 1885, when a German psychologist named Hermann Ebbinghaus introduced the strategy of testing memory accuracy under conditions where the learning events could be verified. He tested himself on a set of to-be-remembered materials, a listing of nonsense syllables. He would check the reliability of his recollection against the documented list of syllables that he originally presented to himself to learn. In short, if you can't know for sure what the learning event was, you can't know for sure if it was remembered correctly.

Most of the research in the early 1900s was done with children, and abundant evidence was accumulated to show that asking misleading questions during recall testing could readily elicit false memories. Sigmund Freud got into the false memory business too. Indeed, a centerpiece of Freud's thinking was that false memory arises because emotionally traumatized people repress memory of the painful events. Suppression was most likely to occur if the traumatic events occurred during childhood. His therapeutic strategy was to unearth these buried memories and analyze them in the light of adult understanding.

Beginning in the 1920s and 1930s, researchers began to clarify the nature and basis of memory distortion. A seminal study, published under the title of *Remembering* by Sir Frederic Bartlett, suggested that people alter memories of newly learned events by reconstructing them in the light of pre-existing knowledge and experience. Bartlett's experimental paradigm was to tell people an old Indian legend and then ask the experimental subjects to recall the story on several different occasions. Subjects rarely got the story completely right. Moreover, the recall errors were usually reconstructions that made the most sense or that fit the subject's expectations of what should have happened. The specifics of the recalled story also changed upon repeated re-telling.

In 1959, J. Deese introduced a classic testing technique for false memory. The procedure is to present a list of words (pillows, sheet, bed, rest) that have a strong natural association to non-studied words (such as sleep, sex, etc.). During recall tests, subjects were likely to include related but non-studied words on their recall list.

Between 1920 and 1970, the predominant view of false memory was based on an "interference theory," which held that recall was corrupted by events that occur between the time of learning and the time of recall. Most scientists now believe that interference is only part of the explanation.

Neisser in 1967 expanded on the earlier themes by proposing that we "construct" memories, much as a paleontologist constructs an idea of a humanoid skull based on a few bone fragments. This view had been anticipated earlier by a French sociologist, Maurice Halbwachs, who had argued in 1925 that social pressures and norms affect what is remembered, both by individuals and the cultural groups in which they live.

Another key idea is known as *source memory*. This is the memory of the conditions under which a learning event occurred, such as when, where, how, and why the event occurred. Recall of the source of a memory helps to assure the validity of the memory, distinguishing it from imagined events. When people forget the source of their memories, they become susceptible to distorting influences.

In the 1980s, Tulving and others introduced the idea that the environment during memory retrieval was important. That is, memory accuracy was greatly influenced by the conditions and place in which retrieval was attempted. Hypnosis is a well-known example of an environment in which memories can be more effectively retrieved. However, because hypnotized people are so susceptible to suggestion, hypnosis is a powerful way to elicit false memories.

In recent years, studies have documented the role of emotions on false memory. Information that is congruent with the current mood or feeling is much more likely to be remembered correctly than when mood does not match the information.

All of these ideas have a degree of validity, and they are not mutually exclusive. The practical point is that the accuracy of memory is affected by both the environment during initial learning and during recall attempts.

Nature of False Memory

False memory, as usually defined, is not lying. People with false memories really believe in their recollections. False memories are believed just as much as true memories. The difference lies in that false memories arise from learning experiences that are mis-registered, mis-interpreted, or mis-preserved.

False memories may be explicit or implicit. False explicit memories are those which a person states as being true when in fact they are not. False implicit memories are misremembered events that become evident when a person is not specifically asked to recall but rather to perform some other task, such as completing a word fragment. Elizabeth Loftus and colleagues[10] describe some experiments that compared explicit and implicit false memory. In one design, college-student subjects watched a series of 51 slides that depicted a female college student, "Kristine," visiting a department store. Kristine was seen to visit six departments in the store, putting a few items from each station in her shopping basket, while surreptitiously slipping a few of the more expensive items inside her oversized purse. After seeing the slides, subjects read a narrative review of the slides that contained some errors. For example, the slides may have shown Kristine handle a hammer that was described in the narrative as a screwdriver or neutrally as a tool.

Later, students were quizzed about what they saw. Explicit recall was tested by direct questioning, such as "What was the tool that you saw Kristine handle?" Accuracy was much higher (72%) when no misleading information was presented in the narrative. When questions dealt with events distorted by conflicting narrative, correct responses fell to 55%. Other experiments disclosed that the subjects with false memory truly believed in the veracity of their memory.

The implicit test involved a degraded picture test in which subjects had to identify pictures of common objects associated with the slides that appeared as fragments on a computer screen. A succession of progressively less fragmented images was shown until the subjects recognized the item and typed in an identification. The implicit test issue was whether misinformation in the narrative also degraded performance on recall, as it did upon explicit testing. Results indicated some degrading of implicit memory as a result of misinformation in the narrative. However, the magnitude of error was much less than in explicit testing. This kind of evidence suggests that implicit memories may be less susceptible to distortion and misremembering. If true, there could be many important practical applications, such as confirming eye-witness testimony in crime scenes and in psychiatric examination of childhood traumas. Implicit tests for recall might be more reliable than asking people to recall explicitly what they remembered.

The demonstration of memory distortion by misleading information highlights the role of suggestibility in memory. Nowhere is this effect more evident than in hypnosis, which paradoxically has been implicated as a cause of and a cure for false memory. Hypnosis can influence memory at all levels: encoding, storage, and retrieval[11].

Take the case of encoding. Hypnotized subjects have an intense, narrow focus, making it much more likely that events of such focus will be firmly registered and remembered. One study[12] demonstrated this effect in non-hypnotized people who had been mugged. They typically developed a gun focus, remembering every detail about the weapon that was used in the mugging, but unable to remember much of use about the assailant.

The power of hypnosis in false memory has been recently investigated by E. C. Orne and colleagues at the University of

Pennsylvania.[13] In one experiment, subjects completed seven recall trials in which they tried to remember a series of pictures that had been shown one week earlier. For half of the subjects, the middle five trials were carried out under hypnosis. The more hypnotically susceptible subjects produced many recall errors, irrespective of whether the trial involved hypnosis. But the less hypnotically susceptible subjects were clearly made more likely to remember incorrectly during hypnosis.

The power of suggestion makes it relatively easy to implant false memories. Elizabeth Loftus spoke of this problem at the 2003 annual meeting of the American Association for the Advancement of Science. She, and many of her peers, expressed concern over police interrogation practices, where false memories may be implanted, even unintentionally, in the minds of suspects or witnesses. If one wanted to deliberately implant false memories, it is not that difficult. The trick is to convince a person that a certain event *could* have happened and then suggest that the event *did* happen to them, even if they don't remember it.[14]

Loftus has described experimentally implanting false memories in 20,000 research volunteers, who were made through suggestion to misremember accidents, leisure activities, and childhood trauma. One particularly telling example of implanted false memory was that in one group of subjects more than one third remembered being hugged by Bugs Bunny at Disneyland. This is not possible, because Bugs Bunny is not a Disneyland character. This ruse was accomplished by recruiting volunteers who had been to Disneyland as children. They were shown a Disneyland advertisement in which Bugs was seen hugging children at Disneyland. Upon quizzing the subjects weeks later, many of them reported that they too had been hugged by Bugs and had shaken hands with him during their visit to Disneyland.

Given the main role in memory of emotion-controlling parts of the brain, it should come as no surprise that emotions can reinforce false memory.[15] In the case of the Bugs Bunny false memory, mentioned above, the feelings of warmth and acceptance made people *want* to believe that they actually had the experience. But negative emotions also promote false memory. For example, at the same AAAS meeting just mentioned, Richard McNally of Harvard reported on ten people who claimed they had been abducted by space aliens. The research team tape recorded each person's story and then monitored body signs of stress while playing back the recording. All signs of stress increased during playback, to a level seen also with people remembering Vietnam combat or childhood sexual abuse. Thus, the association between anxiety and fear and the presumed event was so powerful that it made the abduction event believable. No doubt, as such memories are replayed, the associated emotions strengthen the false memory making it all the more believable.

In everyday life, our most common experience with emotion-mediated false memory is in our personal relationships: parent-child, male-female, and dealing with authority figures. Deep emotions pervade all such interactions. It is chilling to ponder the question of how many of those memories are exaggerated or even altogether false.

Memory Filters

"You hear what you want to hear," I have said to my children on occasion. But we adults do that too. Our brains use past memories, in the forms of prejudices, emotions, preferences, or habits, to filter information that does not fit with our mind set. One of the most prominent memory researchers, Larry Squire,[16] likes to quote Charles Darwin to illustrate this point:

> *I had during many years followed a golden rule, namely, that whenever a published fact, a new observation or thought, came across me which was opposed to my general results, to make a memorandum of it without fail and at once; for I had found by experience that such facts and thoughts were far more apt to escape from the memory than favorable ones.*

Note the role of ego here. Squire as a scientist realizes that he is more likely to believe his own experiments and data than those of others that are at variance. Squire – and everybody else – are stars at the center of a personal universe. We remember ourselves as important. We remember what we did right. We try to filter out failure and blame. We try to become better than what we are. We mentally edit events. Police and insurance adjusters involved in investigating car accidents commonly report how people make excuses and try to shift blame.

Presumably, this filtering effect affects both explicit and implicit memories, as well as possibly operating at all levels of the memory process (encoding, consolidation, storage, and retrieval). However, I have not found much relevant research literature.

Adult Memories Of Childhood Are No Greater Than Chance

We all have memories of our childhood. Some memories are happy, some are sad, and some even painful. False memories of childhood are to a certain extent inevitable. Children are especially prone to co-mingle fantasy and reality, and both become inevitably entangled in memory.

Controlled experiments showed that many of these memories were wrong, according to a group of Northwestern University Medical School psychiatrists. Daniel Offer and colleagues[17] described a study they conducted to determine how well persons at middle age recalled events and relationships that occurred during adolescence. The researchers questioned 67 normal, mentally healthy male participants twice, initially at age 14 and again at age 48, regarding family relationships, home environment, dating and sexuality, religion, parental discipline and general activities.

The answers to the questions were not always the same during the two stages of life when the subjects were interviewed some 34 years later. Memories of what happened during adolescence were not reliable. Emotionally laden items, such as the type of discipline and personal relationships, were not usually remembered any more reliably than items that had no emotional component.

"It is often said that adolescence is the period in the life cycle that is most difficult to see (*and remember,* I would add) clearly," Offer said. "Our study of the emotionally laden experience of adolescence as seen through the lens of 48-year-olds demonstrated that this may indeed be so." Not only is the problem of clinical significance to counselors and psychiatrists who treat patients with childhood traumas, but everyone is potentially affected. What we remember of our childhood may be wrong. How can we be certain of our justifications for our prejudices, grudges, and animosities that we harbor toward parents, teachers, and children with whom we grew up? Offer concludes, "If accurate memory of past events and relationships is no better than chance for normal, mentally healthy individuals, we might expect that the reports of past experiences by people who are currently medically ill, psychologically disturbed or otherwise mentally compromised would be even less accurate," he said.

Practical consequences of false memory in children are huge. One obvious consequence is when as an adult, the person "remembers" being sexually abused by a parent or relative. Daniel Schacter[18] provides plenty of evidence that sometimes such memories are false, causing devastating effects on the families involved. The possible misremembering of childhood events contributes to the emotional scars and broken relationships that adults carry with them all their lives.

Child Testimony

In cases of child abuse, sometimes the only witness to the crime is the child victim. But nowhere is the problem of false memory greater than it is with young children. Sometimes, even the experts can't tell if a child is remembering events correctly. And if those events are traumatic, the possibility of false memory may be greater. In one experiment conducted at Cornell University,[19] preschool children were asked weekly about whether a fictitious event had ever happened to them. By the tenth week, more than half the 3- and 4-year-old children reported that it had and provided clear details. Even when the researchers and parents explained that the events never occurred, more than one fourth of the children could not be convinced otherwise. When professionals who specialize in interviewing children were shown videotapes of the children recalling the events, it was not clear whether the children were giving false or true accounts.

"So compelling did the children's narratives appear that we suspected that some of the children had come to truly believe they had experienced the fictitious events. Neither parents nor researchers were able to convince 27 percent of the children that the events never happened," said Thomas Ceci, one of the research psychologists who conducted the study.

Ceci suggests that when children are asked to think periodically about a fictitious event, they imagine a fictitious scenario, initially rejecting its authenticity because it is unfamiliar. Weeks later, when asked about it again, however, they may have falsely accepted the event's validity because it was now familiar as a result of having imagined the scenario earlier.

"Consequently, it is exceedingly devilishly difficult for professionals to tell fact from fiction when a child has been repeatedly suggestively interviewed over a long period of time," Ceci said. "These children frequently display none of the indicators of lying or tricking; they look and act the way children do when they are trying to be accurate and honest."

In an experiment with colleague Michelle Leichtman,[20] Ceci again demonstrated false testimony in children and, in addition, showed a powerful effect of stereotyping and suggestion. In this experiment, 176 preschoolers enrolled in private day care centers were exposed to a visit by a Sam Stone, who enacted the same scripted event at each center. Two experimental manipulations were involved, one before the visit and interviews once each week for the first three weeks and again at 10 weeks after the visit. Children were divided into four experimental groups. Children in the control group were simply asked questions about what Sam Stone did during his visit to their school. They were not primed with any information about the visit beforehand, nor were any suggestions given after the visit about what he might have done. Another group of children, the *stereotype* group was given a personal profile on Sam before the visit; he was depicted as kind, well meaning, but very clumsy and bumbling. All interviews for this group were neutral, that is, with no leading questions or prompting.

Prompting was given to a third group, the suggestion group, which was treated as were the first two groups except that were not given a pre-visit profile and during interviews they received two erroneous suggestions. The fourth group, stereotype-plus-suggestion, received a combination of pre-visit profile and post-visit suggestion. The results are for 3-4 year olds are shown in the figure (re-drawn from data in the Leichtman and Ceci paper). Data for 5-6 year olds were qualitatively the same, although they made slightly fewer errors.

The results make clear the prejudicial effect of having a pre-visit profile and of post-event suggestions on events that did not actually happen. Not only were errors frequent, but children even insisted that they had actually witnessed first hand the erroneous events. Combining pre-visit profiles with post-visit suggestion magnified the errors. These errors were not simple yes or no errors to interview questions. Children commonly embellished the errors with richly detailed narratives that elaborated and expanded the error. When videotapes of the children described what had happened were played to a test group of 119 researchers and clinicians who work in the area of children's testimony issues, the majority could not discriminate between true tales and tall tales.

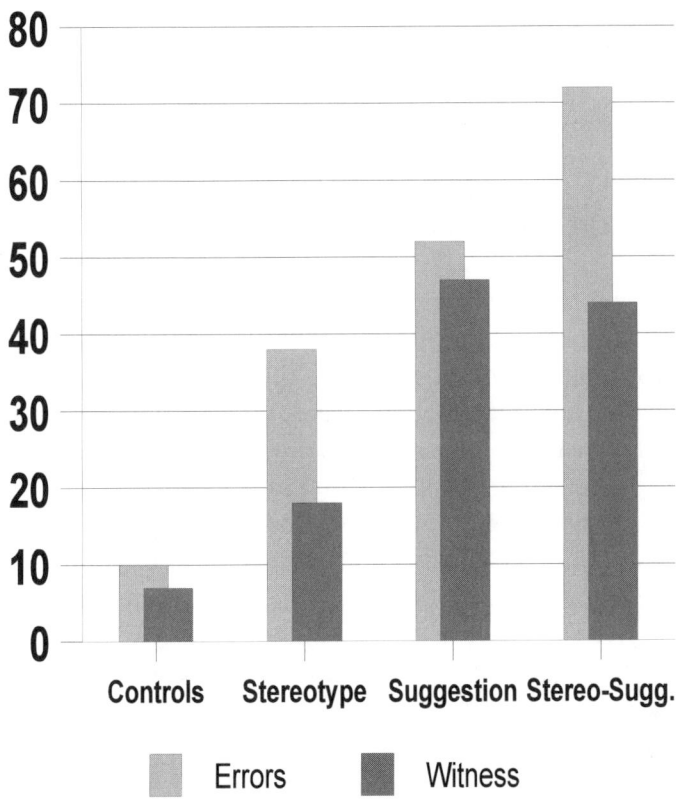

Erroneous answers, as % of total answers, during interviews about a visitor to the day-care center. Data shown are the total errors and the errors where children believed they actually witnessed the non-existent event.

In legal hearings and trials, children's testimony can be influenced by suggestions, especially if given in repeated interviews. Ceci concludes that the sad truth is that when bad things have happened to children, suggestive interviewing is often necessary to get correct disclosure from the child. Unfortunately, suggestive interviewing can also increase the chances of false memory.

Lest we adults become too judgmental about child memory, let us remember the old cliché, "Tell somebody a lie often enough, and they may come to believe it." There are whole cultures and areas of the world where this adage is painfully apparent.

How Does the Brain Get It Wrong?

Emotional trauma may cause the event to get incorrectly registered, as mentioned earlier about the September 11 suicide attack. In addition to that problem, we know that memory traces are reconstructed with each recollection. Retrieving a memory co-mingles events of the past with events of the present.[21] One experiment with rats sheds some light on how a memory can get changed during retrieval. Rats were conditioned to associate a tone with foot shock. The electric shock presumably elicited anxiety and fear in rats. After one training session, rats will freeze when they hear the tone, even if they don't get a shock. This shows that the memory was consolidated. But this memory is disrupted even after consolidation if such rats were injected with a protein synthesis inhibitor, anisomycin, into the part of the brain (the amygdala) that is crucial for fear conditioning. The protocol went like this: rats were fear conditioned, as described above. Then when they froze in response to the tone, the anisomycin was injected. The next day when the same rats were re-tested, the time spent in freeze responses was greatly reduced. Similar results were obtained even when re-testing was done as long as 14 days after the protein synthesis inhibitor. So, even though the memory had been consolidated, it was also vulnerable at the time of recall. That vulnerability period is short, because the anisomycin disrupted subsequent performance only if rats were injected within a hour or two after memory reactivation.

The mechanism for this effect is speculative, but leads to

provocative new thinking about memory. Conventional wisdom says that consolidated memories are preserved in the brain by a change in protein in the junctions (synapses) between certain neurons. Because protein molecules survive no longer than a few weeks, the learned event must also modulate gene expression in the affected neurons. The protein products of these activated genes then allow the synaptic changes to be preserved. Perhaps during recall this process is re-instituted, and can be thwarted by interventions that disrupt protein synthesis. Thus, other external events or mental processes can modify the consolidated memory each time the learned event is recalled.

False Recall In Older Adults and Alzheimer's Disease

As we discuss in the chapter on aging, memory ability commonly deteriorates with age. Even things we think we remember may be remembered wrong. Mark Twain once said, "When I was younger, I could remember anything, whether it had happened or not; but my faculties are decaying now and soon I shall be so I cannot remember any but the things that never happened. It is sad to go to pieces like this but we all have to do it."

Today, formal studies of false memory in the elderly are under way. In one such study by David Balota and colleagues at Washington University,[22] the authors concluded that Mark Twain was right: older adults do appear more likely to remember things that never happened. But this problem is not inevitable. Many healthy older people have very good memories (see the book's last chapter on aging). Moreover, results of experiments suggest that the cause of false memory in older adults may be a breakdown in attention rather than a primary memory failure.

The Balota study was based on an analysis of false recall and recognition rates in 159 people who were divided into five groups: healthy college students, healthy older adults about age 70, healthy older adults about age 85; and two groups of older adults with either very mild or mild symptoms of Alzheimer's related dementia. Subjects were read a list of 12 associated words that strongly suggested another non-presented critical target word. As an example, suppose you were read a list of words such as Excited, Activated, Interested, Agitated, Stimulated, Alert, and Energized. This list does not contain "Aroused," but many people would later recall that Aroused had appeared in the list. In the experiment, multiple trials of this type were conducted and the researchers found that young adults recalled the presented words about 70 percent of the time, but mistakenly recalled the non-presented word in about 30 percent of the trials. Healthy older adults recalled the presented words about 55 percent of the time, and the non-presented words about 37 percent of the time. But people with mild Alzheimer's related dementia actually recalled the item that was not presented slightly more often (35 percent) than they recalled words that were actually presented (only 32 percent).

Memories are created and stored in logical, semantic, or visual association with other events, experiences, or knowledge. Any given thought or idea may trigger a flood of associations, not all of which are accurate reflections of the components of a learned task (the word list in the case of the experiment just mentioned).

Clearly in a task such as this, the subject has to pay attention to what was said and "edit out on the fly" any internally generated words that were not actually presented. This is an attention problem. It is also a working memory problem. So Balota and colleagues assert that at least in early Alzheimer's disease, diminished attention and information processing capability may both be the basis for the apparent decline in memory.

The increase in false-memory susceptibility among healthy older adults and individuals with Alzheimer's seems to indicate that the mind is somehow overwhelmed by the flood of jumbled recollections still pouring in from an active network of knowledge-based associations. False memories result not from a lack of information, but from the mind's diminished ability to process the information and reach sound conclusions. This also implies that highly educated people and people who have spent a lifetime learning how to deal with massive amounts of information may not have as many memory problems as they age.

Stress Can Fool You

We all experience some events in our lives that occur under stressful circumstances. Our memories of those events may be confounded by that stress. Stress most assuredly accompanies the traumatic experiences in the real world that can lead to false memories (such as sexual and other types of abuse, horrific eyewitness situations). See also what I had to say about this in the chapter on emotions.

More specifically, it is the physiological results of stress that can confound our memories of stressful events. Stress causes the release of glucocorticoid hormones, and these hormones are bound by neurons in certain parts of the brain, particularly the hippocampus (which helps us remember) and the prefrontal cortex (which helps us think). This binding of stress hormone to neurons should enhance their function, but it seems that we are designed so that it easier to forget stressful situations.

This phenomenon becomes a particular problem in law and medicine. When we see or are involved in a crime, the stress of the situation may cause us to mis-remember key events.

The possibility that stress itself could corrupt memory formation was recently tested by a group of researchers at the University of Arizona[23]. They divided a group of 84 volunteer undergraduate college students into two nearly equal groups, one stressed and the other non-stressed.

The nature of the stress was psychological. Students were instructed to give a speech in front of a one-way mirror. They were told that there were three trained investigators behind this mirror. The room was set up like a recording studio, giving the impression that the

235

student speech was being recorded for television. The students were given only 10 minutes notice for the speech, after which time their notes were abruptly taken away. The students were then told they would have to begin immediately, speaking extemporaneously. After five minutes of speaking, the students were interrupted and told to subtract aloud and without stopping the number 13 serially from the number 1022.

After the stress events (or time lag in the control group) students were presented with a list of semantically related words (such as candy, sour, sugar, bitter, chocolate, cake, etc.). Twenty such word lists were presented, and students were instructed to remember as many words as they could. Next, for each list students were tested for their recall with four words, only one of which was actually presented in the original list. Of the other non-presented three words, one was a highly related word that might trigger a false memory. For example, for the list above, the false-memory trigger word was "sweet," while the non-presented and unrelated words were "hat" and "cow." The highly related words, though never presented, were most likely to trigger false memories, as had been shown in previous studies by other workers. The hypothesis was that stress, if it had an effect, would cause a higher percentage of errors during re-test, especially with the highly related but not presented words.

Results indicated more errors in the stressed group. Moreover, the false recognition errors were specific: stressed subjects made few errors to unrelated non-presented words. Non-stressed students also made false-memory errors, but significantly fewer than with stressed subjects. Unlike the stressed students, the non-stressed subjects recognized the "trick words" approximately 40% of the time.

You might suspect that the stress impaired memory generally. However, this was not borne out in the control test with unrelated non-presented words, where there were no differences in errors between the stressed and non-stressed groups.

Explanations for selective forgetfulness fall into two categories. One is the possibility that presentation of a new word may create a vague sense of familiarity, given that all the words are well known to most subjects. The second possibility is that subjects may remember the "gist" or theme of the word without remembering the specifics. Both possibilities could exist here. Malfunction of prefrontal cortex and hippocampus could affect the gist mode of operation, because both structures are known to help bind together contextual elements that make up a memorable episode. Stress impairs the contextual binding, perhaps because it introduces other distracting elements.

Why does stress increase this kind of false memory? First, it helps to examine why non-stressed students made so many false memory errors. Because the words are common, everyday words, the problem is not remembering the words themselves but the context in which they are used. Because memory is so dependent on association, it is not surprising that one conjures up memories for a presented word, like sugar, with a related but non-presented word like sweet. This profound sense of familiarity and association makes false memory more likely. So, the real task is remembering whether the related word had actually been presented. There is also the issue of "gist." People who accept imprecise thinking focus on the gist of what is said or seen, as opposed to the nitty-gritty details.

The task for the brain is to "bind together" the elements that go together, as in the presented word list. Thus, it would seem that stress, and the release of glucocorticoid hormones that attend stress, interfere with this binding capability. We don't know why.

What we do know is that stress is not good for your memory. This study shows that stress can selectively cause you to remember the wrong answer.

Role of Education and Intelligence

How much false memory occurs due to recall processes varies with culture, education, and intelligence. This conclusion is illustrated by experiments of Ernest Dube at Cornell University.[24]

Memories That Lie

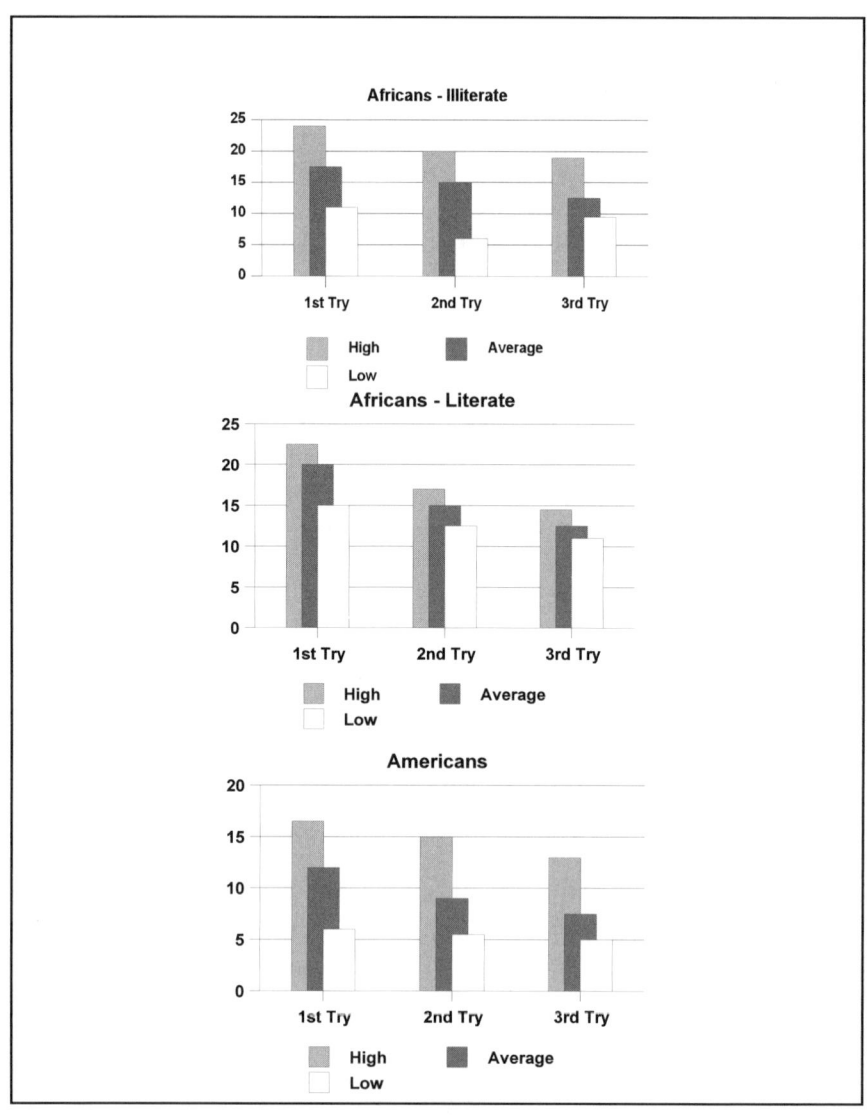

Average recall scores by three groups of people, on three recall attempts after hearing a story. (Data redrawn from *Memory Observed,* 1992)

Dube tested the ability to remember stories as told to illiterate vs. literate Africans in Botswana. Similar stores and recall challenges were made of Americans.

Intelligence ratings of the Africans were necessarily determined informally, given that standard IQ tests were not appropriate. But the African subjects were interviewed by adults who had known them for a long time. Interviews included asking them to distinguish the meaning of thirteen words, such as wise, cunning, intelligent, clever, all in their native language. The raters then assigned subjects to either a "high intelligence" or "low intelligence" category. The number of subjects were all of junior high school age, numbering 36 in each group of Africans and 24 U.S. young people.

The protocol consisted of telling 5 complicated stories to the subjects. Each story was translated into the appropriate language, and the story was presented verbally by a speaker whose first language was the language used in the story. Stories were presented one at a time, with recall of specific themes and episodes tested immediately afterward and again also at one week and one month later.

Ability to recall stories varied widely, depending on culture, education, and intelligence. Not surprisingly, the more intelligent youngsters recalled more accurately. The intelligence effect seemed relatively independent of education and culture. Indeed, the intelligent Africans performed slightly better than intelligent Americans. In fact, in all intelligence groups, Americans remembered stories less well, perhaps indicating a cultural influence. Education does seem to improve the ability to recall in the average and low intelligence groups (compare literate and non-literate African data).

Pictures are Not Always Worth a Thousand Words

Going through the family album brings back many memories. Look at any picture. Grandma remembers one thing, granddad remembers another, mom remembers yet something else, and so it goes. But not only do people remember different things from visual scenes, some of what they remembered never occurred, at least according to studies by Daniel Schacter. After watching a video, subjects remembered best those scenes that had been reinforced by photographs. And when shown related photos that were not in the video, subjects often confused these photo scenes with those in the video. This finding may confirm the popular idea that some memories may be based on photographs, not real events. Photos need a context, and we supply stories to go with the photos that may not be true. Seeing the photo calls up the false memory.

This relates to the power of visual imagery to act as a handle to recall associated memories. Many popular memory gimmicks are based on this idea, as I discussed in the chapter on association.

* * * * *

We hear what we want to hear. We remember what we want to remember. Worse yet, what we want to remember is sometimes reconstructed erroneously. Children are especially prone to false memory when subjected to selective questioning. Adult memories of their childhood are also often distorted.

The point of this chapter is to caution the reader that many memories, including their own, are untrustworthy. This seems to contradict the theme of the first chapter that our brains are reliable memory machines. I guess the point is that our brains can be very good at remembering what they construct as our memory, but we have to take special pains to be certain that the constructed memory is correct. This effort is especially needed in times of emotional stress. Both positive and negative emotions can create false memories.

Intelligence minimizes memory error. Independently of intelligence, education also reduces false memory.

Key Ideas:

1. Make a special effort to "get it right" when you must remember something that occurred under distressing or confusing circumstances.

2. Be aware that a memory may have been mis-registered, mis-interpreted, mis-preserved, or mis-retrieved.

3. Consider the possibility that some of your attitudes, emotions, or habits may reflect false memory, including unconscious conditioning.

4. Implicit tests for recall may be more reliable than asking people to recall explicitly what happened.

5. The "power of suggestion" is a major cause of false memory.

6. Both positive and negative emotions can promote false memory, strengthening the false memory to make it all the more believable.

7. Our past memories, in the form of emotions, prejudices, preferences, and habits, act as a filter that excludes information that does not fit with our mind set. Such filtered information is hard to remember.

8. Realize that children and adolescents are especially prone to false memories that may persist throughout adulthood. Older adults are likewise prone to false memory of events learned as children.

9. Lies repeated often enough may come to be remembered and believed. This is why propaganda and "brainwashing" work so well.

10. Stress increases the odds of false memory.

11. Education and intelligence can reduce the incidence of false memory.

Sources:

1. Begley, Sharon. 2002. The memory of Sept. 11 is seared in your mind; but is it really true? Wall Street Journal. Sept. 13, page B1.

2. Gazzaniga, Michael S. 1998. The Mind's Past. University of California Press, Berkeley, Ca.

3. Ceci, S. J., Huffman, M. L., and Smith, E. 1994. Repeatedly thinking about a non-event: source misattributions among preschoolers. Consciousness and Cognition. 3: 388-407.

4. Bahrick, H. P., Hall, L. K., and Berger, S. A. 1996. Accuracy and distortion in memory for high school grades. Psychological Science. 7: 265-271.

5. Robbins, L. C. 1963. The accuracy of parental recall of aspects of child development and of child rearing practices. J. Abnormal and Social Psychol. 66: 261-270.

6. Anderson, M. 2001. U.S. News and World Report, March 26, p. 55

7. Jacobs, W. J., and Nadel, L. 1998. Psychology, Public Policy, and Law, Vol. 4, page 1110

8. Story by Associated Press. 2001. Houston Chronicle. March 28, p. 12A.

9. Buckhout, R. 1974. Eyewitness testimony. Scientific American. 231: 23-31.

10. Loftus, E., Feldman, J., and Dashiell, R. 1995. The reality of illusory memories, p. 47-68. In Memory Distortion, edited by Daniel Schacter. Harvard University Press, Cambrdige, Mass.

11. Spiegel, D. 1995. Hypnosis and suggestion, p. 129-149. In Memory Distortion, edited by Daniel Schacter. Harvard University Press, Cambrdige, Mass.

12. Loftus, E. F. 1979. Eyewitness Testimony. Harvard University Press, Cambridge, Mass.

13. Orne, E. C., Whitehouse, W. G., Dinges, D. F., and Orne, M. T. 1996. Memory liabilities associated with hypnosis: does low hypnotizability confer immunity? Int. J. Clin. Exp. Hypn. 44 (4): 354-369.

14. Woods, M. A. 2003. It's easy to plant false memories, study finds. Pittsburg Post Gazette, Feb. 17, pg. A6.

15. Beckman, Mary. 2003. False memories, true pain. Science. 299: 1306.

16. Squire, L. 1995 Biological foundations of accuracy and inaccuracy in memory, p. 197-225. In Memory Distortion, edited by Daniel Schacter. Harvard University Press, Cambrdige, Mass.

17. Offer, Daniel, Kaiz, M., Howard, K. I., and Bennett, E. S. 2000. The altering of reported experiences. J. American Academy of Child and Adolescent Psychiatry 39: 735-742. See

http://nuinfo.nwu.edu/univ-relations/media/news-releases/1999-00/*sci
med/memory-scimed.html

18. Schacter, D. L. 1995. Memory Distortion. Harvard University Press. Cambridge, Mass.

19. Ceci, Thomas, S. J., and Huffman, M. L. C. 1997. How suggestible are preschool children. Cognitive and social factors. Journal of the American Academy of Child and Adolescent Psychiatry. 36: 948-958. See http://www.sciencedaily.com/releases/1997/09/970919061741.htm

20. Leichtman, M. D., and Ceci, S. J. 2000, Preschoolers remember Sam Stone, p. 232-247. In Memory Observed, 2nd edition, edited by Ulric Neisser and Ira E. Hyman, Jr. Worth Publishers, N.Y., N.Y.

21. Yadin, D. 2000. Neurobiology: the shaky trace. Nature. 406: 686-687.

22. Watson, J. M., Balota, D. A., and Sergeant-Marshall, S. D. 2001. Semantic, phonological, and hybrid veridical and false memories in healthy older adults and in individuals with dementia of the Alzheimer type. Neuropsychology. 15: 254-267.

23. Payne, Nadel, Allen, J. J. B., Thomas, K. G. F., and Jacobs, W. J. 2002. The effects of experimentally-induced stress on false recognition. Memory 10(1) 1-6.

24. Dube, E. F. 2000. Literacy, cultural familiarity, and "intelligence" as determinants of story recall, p. 426-443. In Memory Observed, ed. by U. Neisser and I. E. Hyman, Jr., Worth, N.Y.

Sleep: Perchance to Dream

Perchance to Remember

- New Reason to "Sleep On It"
- Learning By Sleepy Students
- Learning During Reverie
- A Role for Dreaming that Freud Never Knew
- What Do Rats Remember in Their Dreams?
- Memory's Best Window of Opportunity
- What Video Game Images in Your Dreams Tell Us
- Jet-Lag and Memory

Sleep is to remembering as rain is to grass
- W. R. Klemm

Jay Leno, during one of his comedy monologs, quoted a sleep researcher who claimed that sleep helps memory. *Well, ... duh ... the more you sleep the less you have to remember!*

But we really do know that sleep helps memories to form. Most people think that the purpose of sleep is to rest the brain. There is clear evidence that the brain is still busy at work during sleep. Decades ago, researchers demonstrated that many neurons fired just as much during sleep as during wakefulness, and some neurons were even more active during sleep.

Brain waves, which are derived from neuronal firing but not equivalent to neuronal firing, change during different levels of sleep. In the early stages of sleep, the brain waves (electroencephalogram, EEG) become large and of low frequency. This is called the stage of "slow-wave sleep." Then there are episodes of sharp spikes, called spindles, that are intermixed with the slow waves. As the night wears on, sleep is periodically punctuated by dream episodes, in which the brain waves become small and of high frequency, looking much as they do when you are awake and mentally active.

Recent studies indicate that one of the things the brain is doing during sleep is forming memories of the day's events. Numerous studies have shown that sleep promotes the consolidation of declarative memories. In exploring how sleep might facilitate memory, Steffan Gais and colleagues in Lübeck, Germany found EEG changes during nocturnal sleep after human subjects had been extensively trained on a declarative learning task.[1] They measured the time spent in each sleep stage, the density of spindles during slow-wave sleep, and the EEG power spectra from 28 electrode locations. During sleep after training, sleep spindles were more prominent than in control subjects that had been given the same amount of daytime stimulation, but without a learning requirement. The spindle effect was most prominent during the first 90 minutes of sleep. A related key observation was that recall ability during awake re-testing correlated with the degree to which spindles were prominent during sleep. Thus, it would appear that important memory-forming processes are underway during the spindle portion of the slow-wave stage of sleeping.

The same beneficial effect on procedural memories may also

occur, although not much research in this area has been reported. One procedural memory test showed a profoundly beneficial effect of sleep. Stefan Fischer and colleagues[2] at the University of Lübeck in Germany taught a sequential motor task involving the thumb and finger. No matter whether sleep occurred in the daytime or at regular nighttime, sleep after practice of hand movement enhanced the speed of sequence performance by 33.5% and reduced error rates by 30% as compared to corresponding intervals of wakefulness after the training. The effect of sleep was stable and was still demonstrable when testing was delayed another night to assure that everybody in the control group got enough sleep. So, if you want to learn to play the piano or any other complex motor task, you will probably do better if you sleep after each practice session.

New Reason To "Sleep On It"

School kids may be cutting back on sleep to finish ever-mounting piles of homework, but it could be a self-defeating strategy. Sleep loss degrades many neural functions. In one study,[3] sleep loss degraded visual vigilance and memory for words, and time-of-day fluctuations were found in choice reaction time, logical reasoning, and word memory. Exercise also seemed to play an effect in that non-exercising subjects degraded sooner than did exercising subjects. So, sleep-deprived couch potatoes beware!

Harvard Medical School researchers have found that people who stay up all night after learning and practicing a new task show little improvement in their performance.[4] And the study suggests that no amount of sleep on the following two nights can make up for the toll taken by the initial all-nighter. "Our research shows that you need sleep that first night if you want to improve on a task," says Robert Stickgold, Harvard Medical School assistant professor of psychiatry at the Massachusetts Mental Health Center.

The study adds a critical piece to a growing body of work by Stickgold[5] and others showing that sleep is necessary for learning.

Previously, Stickgold and his colleagues found that people who learned a particular task did not improve their performance when tested later the same day but did improve after a night of sleep.

To see whether the night of sleep actually caused the improvement, Stickgold trained 24 subjects in the same visual discrimination task, which consisted of identifying the orientation of three diagonal bars flashed for a sixtieth of a second on the lower left quadrant of a computer screen full of horizontal stripes. Half of the subjects went to sleep that night while the other half were kept awake until the second night of the study. Both groups were allowed to sleep on the second and third nights. On the fourth day, both groups were tested on the visual discrimination task. Those who slept the first night identified the correct orientation of the diagonal bars much more rapidly than they had the first day. The other group showed no improvement, despite the two nights of catch-up sleep.

"We think that getting that first night's sleep starts the process of memory consolidation," says Stickgold." It seems that memories normally wash out of the brain unless some process nails them down. My suspicion is that sleep is one of those things that does the nailing down."

Another compelling study was published by Sean Drummond and his colleagues at San Diego State U. And the U. C. San Diego[6]. They combined memory performance with magnetic resonance imaging (MRI) to study sleep deprivation of young, healthy adults. After a sleepless night, free recall fell by about half, and the brain imaging analysis showed reduced blood oxygen activity in the temporal area. However, the areas of the prefrontal cortex that had been activated during remembering after normal sleep worked even more after sleep deprivation. What's more, the bilateral parietal lobes and two additional areas in the prefrontal cortex, usually not activated after normal sleep, became active.

These observations led the researchers of the study to suggest that cortical regions not normally involved in some cognitive tasks like verbal learning can be recruited to help out the regions already involved in these tasks. The researchers of the study also emphasize that the cortical areas that work the hardest during wakefulness might have a greater need for sleep. In other words, only sleep seems to provide real rest to these cortical areas.

What about a *little* sleep loss? A University of Pennsylvania study[7] showed that even a little sleep loss can devastate memory. People were assigned to sleep regimens of four, six, or eight hours of sleep each night for two weeks and tested periodically during the daytime for mental performance. Subjects who got four or even six hours of sleep performed as poorly on brain function tests as they did when kept from sleeping at all for three consecutive days. So, short-changing your sleep each night by an hour or so builds up a sleep debt that affects attention and working memory. In the study, performance decline was cumulative. An interesting aside from the study was that none of the 48 people in the study realized that their mental performance had deteriorated from the mild sleep loss. As a college professor, I wonder about the performance loss going on in students who short-change their sleep for months at a time.

Learning by Sleepy Students

It should come as no surprise that sleep deprivation impairs learning, as any teacher knows who has students who sleep in class. What may be surprising is how the brain attempts to compensate for the mental handicap created by sleepiness.

A team of researchers from the UCSD School of Medicine and the Veterans Affairs Healthcare System, San Diego used functional magnetic resonance imaging (fMRI) technology to monitor activity in the brains of sleep-deprived subjects performing simple verbal learning tasks.[8]

They were somewhat surprised to learn that regions of the brain's prefrontal cortex displayed more activity in direct correlation with the subject's sense of sleepiness; the sleepier the subject, the more active the cortex. Also, a region of the brain called the parietal lobes, not activated in rested subjects during the verbal exercise, was more active when the subjects were deprived of sleep. The parietal region normally performs somewhat different functions in the learning process than the temporal region. Although subjects' memory performance was less efficient with sleep deprivation, greater activity in the parietal region was associated with better memory. It is as if the prefrontal and parietal lobes have to work harder during sleepiness. On the other hand, the temporal lobe, a brain region involved in language processing, was not activated during verbal learning in sleep deprived subjects, but was active in rested subjects.

"Only in recent years have we begun to realize the prevalence and severity of sleep deprivation in our population, with a significant number of people doing shift work, suffering from jet lag and so forth," said one of the investigators, J. Christian Gillin, M.D., professor of psychiatry at the UC San Diego. "Yet, we don't know very much about how sleep deprivation impairs performance, and how precisely the brain reacts to lack of sleep. These findings are just a beginning, and as we learn more, perhaps will be able to devise interventions to alleviate the behavioral impairments associated with lack of sleep."

For this study, thirteen normal healthy subjects were first evaluated in a sleep laboratory to determine that their sleep patterns were normal. They were then kept awake and carefully monitored in a hospital sleep laboratory for over a period of about 35 hours. During this experiment, they were given separate mental tasks which they performed while undergoing fMRI scans which produced images revealing brain activity. These images revealed increased and decreased activation of specific regions of the brain in each subject from a rested state through various stages of sleep deprivation.

This study and another study published by Gillin's team indicated that the brain is extremely dynamic in its efforts to function when deprived of sleep, though the consequence for the subject is diminished ability to perform basic mental tasks. It is also apparent that the effects of sleep loss are different depending on the mental task that the brain is asked to perform.

In the earlier study, the team studied sleep-deprived subjects performing a task involving subtraction. In that study, they observed that the brain regions activated in rested subjects doing the arithmetic problems were not active in the sleep-deprived subjects. No other region of the brain became activated when subjects performed arithmetic when sleep-deprived. Subjects had fewer correct answers and omitted more responses when sleepy than when rested.

We don't know why the sleepy brain displays increased activity in certain regions when confronted with verbal problems, but in general shows less activity when challenged with arithmetic problems. "It is possible that when the prefrontal and temporal regions were affected by sleepiness, the brain shifted the verbal processing to another system in the parietal lobes that could compensate for the loss of function. This suggests that parietal lobes might play a special role in the brain's compensation for sleepiness," said Gregory G. Brown, Ph.D., a member of the team. "However, the parietal lobes are the system primarily associated with arithmetic performance when subjects are well rested, so when it becomes less responsive with sleeplessness, there is not a brain system available to come online to compensate for the negative effects of sleep deprivation," he said.

"It is important to remember that sleep deprivation does have detrimental effects, which we sometimes forget as we push workers, students and others to perform even when they are functioning with a lack of sleep," said Gillin.

Learning During Reverie

Back in the 1960s and 70s, a popular fad was "sleep learning." The idea was to play a tape recording of what you needed to memorize while you slept. Formal studies tended to indicate that this did not work. Memory usually did not improve.

However, since that time some new research discoveries reveal that sleep and learning do go together, but in different ways than we originally thought.

Does it help to study just prior to going to sleep? I remember as a young veterinary student how I stumbled upon what seemed to be an effective learning strategy. Veterinary students have an enormous amount of material to memorize - normal and disease data from multiple species with multiple species-specific diseases. I would study hard all day, as did my peers. Then on nights before an examination, a group of us would gather in one room of the fraternity house and go over old exams and discuss complicated issues. Only I was usually so tired (or lazy) that I just lay on the top of a bunk-bed and listened to everybody. In my reverie I would think leisurely about everything the other fellows were saying. Then I would go off to bed, thinking about the material as I fell asleep. Everybody else what staying up several hours longer. Yet I consistently outscored these guys. They were infuriated. Here they worked so hard, and I loafed along and still got higher grades. Physically, I was loafing, but mentally I was focused on what was being said, integrating and using it to promote my memory consolidating processes. The good night's sleep helped me a lot more than the cramming helped my buddies.

A Role for Dreaming that Freud Never Knew

Dreaming is so integral to human life that it pervades our culture and our history. The Bible and the Koran treat dreaming as a primary source of divine inspiration. Shakespeare treated dreams as omens. Julius Caesar's wife foretold his assassination in her dream. Sigmond Freud called dreams the "royal road" to the subconscious. Today's experimental psychologists tell us that dreams are a royal road to memory.

Where does the mind go when we sleep? As dreamers, we have long suspected this mysteriously sealed condition leads a purposeful life of its own. Science, however, has only lately supported a specific role for brain activity during sleep, which is to cement the memories that we acquire while awake. Sidarta Ribeiro and colleagues at Rockefeller University have shown that exposure to a "memorable" environment causes the brain to turn on a gene called zif-268 during subsequent sleep.[9] Because activation of zif-268 can alter nerve cell behavior, this discovery offers an intriguing glimpse of how the sleeping brain could consolidate recently formed memories.

In rats, certain brain cells that activate during daytime exploration tend to reactivate during sleep. Scientists speculate the sleeping brain reenacts waking activity in order to lay down lasting memories, but the way it might do this is unknown. Ribeiro and colleagues focused on the contribution of zif-268, which turns on after heightened brain activity and is associated with strengthened communication between nerve cells.

The researchers exposed a group of rats to novel, enriched environments (labyrinths with toys) and another group of rats to their normal home cages. Afterwards, the rats went to sleep, passing through successive stages known as slow wave and rapid eye movement (REM) sleep. During slow wave sleep, zif-268 turned off in all rats, regardless of which environment they had experienced. During REM sleep, however, zif-268 turned on in rats that had explored the labyrinths and stayed off in rats that had not. This retrieval of zif-268 activity during REM sleep may couple with other reactivated brain mechanisms to "process" memories of novel experiences. Such processing may in turn prove important for memory consolidation. So sleep well. Nature's sweet restorer has a job to do.

What Do Rats Remember in Their Dreams?

Yes, rats dream. Or at least they show the same bodily signs of dreaming as do humans: rapid eye movements, activated brain waves, absence of muscle tone with superimposed episodes of muscle twitches. If you have ever had a pet dog, you most probably have seen it dreaming; the rapid eye movements are not obvious unless you pry open the eyelids and look at the eyeballs. But the limb twitches punctuated by episodes of barking suggest that the dog is chasing something in a dream.

Interesting correlations have been noted between capability for bodily signs of dreaming and animal phyla. Fish and amphibians show no signs of dreams. Reptiles and birds show only partial signs and the "dream" episodes are short and infrequent. When you get to mammals, however, the picture changes dramatically. All but the most primitive

253

animals exhibit dream signs, and the dreaming is frequent. The most robust dreamers are predators (cats, dogs), while the least dreaming occurs in animals that are vulnerable to predation (rabbits, sheep, cattle). Dreaming is a very deep state, in the sense that outside stimuli have less arousal effect during dreaming than during regular sleep. Predators can afford the luxury of dreaming. What all this has to do with the ability of animals to remember has never been studied. I would predict that predators have better memory ability than prey species. However, I don't believe that has ever been tested by experiment.

Perhaps of more relevance is the key correlate of dreaming; namely, that it is most abundant in the young (of all species). Dreaming has even been documented via implanted electrodes in late-term fetuses. Why do babies dream so much? After all, you would think that they have little to dream about. One answer is that dreaming is one of nature's ways to keep the brain stimulated. Stimulation is necessary to sculpt the circuitry in a developing brain. The newborn brain is a blank slate, ready to have learning experiences inscribed upon it by the formation of circuitry to represent those memories.

Many experiments have demonstrated that if you keep rats from dreaming, you will interfere with consolidation of learning tasks performed during the day. How do you keep rats from dreaming? A common method is the inverted flower pot technique. You place the rat on a small island, an inverted flower pot, in the middle of a tank of water. There is just enough room on the flower pot base to allow the rat to curl up to go to sleep. However, as soon as the rat enters dream sleep, all the muscles relax, and the rat falls off into the water. Thus, the rat can sleep all he wants, but he can't dream.

The inverted flower pot method of keeping rats from dreaming. Rats can curl up on the top of the pot to sleep, but when they enter dream sleep, their muscle tone totally collapses and they fall off into the water and wake up.

Depriving Rats of Dream Sleep

A recent experiment in rats suggests a link between dreaming and daily experiences. At MIT, Matthew Wilson and Kenway Louie[10] trained rats to run a circular maze, with stops for food reward. They used surgically implanted electrodes in the hippocampus, the part of the brain that is most central to memory formation, to monitor neuronal activity during maze performance and during sleep. Most of the neurons fired in the same patterns during the presumed dream stage of sleep and during maze running. This suggests that rats are replaying the memories in their dreams, which of course provides an automated way to reinforce the memorization process. To my knowledge, no such studies have been done in humans (who don't volunteer for implanted electrodes), but there are ways to detect brain wave patterns that could correspond to learning events and memories of them. Humans should be studied, because as we know, our dreams are often symbolic. In such dreams we do not directly relate dream content to realities of wakefulness. Presumably, rats are incapable of symbolic dreams. The extent to which humans replay daily events in their dreams could well differ depending on whether dream content was literal or symbolic. Because so much of our dream life is symbolic, we have to wonder if symbolic dreams provide a more powerful way to reinforce memories. If so, why?

Brain imaging techniques, such as positron emission tomography (PET), are beginning to be used to test such questions. These techniques do not show activity of individual neurons, but rather clusters of many neurons. Nonetheless, P. Maquet and colleagues[11] have reported that certain brain regions that were activated when people were trained in a task, became more active during their dream sleep.

Critics have argued that replaying daily events during dreams has no practical value. In real life, a rat would not normally run a maze, much less run it two or more times. More likely, it seems to me is that replay during dreaming is consolidating a memory of learning how to learn in a given context.

Memory's Best Window of Opportunity

Apparently, the early morning hours are the important time for sleep to promote memory. If you cut your night sleep short by getting up early, memory is impaired. At least that is the finding of Dr. Robert Stickgold at Harvard Medical School and his colleagues at the Massachusetts Mental Health Center in Boston.[12] Their study tested memories of college student volunteers under conditions where they spotted targets on a computer screen and pressed a button as soon as they realized they had seen a target. At first, it may have taken up to 400 milliseconds to realize a target had appeared, but with practice, the response time went down to less than a 100 milliseconds. When trained students were re-tested 3 to 12 hours later on the same day, there was no improvement over their best time during the earlier training session. Also, students who slept less than 6 hours showed no improvement the next day. But improvement did occur if students slept more than 6 hours, and the improvement was proportional to the length of time beyond six hours. For those who slept more than 8 hours, improvement of the skill was proportional to the amount of slow wave sleep that they got in the first quarter of the night's sleep and to the amount of dream sleep that occurred in the last quarter of the night's sleep. Thus, both phases of sleep have an important effect on memory formation in the tests. The enhanced performance grew over time, with the well-rested students performing even better when re-tested two days to a week after the initial training session. Another important observation was that the degree of improved memory on this test had no correlation with what prep school the students had attended, their SAT scores, or how hard they tried. It all depended on how well they slept.

A role for both slow wave sleep and dream sleep was also documented in a study by Werner Plihal and Jan Born[13]. They tested twenty healthy men on a declarative memory task and on a procedural memory task. The benefit from sleep on recall depended on the phase of sleep and the type of memory. The declarative memory task improved more during early sleep, the phase when slow-wave sleep dominates. The procedural task improved best after dreaming (note that the task in the Stickgold study mentioned above was a procedural task).

What Video Game Images in Your Dreams Teach Us

The video game Tetris can be found on in almost any college dorm room. College students need their entertainment, after all. But the game has attracted the attention of brain researchers too. Robert Stickgold[14] and his colleagues at Harvard Medical, for example, used the game to study memory.

The game appears on a video screen. The player uses a computer mouse to align falling blocks of different design patterns to fill gaps as layers build up on the screen from the bottom. Images of these blocks taunt a player in the reverie before going to sleep. Similar replay of intense stimulation can occur as we go to sleep anytime we have an intense sensory experience, such as hearing in our mind's ear the music that we heard at a concert that evening. This is a common response to any kind of intense learning experience. For example, I am a jazz fan, and if I go to a concert or listen to jazz CDs I will often hear the music in my mind's ear afterwards, keeping me awake. I not only hear parts of what was actually played by specific instruments, but I can hear myself improvising on top of what I actually heard.

Strickgold and co-workers studied this phenomenon in normal people and in amnesics, people who had damage to their hippocampus and therefore had difficulty in forming memories. A prior brain imaging study by Richard Haier of the University of California at Irvine had shown that brain activity increased during Tetris game playing, but the activity decreased as the player became more proficient. In Strickgold's experiment, the subjects played Tetris for seven hours per day for three days. Then, in a sleep lab each evening, researchers awakened them repeatedly during the first hour to ask what was on their minds. The subjects were divided into three groups: 1) expert players who had played Tetris many times before, 2) novice players who had never played it before, and 3) novice players who could not form new memories because of disease in the medial temporal lobes of their brains. The first thing the experimenters noticed is that many subjects in the first two groups had visual playback of the Tetris game as they went to sleep. Nine of 12 normal subjects reported seeing the falling Tetris blocks. Three of the five amnesic subjects also reported the falling blocks, even though they had no memory of having played the game, nor had their ability to play it improved much over the three days.

In the normal subjects, imaging in sleep progressed in parallel with memory of the game and performance scores. Only 10% of the total reported images occurred on the first night of sleep. Ninety percent occurred on the second night.

Intense practice on the Tetris game allowed the researchers to examine 17 different people who had similar dream content. They had their subjects (12 novices, 10 experts, and 5 amnesiacs) play the game over the course of three days for two hours in the morning and one hour in the evening of the first day and for an hour in the morning and the evening of the following days. All subjects reported dreaming of falling Tetris game pieces. Even the amnesiac subjects recalled seeing the pieces in their dreams, even though they had no explicit memory of the game during wakefulness because they had brain lesions that made them unable to create new memories. What the researchers found was that the amnesic patients did not improve their Tetris scores with practice. No surprise there. What was not expected was that amnesics, when awakened, sometimes reported seeing Tetris object images, but did not know what the context was or the rules of the game for manipulating the objects. With each successive day, the number of reported imagery increased, but there was no increase in any thoughts associated with the images. The other two groups of subjects showed a progressive increase in both imagery and Tetris thoughts with each successive day. In short, it seems as if the amnesic patients were rehearsing (and learning) the procedural component of Tetris, but not the declarative part. Tetris scores of the novice players increased each day in parallel with the increase in imagery and Tetris thoughts after the awakenings. Performance in the experts did not improve each day, presumably because they were already functioning at maximum capacity.

In dreaming, the brain does not merely replay memories but transforms them by associating them with old images and memories. "It's actually hunting around and finding other relevant information to connect to, which is the integrative process – which over time, I would argue, is a critical function of sleep," Stickgold concluded.

The imagery seems to be wandering around in the brain, and it is probably serving as rehearsal to help strengthen memory formation and improve skill. Note that this occurs while subjects slept, raising the possibility that sleep is actually necessary for memory and skill formation. The fact that this wandering also seems to be occurring in amnesics who do not remember the game and who do not get better at playing it, suggests that the images have to be processed through the hippocampus (which was not functioning normally in these subjects) in order to make a permanent change.

These observations also relate to our understanding of the difference between declarative memory (that which is consciously remembered) and procedural memory (that which is not recalled, but nonetheless reflected in enhanced performance). The imaging in amnesics show that there is a memory for the game in their brains that they cannot normally access.

Such wandering images, not only from the Tetris game but other experiences, may also contribute to our dreams. Suppose that declarative processes during dreaming, even in normal people, are not working to provide the anchors for making associations. Such untethered images would then free to be seen in the dreaming mind in bizarre recombinations of image and associations. Since the dreaming stage of sleep is uniquely important to memory formation, these untethered recombinations of association are apparently very necessary, for reasons we do not understand.

What if the actual learning occurred just prior to sleep? That was not tested, but it might not work very well. Others have reported in a word recall task that explicit recall of the words was impaired if the words were presented within three minutes of sleep onset. This should not be any surprise. Sleep is such a major disrupter of normal brain function that it could prevent the consolidation process from getting under way if sleep comes too soon after learning. But it would appear that if the consolidation process is well under way, sleep might actually help it along by allowing a kind of rehearsal to continue at some unconscious level.

Because dream sleep is especially important for memory formation, some residue of the memory trace must survive during sleep until the dream stages of sleep begin, which typically come later in the night and especially in early morning.

So, what lessons do we draw? First, our brains do not go to sleep just because we do. In fact, the brain seems busily at work during sleeping and dreaming to help create the memories and skill sets that we use during waking hours. It is as if the purpose of sleep is to prepare us for non-sleep. It is also possible that the purpose of sleep is to prepare us for dreaming, inasmuch as the brain does not normally enter the dream stage until after a preceding stage of regular sleep. These ideas were actually proposed in my book about the brain (p. 194),[15] but in the context of a physiological readiness for the bodily activity that would occur upon awakening. Finally, we will want to reflect on Strickgold's comment about the implications for our conscious control over our mind. "We think of our mind as being ours. But there are real ways in which the brain has a set of rules of its own. We're getting an idea of what the brain uses as its rules for picking out cortical memory traces to reactivate and bring into our conscious mind, and, we're trying to see across wake-sleep cycles how that process happens."

Jet-Lag and Memory

If you have ever flown through several time zones, you know the feelings of fatigue, mental fogginess, and general discomfort that goes with so-called jet lag. It should not be surprising that jet lag adversely affects memory. This is confirmed in a recent study of 20 flight attendants, whose brain images were compared with other people that did not have repeated jet lag experiences.[16] Kwangwook Cho, a neurologist at the University of Bristol in England, has found actual structural deterioration in these subjects in the area of the brain that is involved in spatial orientation and processing. All the subjects, aged 22-28, had worked for at least five years and experienced regular flights across at least seven time zones. He recorded fMRI images and also tested visual memory with a test that required subjects to recall the location of black spots flashed on a computer screen. Subjects were sub-divided into two groups: those who routinely had long recovery periods between jet-lag trips (more than 14 days in the home time zone) and those who had short recovery periods (5 days or less in the home zone). The total number of work hours did not differ between the groups.

The subjects who had short recovery times exhibited reduced brain size in the right temporal lobe, an area important to visual and spatial memory. In the memory test, short-recovery subjects had longer reaction times. Although stress hormone levels (cortisol) did not differ between groups, there was a correlation between cortisol level and size of the temporal lobe. In the previously mentioned information on stress, I mentioned the potential destructive effect of stress hormones on brain tissue.

The Cho group led another troubling study of jet lag in which they used salivary cortisol levels as a measure of stress in 62 women, aged 24 to 29, working for international airlines. They compared cabin crews and ground crews.[17] The cabin crews had an average of 8 hours per week of jet lag, while of course the ground crews had no jet lag. The cabin crews had significantly higher cortisol levels during an average working day, indicating that their bodys were chronically stressed.

Memory was tested with delayed match-to-sample tasks. Each visual memory task started with a short (2.5 seconds) presentation of an identical pair of stimulus pictures, followed by the presentation (5 seconds) of a black dot in the center of the screen to hold the subject's attention, and then after a 5 or 25 second delay, the test picture was presented for 2.5 seconds. Four different types of stimuli were used; symbol, meaningful word, and Arabic numerals. In the case of a word stimulus, the pair of words comprised a meaningful word pair (three to eight letters in length), and the pair of number stimulus pictures comprised one or two digits of Arabic numerals. Each subject was presented with a total of 80 trials (i.e., 20 items times four types of stimuli), and the different types of stimuli were presented in a pseudorandom order. After the test picture, the subject had to choose the correct response by pressing a key. If the test pair of pictures was exactly the same as the stimulus pair of pictures, the subject had to press one key, and if not, then they had to press another key. The next stimulus picture was presented after the subjects had pressed any response key after the preceding test picture. The cabin crews who had been working for less than three years had no memory deficit, but those with four years of service had significantly fewer correct responses at both the 5 and 25 second delays. In the cabin crews, cortisol levels were positively correlated with impaired memory scores. The research of Newcomer and colleagues has also shown that use of cortisol as medication causes memory deficits.[18]

The Washington Post reports a convincing anecdote from Lesley McKeever, a flight attendant who lives in Annandale, said that she had memory problems during trips and a couple of days thereafter when her flights were bunched so that she was home for only a day or two between jet-lag flights. "I had difficulty remembering my room number," she is quoted as saying. "I kept forcing myself to make sure

I put things in the same spot, because otherwise I would have no clue as to how to retrace my steps." Note that these are working memory problems and that the temporal lobe is particularly involved in converting working memory to permanent memory. Such memory changes may be more than transient. Dr. Cho said that cabin crew who had more than four years in service reported that their memory was getting worse. These data do not deal with the issue of whether or not the effects are caused by jet lag itself or by the lack of sleep that typically accompanies jet lag. But this study, if it can be confirmed, means that work schedules of pilots and flight attendants need to be adjusted to make certain there is sufficient recovery time between jet lag episodes.

In the U.S., cabin crew and flight attendants' work schedules are regulated by the Federal Aviation Agency. Rules in force at this writing allow international crew to be on duty for as long as 20 hours at a time and to have as little as eight hours of rest between duty periods.

Now, what does this suggest about astronauts who undergo continual jet lag for many consecutive days or months if they are in a space station? And what about medical residents and interns who may be required to work 36 or more hour-shifts without sleep?

* * * * *

I hope these studies convince you of the importance of sleep for better memory. We don't know why the brain needs to sleep, but the need has been compellingly demonstrated in many experiments. The implications regarding memory are far-reaching. Not only is a full night's sleep necessary for students to perform optimally, but good sleep is important to anyone whose job requires them to learn and remember well. And it is not only the amount of sleep that is important. Sleep that ensues after drug taking, such as alcohol drinking, will still disrupt memory, even though the amount of time in sleep is more than adequate.

Key Ideas

1. The brain is still active in sleep, busily consolidating memories. As mentioned elsewhere, many drugs, such as alcohol, interfere with memory. There is the possibility that these drugs taken before bedtime interfere with memory. Such drugs do reduce dreaming, which we already know interferes with memory.

2. Both dreaming and non-dreaming stages of sleep contribute to memory formation. You can't dream if you don't sleep.

3. Cutting sleep short by an hour or so degrades memory formation.

4. Staying up all night to study is counter-productive. While you might remember a lot for the next day's examination, you probably won't think clearly and you certainly have low odds for consolidating that memory for later examinations.

5. Sleep should not be delayed after a day of intense learning. Sleep promotes consolidation, and delaying sleep may close the window of opportunity for optimal consolidation.

6. Intense learning experiences are more likely than casual experiences to induce automatic rehearsal processes, which presumably increase the likelihood of memory formation.

7. If the learning experience has both declarative and procedural memory components, the procedural component may be remembered easier because it does not involve the same consolidation system that operates in the medial temporal lobe and the hippocampus. Therefore, intentionally contriving procedural aspects for the learning material may enhance memorization because both consolidation processes are put into play at the same time.

8. One simple way to contrive procedural aspects is to make drawings and diagrams that have little or no explicit verbiage. This is another way of saying that "a picture is worth a thousand words."

9. If the automated rehearsal that occurs just prior to sleep and during the early stages of sleep is important to memory, then deliberately rehearsing just before going to sleep may be even better.

10. Conversely, failure to rehearse the day's learning effort before bedtime may make memorizing more difficult. This is particularly true if activities just prior to sleep are highly distracting and induce conflicting rehearsal of other things.

> 11. Dreaming may also be necessary for development of fundamental learning skills, such as knowing how to learn under different conditions.

Sources:

1. Gais, S. et al. 2002. Learning-dependent increases in sleep spindle density. J. Neuroscience. 22: 6830-6834.

2. Fischer, S., Hallschmid, M., Elsner, A. L., and Born, J. 2002. Sleep forms memory for finger skills. Proc. National Academy of Science. 99: 11987-11001.

3. Englund, C. E., Ryman, D. H., Naitoh, P., and Hodgdon, J. A. 1985. Cognitive performance during successive sustained physical work episodes. Behav. Res. Methods, Instr. Comput. 17: 75-85.

4. This story has been adapted from a news release issued by Harvard Medical School for journalists and other members of the public. Source: Harvard Medical School (http://www.hms.harvard.edu/) Original source of story:
http://www.sciencedaily.com/releases/2000/11/001122075125.htm

5. See http://www.med.harvard.edu/publications/Focus/Oct27_2000/index.html

6. Drummond, S., et al. 2000. Altered brain response to verbal learning following sleep deprivation. Nature. 403: 655-657

7. Van Dongen, H.P., Maislin, G., Mullington, J. M., and Dinges, D. F. 2003. The cumulative cost of additional wakefulness: dose-response effects on neurobehavioral function and sleep restriction and total sleep deprivation. Sleep. 26 (3): 247-248.

8. Source: University Of California San Diego School Of Medicine (http://health.ucsd.edu). The original news release, based on a paper in the Feb. 10, 2001 issue of Nature, can be found at http://health.ucsd.edu/news/2000_02_09_Sleep.html

9. Note: This story has been adapted from a news release issued by Cold Spring Harbor Laboratory for journalists and other members of the public. Source: Cold Spring Harbor Laboratory (http://www.cshl.org/) http://www.sciencedaily.com/releases/1999/10/991026074517.htm

10. Wilson, Matthew, and Louie, Kenway. 2001. Temporally structured replay of awake hippocampal ensemble activity during rapid eye movement sleep. Neuron. 29: 145-156.

11. Maquet, P. 2000. Experience-dependent changes in cerebral activation during human REM sleep. Nature Neuroscience. 3: 831-836.

12. Stickgold, R., Whidbee, D., Schirmer, B., Patel, V., and Hobson, J. A. 2000. Visual discrimination task improvement: a multi-step process occurring during sleep. J. Cognitive Neuroscience. 12: 246-254.

13. Plihal, W., and Born, J. 1997. Effects of early and late nocturnal sleep on declarative and procedural memory. J. Cognitive Neuroscience. 9: 534-547.

14. Stickgold, Robert; Malia, April; Maguire, Denise; Roddenberry, David; and O'Connor, Margaret. 2000. Replaying the game: Hypnagogic images in normals and Amnesics Science. 290: 350-353. Quotes are taken from a news release issued by Harvard Medical School for journalists and other members of the public. See http://www.sciencedaily.com/releases/2000/10/001013073843.htm

15. Klemm, W. R. 1996. Understanding Neuroscience. Mosby, St. Louis.

16. Cho, K. 2001. Chronic 'jet lag' produces temporal lobe atrophy and spatial cognitive deficits. Nature Neuroscience. 4: 567-568.

17. Cho, K., Ennaceur, A., Cole, J. C., and Suh, C. K. 2000. Chronic jet lag produces cognitive deficits. J. Neurosci. 20: RC66: 1-5.

18. Newcomer, J. W., Selke, G., Melson, A.K., Hershey, T., Craft, S., Richards, K., Anderson, A. L. 1999. Decreased memory performance in healthy humans induced by stress-level cortisol treatment. Arch. Gen. Psychiatry 56:527-533.

Sleep. Perchance to Remember

Why Old Dogs Can't Learn New Tricks (Or Can They?)

- Senior Moments
- Declining Mental Skills Can Catch You Unaware
- Documenting Memory Decline
- A Stroke of Bad Luck
- Alzheimer's Disease - The Beginning of the End
- Lifestyles of the Old and Forgetful
- Diet and Drugs
- Forgetful Neurons
- New Neurons
- Becoming Nimble Minded
- Exercising the Body Exercises the Mind
- Rehab Can Work
- Workouts That All Elderly Can Do

There is a wicked inclination in most people to suppose an old man decayed in his intellects. If a young or middle-aged man, when leaving a company, does not recollect where he laid his hat, it is nothing; but if the same inattention is discovered in an old man, people will shrug up their shoulders, and say, "His memory is going."

- Samuel Johnson

Life "may begin at 40," but that doesn't apply to memory. For most folks, memory begins a steady decline around age 40, according to psychology professor Keith Wesnes[1]. This conclusion was based on his review of 2,300 healthy people aged 18 to 87. Is wasn't the memory as such that was impaired; rather it was the speed at which memories could be recalled. This finding was accompanied by an observed age-related slowing in general reaction times and concentration span. The most obvious example from everyday life was a slowing in the ability to recall names.

Senior Moments

"Having a senior moment" has become a standard cliché in our language. We live in an aging society. Whereas in 1900 about 4% of the population of the United States exceeded the age of 65, in 1980 the figure approximated 12%. By year 2000, an estimated 15% of the population (at least 35 million people) is over 65.

With aging comes the grim possibility of senility. But senility and aging are not synonymous, although both share in common a progressive loss of memory capacity. Obviously the memory loss in senility is much more serious. The memory loss of aging can be overcome in part by healthy life styles and the practice of "healthy" memory habits, which we summarize at the end of this chapter.

Some, if not most, memory deterioration that occurs with age is attributable to disease. Common causes of memory decline include diabetes, hypertension, and alcohol abuse. Diabetes regulates blood sugar, and sugar is the sole direct source of energy for the brain. But too much blood sugar is bad, which is the problem in so-called type 2 diabetes. Insulin, the release of which is triggered in response to a spike in blood sugar, normally drives sugar into the body cells. But in diabetes, the transport process becomes resistant and sugar accumulates in the blood. Everybody knows that long-term obesity is a major cause of diabetes, and we can expect a major "epidemic" of diabetes as many more people are overweight than in times past. Some 16 million people today have type 2 diabetes. What you may not have known is that diabetes impairs memory.

Antonio Convit, a neuroscientist at New York University School of Medicine, has reported results of a memory study with 13 men and 17 women with poor glucose regulation but who had not yet reached the stage of diabetes. Participants were asked to recall the contents of a paragraph immediately after reading it and 10 minutes later. Then experimenters compared results of a glucose tolerance test with memory formation. The higher the glucose (due to failure of insulin to work well) the lower the memory scores. Earlier research has shown that the hippocampus, which we know to be crucial in forming memories, is smaller in diabetics.

Hypertension commonly results because arteries are plugged. When this involves arteries to the brain, blood supply to the brain is impaired. Thus, it is not surprising that hypertension and memory deficits often go together.

Alcohol impairs memory because it lowers attentiveness and focus, and it directly impairs the neurons that mediate memory formation and recall. One apparent exception is the state dependence of memory that can be seen with moderate doses of alcohol. Things learned during a moderate exposure to alcohol are best recalled when in that same state. Continuous use of large amounts of alcohol kills nerve cells. In older chronic alcoholics the memory loss can be devastating, and there is no recovery. With only a few minor exceptions, dead neurons are not replaced.

The popular view that we lose hundreds of thousands of neurons as we age may be a myth, at least as it applies to normal aging in the absence of disease. While most modern studies do show that the aged brain has some loss of nerve cells, the loss is modest and should be largely offset by the positive effects of the accumulated knowledge and enhanced coping strategies that come with age. Also, there is a tendency for normal aged brain to compensate for loss of neurons with enhanced growth of connection points (synapses) among the remaining neurons.

Animal studies make it clear that loss of neurons is most pronounced during early development, when the brain is "sculpting" its circuitry for function in the real world. In normal rats, for example, the only significant cerebral cell losses occur during the first 100 days of life in what might be considered a period of adaptation and fine tuning to the environment. There is very little subsequent loss of neurons, even at 900 days when rats start to die of natural causes.

Declining Mental Skills Can Catch You Unaware

As if having recognizable "senior moments" isn't bad enough, now Penn State researchers[2] say that we may lose some basic mental skills and not even realize it. In a study of 15 normal, healthy aged men and women that is the first of its kind, the researchers found that the subjects were unable to accurately estimate their prowess at reading maps, remaining attentive, or pantomiming tool use. The subjects were accurate in estimating their memory, their ability to recall, and several others functions such as mood and vision.

Dr. Anna Barrett, at Penn State's College of Medicine and the study's principal investigator, believes that people need to know their levels of performance so they can take countermeasures or seek assistance when these skills decline. In the study, nine women and six men who were all about 75 years old and living independently, were asked first to estimate how they would perform on four series of tests and then actually took the tests. The tests included visuospatial skills such as reading a map, copying a design, and matching up lines of different angular orientation. In an attention test, subjects were asked to find all of the As in a sheet of random letters and avoid being distracted as they visually fixated on a target and to inhibit movement responses by holding up one finger when the experimenter held up two. A tool-use test asked them to move their hands, for example, as if they were using a screwdriver, a knife, or a hammer. Pantomime of movement is a familiar test for dementia, and it was included in the test battery.

All of the study subjects were neurologically normal individuals whose performances on all of the tests fell within the normal range. However, their estimates of their performance did not match their competence.

Subjects overestimated their prowess at pantomiming tool use by 10 percent; overestimated map reading and other visuospatial skills by four percent and underestimated their ability to maintain attention by 13 percent. Estimations of memory, mood, vision and naming ability matched actual performance.

Documenting Memory Decline

Of the many ways to quantify memory decline, scientists like to use methods that they can use with both animals and humans. One such approach is called the delayed recognition-memory task. In such tasks, the subject (monkey or human) is asked to view a set of items in a visual field. There follows a delay when the scene is hidden, and then the image is re-presented with a new object added. The task is to identify the added element (which obviously requires one to hold the original pattern in working memory).

In a typical experiment, the diagram below shows that the original set contained three big dots, and the next presentation contained four dots. The task is to recognize which of the four dots was new. The task is made progressively more difficult by adding other dots. Dots are added one at a time on the screen in a series of increasing length. Another advantage of this strategy is that the test can be based on a variety of parameters for the items displayed: spatial location, color, pattern, or even words. Alzheimer's patients do very poorly on this kind of test.[3]

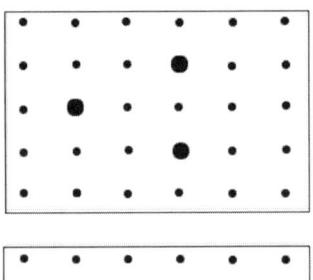

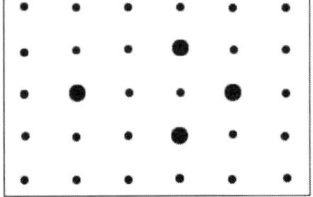

Diagram used for the memory-recognition task

Source: Squire, Larry (1984). Neuropsychology of Memory.

A memory recognition task in which the items to be remembered involve large dots, which are first presented in threes and then successively another dot is added. As a dot is added, subjects may be required to remember which dot is new. Other variations of the task include altering the spatial location of dots, the color of dots, or the dot pattern.

The following graph shows the severe impairment of Alzheimer patients and reveals that the memory deficit is much greater for patterns than for words. The average delay span for remembering which words are new in the test is cut almost in half for Alzheimer's patients. Marked memory deficiencies are also seen with spatial, color, and pattern tests. Re-drawn from original source.[1]

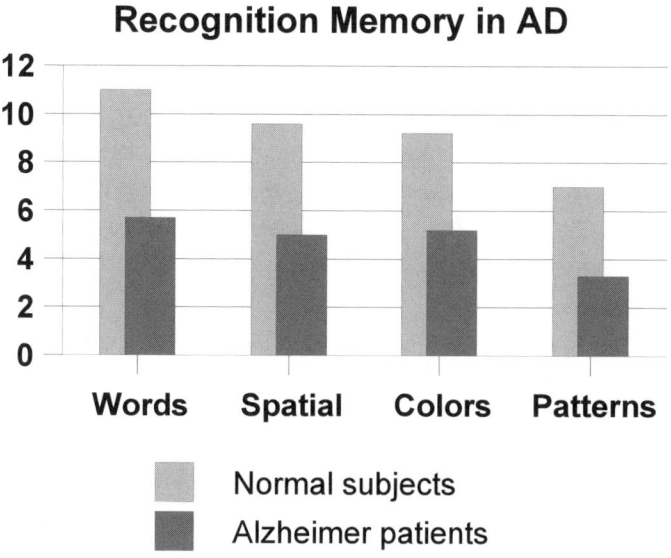

Test results showing decline in memory capacity for words, spatial location, colors, and patterns in the dot memory recognition task shown in the preceding diagram.

A Stroke of Bad Luck

A UC Davis and Department of Veterans' Affairs Health System study[4] may be an important advance in helping doctors correctly identify the cause of memory problems in elderly patients. The researchers report that the impact of minor strokes deep in the brain can be distinguished from the damage caused by Alzheimer's disease. "We found that the brain systems that failed in stroke patients with memory losses were different from those that failed and caused the memory losses of Alzheimer's disease," said Bruce R. Reed, associate director of the UC Davis Alzheimer's Disease Center and lead author of the paper. Reed believes that physicians who are alert to what the memory loss of stroke looks like may be able to treat the root cause, high blood pressure or diabetes, and thereby prevent strokes.

It is not obvious where ordinary forgetfulness leaves off and the early stages of Alzheimer's begin.Complicating the diagnosis is evidence accumulated over the past several years, indicating that small strokes deep in the brain may make the memory loss of Alzheimer's worse. These strokes become more common with age, and their role in causing memory problems, either alone or in conjunction with Alzheimer's, has been puzzling because they often do not occur in "memory" areas of the brain.

Reed and his colleagues studied 15 patients who had suffered small strokes deep in the brain and 15 patients with the diagnosis of mild Alzheimer's Disease and compared these patients with similarly aged control subjects. The subjects took memory tests designed to distinguish between different components of memory, including attention to the task and the ability to retrieve memories after longer or shorter test intervals. The stroke patients were more likely to have problems related to the inability to pay close attention to the task or to remember things after a very short time. Alzheimer's patients, on the other hand, were more likely to have difficulty with retrieving memories after longer intervals.

The researchers also scanned the subjects' brains with positron emission tomography (PET) while the tests were in progress. The scans of stroke patients showed reduced levels of activity in the frontal cortex, a brain area known to be essential for attention. By contrast, the Alzheimer's patients had reduced levels of activity in brain areas (such as the temporal lobe and hippocampus) known to be involved in the coding and storage of memories.

"This shows that it's not simply that stroke pushes people with a little Alzheimer's disease over some sort of threshold for memory loss," said Reed. "The memory loss of deep stroke is more closely related to failures of attention and this makes sense considering the brain circuits that are usually affected by deep strokes."

The results point out the importance of being alert for mild memory loss in elderly patients, Reed said. "These problems may not reflect Alzheimer's Disease, and so it's all the more important to look for and to treat any risk factors for cerebrovascular disease."

Exciting new research also points to a future in which we may be able to restore the learning capability of youth. Recall that I had earlier described the mental processes of aging as "hardening of the categories." It now appears that there is actual physical hardening, in the sense that the space between the active zones of neuronal membranes (synapses) are filled with a matrix of glycoprotein, much like a spider web. This matrix is somehow involved in the establishing the functional connections between neurons. The matrix imposes a degree of rigidity in a neural network, making it difficult for the network to alter its connections. The new research discovered an enzyme which, when injected into the brain, breaks down this rigid matrix and restores the ability of the neural network to make new connections (that is, learn something new).[5]

Tommaso Pizzorusso and colleagues at universities in Piza and Firenze, Italy, tested the idea of restoring plasticity in adults by using an experimental model of visual cortex reorganization after eyesight is blocked in one eye. The visual cortex receives two images of the world, one from each eye. If one eye is forcibly closed early in development, the open eye takes over the visual cortex. That is, neurons that would have developed connections to both eyes now assign these contacts to the one open eye. During a short critical period, such a procedure creates a permanent condition, where rewiring will not occur even if the closed eye is returned to normal. The individual will be blind in the closed eye. In humans, this critical period occurs at age 7 to 8.

The experiments began with raising baby rats in the dark for various times and observing the formation of the synaptic glycoprotein matrix. They observed that during the critical period, the formation of matrix was blocked, meaning that connections in the cortex were not being established.

Next, they tested adult rats to see if presence of this matrix impaired experience-dependent plasticity. Breaking down this matrix with enzyme injection into the visual cortex reduced the inhibitory effect and even stimulated the growth of neurons. Also they tested adult rats by closing one eye, well after the critical period, injected the matrix-breaking enzyme or a control enzyme, and tested ocular dominance 7 days later by recording electrical activity in the cortex. Seven days of blindness in one eye did not shift the dominance in control conditions of no injection or injection of the nonspecific enzyme. But a shift of responsivity bias did occur in the cortex when matrix disrupting enzyme was injected. In other words, the adult cortex could develop new function, but only with enzyme treatment that broke down the synaptic matrix.

Is there an enzyme pill on the horizon? Well not exactly. Enzymes taken by mouth get digested, and in any case they have to get to the target areas of the brain. It does not seem feasible to go around injecting multiple areas of the cortex through holes in the skull. Perhaps, though, a matrix-breaking enzyme, or enzyme precursor, or gene activator, could be injected into the cerebrospinal fluid that would eventually distribute throughout the brain, re-vitalizing the circuits.

Alzheimers Disease - The Beginning of the End

Incidence of Alzheimer's Disease (AD) is increasing. People are living longer, and this disease does have a higher incidence in older people. For example, at age 65, only one or two people out of a 100 have the disease. By age 80, the incidence goes up to one in five. At age 90, half of all Americans have some symptoms. This dreaded disease already afflicts about 4 million people in the U.S. By the year 2050, the number will rise to 7.5 to 14.3 million, depending on the assumptions one makes about the U.S. population growth.[6]

AD insidiously generates neurodegenerative plaques and tangles that spread throughout the brain. Although AD usually appears late in life, it probably begins much sooner. First signs of the disease's onset are usually minor memory lapses. But these memory deficits increase in amount and severity over time, eventually destroying memory of loved ones. AD ultimately destroys the memory of who we are.

Lifestyles of the Old and Forgetful

We know some of the reasons why memory deteriorates with age. Reaction times slow down with age, but there is no evidence that slower reaction times cause memory problems. Older people may not form associations between new and old information as automatically or as well as younger people. Older people have more trouble being mentally flexible. The good news is that when older people make a conscious effort to form associations and to memorize, they can do just as well as youngsters. Because of their vastly larger store of experiences and knowledge, older people have more pegs to hang new memories on.

General health is also a key consideration. Guy McKhann and Marilynn Albert, in their book Keep Your Brain Young, summarize their study of 1,200 older people between the ages of 70 and 80 and tracked their mental changes over the next 10 years. Many of these people did not deteriorate. Those that maintained their mental abilities were those that were:

>   1. Mentally more active.
>   2. Physically more active
>   3. Aware of their own effectiveness in the world, with a sense of being in control over their lives, contributing to their families or society.

Everyone should develop a lifestyle that contributes to good memory. Unfortunately, many people do not. For example, the same factors that make older people prone to heart attacks make them also prone to brain damage that would impair memory. The brains of older people have accumulated years of plaque buildup in the small arteries of the brain. Miniature strokes are common.

Diet and Drugs

A pro-memory diet is one that is nutritionally balanced, low in saturated fats and high in fruits and vegetables. Recent evidence suggests that cholesterol-lowering drugs may reduce the risk of developing AD by as much as 80%.[7] More and more people are taking "statins," such as Lipitor, Pravachol, Lescol, Zocor, and Mevacor, and the beneficial effect these have on blood supply to the heart probably also applies to blood perfusion of the brain.

An aspirin a day can keep forgetfulness away. Just as aspirin protects the heart from blood clots, it also protects small arteries in the brain from clots.

Vitamins and dietary supplements are mostly only hoped-for solutions. A rather exhaustive study of 4,809 nonHispanic white, nonHispanic Black, and Mexican-American elderly tested for correlations between poor memory and serum levels of vitamins A, C, E, beta-carotene, and selenium[8]. Only vitamin E levels showed any correlation with memory. Poor memory was consistently associated with low levels of vitamin E, after adjusting for age, education, income, vascular risk factors, and trace minerals. There was no indication that taking vitamin E would improve a normal memory, but certainly taking vitamin E supplements might help an elderly person with failing memory.

A lifetime of heavy consumption of alcohol also takes its toll on the brain. One of the more sensitive parts of the brain to alcohol is the hippocampus, the very structure that is essential to forming new memories. Heavy alcohol consumption is also associated with vitamin B1 and thiamine deficiencies, both of which are needed for normal function of nerve cells.

On the other hand, it is increasingly clear that a little alcohol (1-2 drinks a day) is probably good for the circulation of the heart and no doubt of the brain as well. Red wine has received the best accolades, but even a bottle of beer is reportedly beneficial.

A lifetime of free-radical attacks on nerve cells also take a toll. Supplemental vitamin E (400 to 1000 units) and vitamin C (1-5 grams) may also help the brain and memory by counter-acting free radicals. This has even been shown to help Alzheimer's patients.

Melatonin, the hormone that helps set the body's daily clock and can help prevent jet lag, is also an antioxidant. The homone is normally made in the pineal gland, which may shrink in older people, creating a melatonin deficiency. Some elderly people find that melatonin pills help their sleep, and as we have seen in the previous chapter, sleep itself is good for memory.

Another over-the-counter medication that might help memory is phosphatidylserine (PS). This compound actually occurs in neuron membranes and the glial cell sheaths that insulate neurons. One dosage regimen is 300 mg daily for six to eight weeks, followed thereafter by 100 mg/day.

Vinpocetine, a derivative of an extract of the periwinkle, has been seen in some studies to dilate blood vessels and reduce blood clotting. Thus, it might assist memory deficits that are caused by impaired blood flow to the brain. One study[9] of 12 healthy females received pre-treatments with vinpocetine 10, 20, 40 mg and placebo (t.d.s.) for two days according to a randomized, double-blind crossover design. On the third day of treatment and 1 hour after morning dosage, subjects completed a battery of psychological tests. No statistically significant changes from placebo were observed on any of the tests, except for the memory test, which was significantly improved at the higher (40 mg) dose of vinpocetine.

There are few really good prescription drugs for the memory problems in AD. Treatments that have been used include anti-inflammatory medications (cox-2 inhibitors), and drugs that mimic or augment the neurotransmitter system that uses acetylcholine. The more promising drugs are the "cholinesterase inhibitors." These drugs inhibit the enzymes that normally destroy a major signaling compound in the brain, acetylcholine. Actually, drugs in this class are the infamous "nerve gases." Low doses of the milder of these agents serve as a general brain tonic. The acetylcholine-promoting drugs include physostigmine, tacrine (Cognex), donepezil (Aricept), rivastigmine (Excelon), and galantamine (Reminyl). None of these drugs is very effective for advanced AD, and their enhancement of memory is not specific but secondary due to an improvement in general brain function. These drugs are not known to help normal elderly people.

Acetylcholine is a neurotransmitter that is fundamental to memory. It is a major transmitter in the cerebral cortex, and the cortex is clearly involved in explicit learning. An interesting study of the possible role of acetylcholine in learning has recently been reported in experiments in pregnant rats by Scott Swartzwelder, a neuropsychologist at Duke and the Durham VA Medical Center[10]. Feeding pregnant rats the essential nutrient, choline, produced offspring that remembered far more efficiently than offspring fed a typical rat diet. The only time the pregnant rats received additional choline was during a five-day period, days 12 through 17, of their 22-day gestation period. The control group received a normal dietary amount of choline, and a third group was virtually deprived of choline.

The Duke group studied the long-term postsynaptic potentiation model of memory formation, using hippocampal brain slices in sacrificed rat pups. In this model, the slice contains intact three-neuron chains that normally process input into the hippocampus. By stimulating intensely the neurons that bring input into the slice, the target neurons in the slice become more responsive to subsequent input, and the extra responsiveness lasts long after the initial stimulation. Slices from pups of mothers that were fed the choline supplement showed increased postsynaptic potentiation, compared to normal controls, and rats deprived of choline indicated a decrease in memory capability. The enhanced signs of memory were found in rats even four months after birth, which is the equivalent of adulthood in people.

Many scientists believe that choline supplements can help memory formation in people, at least in people who have less-than-normal memory ability.

Common dietary sources of choline include egg yolks, milk, nuts, liver and other meats as well as in human breast milk. Human milk contains very high levels of choline on the first day but the amount then decreases more than four-fold.[11] The amount can be increased by taking choline supplements. This source of choline may be one more reason that babies need to be breast fed. Baby milk formulas vary over a 2.5 fold range in the amount of choline present.

Two co-investigators of milk choline research, Christina Williams and Warren Meck, had earlier reported experiments that showed that choline has a behavioral effect on memory in animals. The evaluated rats that had been exposed to choline prenatally and observed that such rats could perform better than controls in both of the tests they used (a task involving learning the location of food in a maze and the ability to locate a hidden safe platform in a water-filled maze). The memory enhancement persisted into the rats' old age.

Recently, some interest has developed for drugs that increase cerebral blood flow. Such drugs do seem to compensate for brain damage due to stroke, where a lack of blood flow is the basic problem. In rats, such blood-flow enhancers have been shown to offset learning impairments produced by scopolamine, a drug that blocks acetylcholine function. The drug that is attracting the most interest now is vinpocetine, which is sold in a variety of nutritional supplements that are sold over the counter and advertised as helping memory.

Memory problems often accompany female menopause. Estrogen hormone suddenly becomes deficient when ovaries cease to function. Estrogen acts not only on bodily tissues, such as secondary sex organs and bone, but also acts on the brain. As we discussed earlier, one of the brain effects of estrogen is to facilitate memory.

Forgetful Neurons

You must remember this: the specter of dying brain cells and an irretrievable loss of memory during old age is a myth. File it away with all of the other old wives' tales.

Michael Gallagher, a professor of psychology at Johns Hopkins University, announced recently at the 28th annual meeting of the Society of Neuroscience[12] that there is now overwhelming evidence showing that cognitive decline in old age is far less common than most people believe.

"It's good news," Gallagher said, "particularly for Baby Boomers who no longer need fear that expiring brain cells are the natural accompaniment of doddering old age, subverting memory and other higher order mental processes."

By studying human data and tracing the neurological pathways of more than 800 healthy rats across their lifetimes, Gallagher has spent much of the past decade illuminating the mysterious processes that link memory and aging.

The dreaded loss of gray matter, which so many people believe is a natural result of growing old, actually is a process that occurs throughout a person's lifetime. Neuron numbers slowly decrease across decades, as cells die off regularly and consistently from youth to old age. The brain demonstrates a remarkable ability to compensate for those losses, forestalling any noticeable effect until the losses become extreme. It now appears that even those neuron losses that do occur are confined to populations of cells that may not play any significant role in memory.

"It represents a real paradigm shift in neuroscience," Gallagher said. "For years, people have been trying to discover what caused the death of brain cells during aging. Our research has quite reversed that idea. We now know it's more important to understand the existing cells than to account for the ones people thought were missing. This idea of rapidly losing neurons in old age just doesn't hold water anymore."

I don't mean to imply that there is *no* memory loss in healthy people as they age. One of the best studies of this matter makes it clear that most healthy people do develop certain memory deficiencies as they age.[13] The study compared 212 healthy people in three age groups (less than 70, 70-80, and 80+) and tested them annually with a battery of mental function tests. On average, an age-related memory decline was observed, but it was restricted to only one specific aspect of memory, the ability to acquire new information and the ability to retrieve this information shortly after acquisition. Total memory capacity did not differ among the groups. This memory deficit in older people had a bimodal distribution. That is, some older subjects do not show any kind of memory decline. It is possible that many of the older subjects in this study had some subclinical neurological disease, perhaps involving blood supply problems to the hippocampus or early-onset Alzheimer's Disease.

The good news from this study is that the investigators could find no age-related differences in performance in other aspects of cognitive functioning, which included five tests of language, two tests of visuospatial ability, and two tests of abstract reasoning.

Some encouraging news also comes from another study.[14] Twenty young people (25 to 30 years old) and 20 elderly (60-79 years old) were tested, and there was no difference in a test of motor skills and both groups learned new skills at the same rate. Even recall from word lists and word-stem completion tests were similar.

New Neurons

One of the central dogmas of neuroscience is that you are born with life's quota of neurons. Worse yet, the neurons die by the thousands with each passing month. By the time you are in old age, you supposedly have lost perhaps a billion or so neurons. The number varies enormously with lifestyle (for instance, bad diets that cause strokes, excessive alcohol that kills neurons)

We can take comfort in knowing that the supporting cells of the brain, glial cells, continue to increase with age. Recall that earlier I pointed out that modern research has shown that glial cells help to form the synapses (junction points) between neurons and thus actively contribute to creation of experience-dependent new circuitry.

The really good news is that adult humans *can* hatch new neurons. Best of all, the place in the brain where this most likely happens in the key memory center, the hippocampus. Elizabeth Gould and colleagues at Princeton broke this field of research wide open in 1999 when they showed that new neurons seemed to be forming in the association cortex of adult macaque monkeys[15]. This result has not been replicated, as of this writing, but many labs have shown evidence of new cells in the key memory structure, the hippocampus. More recently, the

Princeton group has shown that up to 5,000 new neurons can be born in the hippocampus *every day* and that the new cells appear in conjunction with new learning[16]. How do they know? The technique for seeing new cells was to inject a fluorescent chemical, 5-bromodeoxyuridine (BrdU), which gets incorporated into DNA during cell division. Any newborn cells will fluoresce.

The association of new hippocampal neurons with new learning was demonstrated with several learning tasks. One was a water maze, where swimming rats were trained to use various spatial cues to locate a hidden "safe" platform in a pool of water. This task had been shown by others to require the hippocampus, which in addition to its general memory functions, has specific spatial processing capability. As a control test, other rats were trained with the safe platform above water and clearly visible; this spatial learning task does not depend on the hippocampus. After learning, the rats were sacrificed and their brains examined for any new neurons. New neurons appeared in the hippocampus when the platform was hidden below water but not when the platform was visible above water.

Similar results were seen in another learning task, a classical conditioning task involving learned eye blink. Rats hear a tone, and then receive stimulation that makes them blink. This stimulus pair repeats until the rats begin to blink when they first hear the tone, *before* the blink stimulus. As I describe in the chapter on "Catch It While You Can," eyelid conditioning can be conducted under implicit learning conditions or under conditions where the task has explicit components that require a normally functioning hippocampus. Microscopic examination of the brain of sacrificed rats revealed that new neurons occurred in the hippocampus in the task that depended on hippocampal function but not when the task was adjusted so that the hippocampus was not required for memory. The practical implications here are astounding. It suggests that no matter what your age, you may acquire new neurons. Learning new things may actually increase your capacity to learn new things. You may not only get older and wiser, but older and smarter!

The earlier report of increased neurons in the thinking part of the brain, the neocortex, has not been replicated. In an examination of this discrepancy, David Kornack and Pasko Rakic[17] found a possible error in the original work. They used a multiple labeling technique that could distinguish between the BrdU cells in new neurons versus any other kinds of new cells. They did confirm that new neurons appeared in the hippocampus (and olfactory bulb) but that the new cells in the cerebral cortex were *glial* cells, not neurons. We can take great comfort in knowing that there is a possibility of generating new neurons and glial cells, even as many of our old ones die.

Becoming Nimble Minded

Remembering requires a nimbleness of mind that can be developed with mental exercise. "Use it or lose it" definitely applies to mental abilities. The most clear-cut examples occur with intense educational experiences, in which the ability to remember (and also to think) improves in order to meet the educational challenges. Unfortunately, most people lose some of this edge when the intense learning experience is over. Over the nearly forty years of teaching college students, I have had many opportunities to observe this phenomenon. Even within a single semester, I have seen students grow conspicuously in mental competence, only to fall back to lesser levels within a year or so.

Abundant neurophysiological research provides the explanation. The brain's processing capability depends on the number of its neurons and the richness of the interconnections among them. Because many people have a net loss of neurons as they age, any improvement in mental performance could depend largely on increasing the richness of connections among the existing neurons. These connections occur through contact points between membranes of one neuron and membranes of other neurons. These connections can grow or shrivel, depending on the level of electrochemical activity occurring in neurons. The junctions between neurons have a characteristic appearance, particularly thickening of membrane and accumulation of chemical vesicles on one side of a junction. Animal studies have shown that rich learning experiences can actually increase the number of synapses in the neural pathways that process the learning stimulus. Conversely, lack of learning stimulation will decrease the number of synapses.

Paying attention is always helpful for memory, but may be more so in the elderly. In a study conducted at the National Institutes of Health,[18] researchers conducted a study on encoding and recognition of faces. Young people (average age of 25) showed increased blood flow in PET scans in the right hippocampus and left prefrontal and temporal cortices during encoding and in the right prefrontal and parietal cortex during recognition of learned faces. In older people (average age of 69), no increase in cortical blood flow occurred during encoding, and only an increase in right prefrontal areas occurred during recognition. Thus, the memory problem in older people may reflect a lack of effective encoding. Maybe as we get older we have to work harder at paying attention so that stimuli that we wish to remember get encoded in the first place. You can't remember something that never registered.

Exercising the Body Exercises the Memory

A team of Duke University Medical Center researchers, led by James Blumenthal, reported in 1999 that aerobic exercise significantly improved higher mental processes of memory and the so-called executive functions, which include planning, organization and the ability to juggle different intellectual tasks at the same time.[19] These changes were an unexpected by-product of the exercise regimen that was designed to help older people fight depression and to improve their physical health. The memory enhancement appeared to be specific: it was greater than what would have been expected from eliminating depression and could not be attributed to greater attention or concentration.

Blumenthal concluded that "The implications are that exercise might be able to offset some of the mental declines that we often associate with the aging process." We do not know why memory improves, but Blumenthal believes that it could be influenced by the improved flow of oxygen-rich blood to specific regions of the brain... "just as exercise improves muscle tone and function, it may have similar effects on the brain," he said. Blumenthal's original exercise and depression study involved 156 patients between the ages of 50 and 77 who had been diagnosed with major depressive disorder (MDD). They were randomly assigned to one of three groups: exercise, medication, or a combination of medication and exercise.

The exercise group spent 30 minutes either riding a stationary bicycle or walking or jogging three times a week. The anti-depressant used by the medication group was sertraline (trade name: Zoloft), which is a member of a class of commonly used anti-depressants known as selective serotonin reuptake inhibitors.

After 16 weeks, all three groups showed statistically significant and identical improvement in standard measurements of depression. In other words, the exercise was just as effective in alleviating depression as was the drug. When these same subjects were given mental performance tests, the researchers found that exercise benefitted selective areas of mental functioning. Less improvement occurred in the more depressed subjects.

Exercising the Mind Exercises the Memory

The belief that the mind starts to decline after age 60 or 70 had a lot to do with the long-held standard of 65 as the age for retirement. We now know that is not true, at least for people who stay healthy and mentally active. Scientists are particularly noted for being sharp and productive long into the late 80s and 90s.[20] It seems that the level of education and independent of lines of work are key factors. The National Science Foundation reports that at age 69 more than 29% of scientists and engineers with PhDs work full time, compared to 13% of scientists with a M.S. or B.S. degree. Linus Pauling was actively publishing just before his death at age 93. Eighty-nine year old Britton Chance at the University of Pennsylvania arrives at his lab everyday at around 9 AM and works till 5 PM, with a break for exercise and lunch. He takes a short pre-dinner nap and spends most of the evening until 11 writing. He also works a half day every Saturday. He is not just busy. He still wins competitive research grants and his most recent work has led to "molecular beacons," which are injectable molecules that attach to early-stage cancer cells and light up in MRI scans to show where the cancer is. The method is now awaiting approval from the Food and Drug Administration.

Other examples of great mental performance in the elderly are found in Rebecca Rupp's book, *Committed to Memory:*

- Leo Tolstoy learned to ride a bicycle at 67
- Queen Victoria began learning Hindustani at 68
- Giuseppe Verdi was still composing operas in his 80s
- In their 90s, Robert Frost was writing poems and George Bernard Shaw was writing plays, Georgia O'Keefe was painting pictures, and Pablo Casals was playing cello
- Oliver Wendell Holmes was still dominating the Supreme Court until he retired at 91
- Somereset Maugham wrote his last book at 84
- Frank Lloyd Wright designed his last building at 89
- Leopold Stokowski recorded 20 albums in his 90s and signed a six-year contract at 96

None of this comes as a surprise to neuroscientists familiar with the literature on brain plasticity. Marion Diamond, another active senior scientist at 75, had published data from experiments in rats showing that brain cells can grow and learning can improve at any age, provided the rats were kept mentally active.[21]

Rehab Can Work

Rehabilitation after stroke or other injury to the brain may not create any more neurons for you, but it can re-organize existing neural circuits so that they can partially compensate.

One of the more dramatic demonstrations of this effect was performed in monkey experiments where there was no specific rehabilitation program. The investigators[22] mapped the sensory cortex by recording which neurons in the sensory cortex responded to electrical stimulation of the major nerves of the arm: radial, medial, and ulnar nerves. Then they cut the median nerve during anesthesia and repeated the cortical mapping studies at various times after surgery. They saw an astonishing re-organization of the cortical maps. As expected, the area previously devoted to median nerve input no longer existed. Much of that area had become responsive to stimulation of skin areas that supplied radial and ulnar nerves. The radial and ulnar maps also changed.

With explicit post-damage training programs, one should expect even more robust changes. And this is what scientists have seen. Investigators at the Texas Health Center in Houston[23] created a localized blood clot, as would occur in stroke, in the cortex of monkeys. Such a lesion caused a loss of the hand territory represented in the cortex adjacent to the infarct. But skilled hand-use exercises by these monkeys prevented loss of hand territory adjacent to the infarct. These results, and many others that had set the stage for these experiments, suggest that healthy neural tissue can "take over" to help perform the functions of damaged tissue. In particular in this study, the zone of cells surrounding the clot acquired the ability to perform the skilled hand movements.

So what has this got to do with memory? Remember, skilled hand movements are learned. "Motor memory" is a form of procedural memory, often performed at the subconscious level, that enables performance of learned muscle contraction sequences that constitute skilled movements. For such memory to occur, there must be neural motor circuitry that has a memory for the movements. New circuitry can be created by training.

Workouts That All Elderly Can Do

Older people are much less likely to have major memory problems if they believe in themselves and work to improve their recall, according to a University of Florida study.[24]

The elderly are more likely than younger people to buy into the stereotype that they can't control their memory, and it affects not only their self-esteem but also how hard they try to remember, said Robin West, a UF psychology professor who did the research.

"Some of the research shows that people can improve their memory performance by as much as 50 percent if they work at it, use the right strategies and challenge themselves," said West, author of the book, *Memory Fitness Over 40*. "I really try to convince older people that they need to think of themselves in terms of their potential rather than their losses. Yes, there are losses, but there is also enormous potential at any age to improve memory, just as there is potential to improve strength."

In the study conducted by psychology graduate student Monica Yassuda, more than 200 older and young adults were divided into two groups. One group was told memory is a skill that can be improved with effort, and the other group that the ability to remember is fixed forever at birth.

"There is some indication in the literature that older people tend to see memory as something they can't control -- you either have a good memory or you don't," West said.

The researchers decided to examine how preconceptions affect memory by using an exercise to test a common concern that people have: the ability to remember names.

In four trials, participants were shown videotapes of people telling their names and then were asked to remember the names when the images reappeared on the screen.

People who were told their memory could not be controlled were more apt to report making less effort and using fewer strategies, such as associating a name with an image, to remember people's names.

According to West, older adults were more likely than their younger counterparts to react to the information given to the two groups, probably because they accept the notion that memory can not be improved. "The results show that we need to encourage older adults to think of themselves as a group that has the potential to have a better memory if they work at it."

Other studies, which were sponsored by the John D. and Catherine T. MacArthur Foundation, have found the belief that people can control part of their lives is a good predictor of whether they age well mentally and physically.

West explains: "We used to see it as a chicken-or-egg proposition. Is having control something that allows you to age successfully, or does aging successfully make you feel like you have more control? One thing about our work as well as the MacArthur Foundation research is that it found that having a feeling of mastery predicted whether or not people used strategies that could ultimately make them more successful."

* * * * *

Mental faculties decline with age in most, but not all, people. Indeed, we need to know more about why some old people stay mentally sharp. Certainly, memory ability is helped by a healthy lifestyle of vigorous exercise and a well-balanced diet.

Most commonly, memory and other mental problems in old age are caused by disease, especially diabetes and problems in the cardiovascular system. I have tried to stress in this chapter that there are things the elderly can do to keep their brains in shape. It seems that the most crucial requirement is to stay active mentally, living life with a purpose that makes rigorous mental demands. As our bodies grow weak and flabby with age, a similar deterioration occurs in our mind. Such deterioration is not self-correcting. You have to work at correction. Better yet, work at prevention of mental decline.

Stay active mentally. In the year that this book is released, I will be 70 years old. Though technically retired, I have written in the last few years an average of about 6 scholarly papers each year. I am working on two more books, and I work as a Co-Principal Investigator on three federal education grants. I don't have the memory that I had as a 20-year-old, but my memory is a lot better than that of many of my elderly colleagues. Your memory can be better too.

Key Ideas:

1. Be aware of memory decline and take steps to compensate and improve your memory capability. Make more of a conscious effort to pay better attention, make associations, and memorize.

2. Control your blood pressure. High pressure can lead to strokes that can have devastating effects on memory and all aspects of cognitive function.

3. Prevent diabetes with weight control, or if you have diabetes, keep blood sugar regulated by medication and proper diet.

4. Take vitamin E (400-1000 units/day) and vitamin C (1-5 gms/day). They might help memory. Vitamin E deficiency does impair memory.

5. If you or a loved one has old-age memory loss, consider getting tested for Alzheimer's Disease by a neurologist. If the loss is not due to Alzheimer's Disease, it should be at least partially reversible.

6. Look for more research on vinpocetine and other possible "memory pills."

7. Keep mentally active. Challenge your memory and strive to minimize the need for memory crutches.

8. Eat a pro-memory diet, low in saturated fats and high in fruits and vegetables.

9. If you have high cholesterol, ask your doctor to prescribe a statin.

10. Choline supplements may help. A diet rich in choline includes egg yolks, milk, nuts, liver, meat, but such a diet is too rich in saturated fats and would likely raise blood cholesterol. Breast-feed babies to make sure they get plenty of choline during this critical period.

11. Take an aspirin a day.

12. If you drink alcohol, drink in moderation. One to two glasses of red wine a day is said to reduce blood clotting, and that should reduce the incidence of small strokes in the brain. More alcohol than that may kill neurons.

13. Be optimistic about your ability to improve your memory. Don't buy into the stereotype of the inevitability of memory decline as you age.

14. Learn new things on a continuing basis. This will increase your capacity to learn still more. You may not only get older and wiser, but older and smarter.

15. Work harder at paying attention. This ability normally declines with age.

16. Do aerobic exercise (at least 30 minutes, at least three times a week).

Sources

1. Keith Wesnes, as reported at http://www.arabia.com/life/article/english/0%2C11827%2C35892%2C00.html

2. Barrett, Anna, Eslinger, Paul. J., Heilman, K. M. 2002. Unawareness of cognitive deficit (Cognitive Anosognosia) in aged subjects, proceedings. Annual meeting of the International Neuropsychology Society in Chicago, Ill., Feb. 14.

3. Albert, M., and Moss, M. 1984. The assessment of memory disorders in patients with Alzheimer disease, p. 236-246. In Neuropsychology of Memory, edited by Larry R. Squire and Nelson Butters. The Guilford Press, New York.

4. This story has been adapted from a news release issued by University Of California, Davis - Medical Center for journalists and other members of the public. See also http://www.sciencedaily.com/releases/2000/09/000904122406.htm

5. Pizzorusso, T., Medini, P., Berardi, N., Chierzi, S., Fawcett, J. W., and Maffei, L. 2002. Reactivation of ocular dominance plasticity in the adult visual cortex. Science. 298: 1248-1251.

6. Evans, D. A. Et al. 1990. Estimated prevalence of Alzheimer's disease in the United States. The Milbank Quarterly. 68: 267-289.

7. Fackelmann, K. 2002. Cholesterol drugs may clear mind, too. USA Today, July 9, Pg. D1.

8. Perkins, A. J., Hendrie, H. C., Callahan, C. M., Gao, S., Unverzagt, F. W., Yong, Xu, Hall, K. S., and Hui, S. L. 1999. Association of antioxidants with memory in a multiethnic elderly sample using the third national health and nutrition examination survey. Amer. J. Epidemiol. 150 (1): 37-44.

9. Subhan, Z; Hindmarch, I, 1985. Psychopharmacological effects of vinpocetine in normal healthy volunteers. European Journal of Clinical Pharmacology, 28 (5): 567-571.

10. Source: Duke University Medical Center. http://www.sciencedaily.com/releases/1998/04/980409080807.htm

11. http://www.babysbest.com/choline.htm

12. Note: This story has been adapted from a news release issued by Johns Hopkins University for journalists and other members of the public. See also http://www.sciencedaily.com/releases/1998/11/981125140144.htm

13. Small, S., Stern, Y., Tang, M., and Mayeux, R. 1999. Selective decline in memory function among healthy elderly. Neurology. 52: 1392-1396.

14. Peretti, C.-S., Danion, J.-M., Gierski, F., and Grane, D. 2002. Cognitive skill learning and aging. A component process analysis. Arch. Clin. Neuropsychol. 17: 445-459.

15. Gould, E., Reeves, A. J., Graziano, M. S., and Gross, C. G. 1999. Neurogenesis in the neocortex of adult primates. Science 286: 548-

552.

16. Gould, E., Beylin, A., Tanapat, A., Reeves, T. J., and Shors, T. J. 1999. Learning enhances adult neurogenesis in the hippocampal formation. Nature Neuroscience. 2 (3): 260-265.

17. Kornack, David R., and Rakic, Pasko. 2001. Cell proliferation without neurogenesis in adult primate neocortex. Science. 294: 2127-2129.

18. Grady, C., et al. 1995. Age-related reductions in human recognition memory due to impaired encoding. Science. 269; 218-221.

19. This story has been adapted from a news release issued by Duke University Medical Center. See http://www.sciencedaily.com/releases/2001/01/010117074808.htm

20. Calandra, Bob. 2002. Senior scientists grace their ages. The Scientist. Oct. 14, p. 61-62.

21. Diamond, M. Et al. 1985. Plasticity in 904 day-old male rat cerebral cortex. Experimental Neurology. 87: 309-317.

22. Merzenich, M. M., Nelson, R. J., Stryker, M. P., Cynader, M. S., Schoppmann, A., and Zook, J. M. 1984. Somatosensory cortical map changes following digit amputation in adult monkeys. J. Comp. Neurol. 224: 591-605.

23. Nudo, R. J., Wise, B. M., SiFuentes, F., and Milliken, G. W. 1996. Neural substrates for the effects of rehabilitative training on motor recovery after ischemic infarct. Science. 272: 1791-1795.

24. This story has been adapted from a news release issued by University of Florida for journalists and other members of the public. See also
http://www.sciencedaily.com/releases/1998/07/980723104339.htm

Why Old Dogs Can't Learn New Tricks

Untie That String On Your Finger

So how much of this book do you remember? Maybe a short summary will help. I will try to wrap it all up by modeling what the book has emphasized, in terms of paying attention, making associations, consolidating temporary memory, using retrieval cues, sustaining constructive emotions, recognizing that memory reconstruction during retrieval can lead to errors, and the value of sleep.

On the next page, I give the example of trying to remember my name and face. First notice that this sensory input is distributed to many areas of your brain. Information about my name goes to the speech centers, as well as to multiple areas in the cerebral cortex. I only show a few arrows in order to keep the diagram simple. Likewise, the visual information of the face goes to multiple areas of the visual cortex. The Nobel Prize[1] was given to David Hubel and Torsten Wiesel in 1981 for the elegant way they proved that visual scenes are deconstructed in the brain, wherein very small fragments in the scene are parceled out to individual neurons scattered throughout the visual cortex.

When you saw my name, how well did you notice the spelling? Did you notice that Klemm has two "m"s? Did you notice that the first letter is a "K," not a "C?" With the face did you notice the dimple? ... the sharp nose? ... the moles on the forehead? ...the squinted eyes? ...the bags under the eyes? ... the cheek creases that arise from about the middle of the nose? ...the two lapel pins?

What associations did you make? For the name, you might have associated the sharp nose with a bird's bill ("Bill"). Maybe you visualized the bird trying to peck open a clam ("Klemm"). Maybe you remember the famous baseball umpire (Bill Clem) and associate some features of my face with baseball (the moles that might resemble miniature baseballs, or the angular cheek creases resembling part of a baseball diamond, or the chin dimple reminding you of the recess in a catcher's mitt). Whatever associations you make will register in the

303

Untie That String

brain at still yet other locations, but the neurons there are linked to neurons that receive the original name and face information.

Deconstructing the information to be memorized

Have you been rehearsing these mental images of associations for a few minutes without distractions, so that you will have better odds of consolidating this memory? Will you rehearse again, perhaps later today and several times more on subsequent days?

Untie That String

Have you been using retrieval cues? Perhaps the lapel pins or the suit will provide cues. The main context you have to use is that the name and picture are part of this book, serving, I hope, to summarize by example the main points of the book. But other contexts exist too, such as where you are or what you are doing while going through this exercise. Of what use will the context cues be if you meet me in a different context? Perhaps we meet on the street, and I am dressed in a T shirt. What cues for retrieval will you use then? Did you notice and rehearse enough of the facial features and associations with my name for the memory to survive meeting me in a different context?

These cues are associated with the primary information you are trying to memorize. Because the cues are linked in your brain with the primary information, receiving the cue can help drag out the primary memory that is linked to it, as the linkages in the second drawing on this facing page indicates. If you go fishing for the memory, hooking a cue can drag along the memory you are looking for.

What were your emotions about me? Do you have any real motivation for memorizing my name and face? Are your emotions going to make you want to remember me or to forget me? Do I look like a jerk or a stuffy old professor? Were you pleased with the book? Do you feel as if you got your money's worth? What are your emotions about retrieving the memory? Are you in a bad mood and don't feel like playing this silly game? Are you stressed or embarrassed because you find it difficult to remember? Or are you confident that you went about learning in the right way and that your memory will work for you? Whatever the emotion, consciously make it part of the memory.

No doubt you realize that the process of retrieval is the opposite of getting the information registered in the first place. Originally, the information about the name was broken into pieces and scattered widely throughout the brain. Now, during retrieval the brain has to reconstruct these pieces back to original form. You should recognize the possibility of errors during reconstruction. For example, some of my facial features are similar to those of somebody else you know, and you make a false identification. This problem can happen with many faces you try to memorize.

Finally, are you getting enough sleep so that your brain can work

Untie That String

through all the processes needed to cement the associations and linkages you made and set the stage for a retrieval reconstruction process that will produce error-free recall?

There are seven steps to good memory:

1. Pay more attention
2. Make associations, especially visual
3. Stop interfering with consolidation
4. Use cues to retrieve
5. Avoid stress and negative attitudes
6. Get plenty of sleep
7. Use your memory. Trust it to work

Now how do we remember these seven steps? Let me illustrate with another example of making mental pictures (if my imagery doesn't work for you, make your own pictures). Imagine yourself as a soldier, walking up to your bank's ATM machine to get a withdrawal. You put in your card and pin number, but instead of getting money, you get a "Good Memory Certificate!" You snap to *attention* and salute your Certificate. While holding your salute, you look around the ATM, noticing all sorts of things that you can *associate* with your Certificate (the ATM machine and layout of its buttons, driveway, sign with the bank's name, etc.). You freeze, still holding your salute, and shut out all other stimuli and activity, *avoiding all possible distractions*, giving yourself time for this experience to sink in. You think hard about all the items you have associated with your Certificate, because these are *cues* to help you remember this whole scenario. You see yourself as *calm, happy* with your new memory capability, as validated by your certificate. All is right with the world. You are ready to go home and have a good night's *sleep*. You picture yourself sleeping, snug and happy in your bed. When you get up in the morning, you put your Certificate in your shirt pocket to have with you all day, easily accessible to remind you that you can *trust* your new memory skills to work for you all day.

I can summarize the essence of good memory with what I call the Four Rs. The equation is straightforward:

Remembering = Register + Relate + Rehearse + Recall

- Register the information in the first place
- Relate it to something you know, especially in pictures
- Rehearse new memories, especially right away and even as you are being exposed to them
- Recall with cues.

By now you should be fully convinced that you can improve your memory, irrespective of your previous memory ability, age, sex, health, or station in life. The principles and strategies mentioned in this book can serve you well. This book's 150-plus key ideas for improving memory are easy to review and should be reviewed periodically until they become integrated into your approach to remembering.

I have a word of caution for the students among you: remembering is NOT the same as learning. Professors know this better than anyone. We are continually confronted by students complaining about their test grades, because they studied hard and "knew" the material. What they mean, of course, is that they had memorized the material - but not well enough to apply it in new contexts. A good test asks students to do more than regurgitate memorized facts or recognize a correct answer when it is given along with three or four wrong answers. Learning includes the ability to think critically and creatively with what you have memorized. For help in becoming a better thinker, I recommend John Chaffee's book, *The Thinker's Way*,[2] Ronald Gross's *Peak Learning*,[3] and de Bono's *Six Thinking Hats*.[4]

Learning only begins with memory. Professor Benjamin Bloom at the University of Chicago, has created a "taxonomy" of learning that captures the key distinctions between memory and higher learning. The elements of learning are commonly viewed as a sequential enrichment of remembering, extending to understanding what you have remembered, to applying the information, to analysis that includes perceiving the component parts, to synthesis of information from multiple sources, to judging the value of material for a given purpose. In the real world, these six components of learning do not have to be serially ordered. You can, for example, apply a memorized equation even though you don't really understand it (this is the only way I could get through college calculus). You can judge the value of information without knowing how it was synthesized.

Having taken this journey toward better memory, I trust that you now are motivated and encouraged to enhance your memory skills. You have seen many ways to remember better. How can you fail to implement these ideas? Expend the effort to obtain a better memory and reap the reward of a more orderly, competent, and satisfying life. Untie that reminder string from your finger.

There is a learner within you, able and confident, waiting to function freely, usefully, and joyfully.
- Marilyn Ferguson

1. Langley, Veronica. 1999. The Nobel Prize. Barnes and Noble Books. New York.

2. Chaffee, John. 1998. The Thinker's Way. Little, Brown & Co.. Boston.

3. Gross, Ronald. 1991. Peak Learning. Putnam. New York.

4. Bono, E. De. 1985. Six Thinking Hats. Little, Brown & Co.. Boston.

INDEX

acronymns, 75, 93
acrostics, 187
aging, 270-296
alcohol, 263,273
Alzheimer's Disease, 53, 198, 275-281
ambiguous figures, 195-196
ambition, 4
amnesia, 114, 121
   H.M., 125-127
amnesiacs, 44, 129, 194, 258
amygdala, 150, 152-153
anesthesia, 138
anger, 157
antioxidants, 55
anxiety, 152-159, 187, 206
Aplysia, 57, 131-133
associations, 66-108
attention, 12, 13, 37-65, 249, 257, 262
attention deficit, hyperactivity disorder, 53
auditory nerve, 69
avoidance learning, 167-168
bait shyness, 40
behavior, maladaptive, 82, 84
biofeedback learning, 169
blood pressure, 81, 165, 168, 278, *see also* *hypertension*
blueberries, 55
categorization, 30-31, 89-93
chewing gum, 46

children, and memory, 225-232
child testimony, 228-232
   early childhood, 88, 155, 163-164, 219-220, 228-232
chunking, 93, 125
conclusions, 303-308
confidence, 4, 190, 206, 208
context, learning, *see also* *state-dependent learning*, 87, 187, 206
cortex, cerebral, 9, 47, 69, 126-127, 135-136, 171, 188, 191, 195, 197, 24-251, 278
CREB protein, 57
culture, 237-239
déjá vu, 42, 189
depression, 158, 160, 170, 206, 290
diabetes, 266, 295
diet, 282-285
dopamine, 51
dreaming, 188, 253-260
drug abuse, 98, 169-174, 263
education, 237-238
educational reform, 4, 27, 88, 95-96, 120-122, 149-150
electroencephalogram (EEG), 195, 246
electroconvulsive shock (ECS), 40, 111-112, 114-

115
emotions, 20, 145-180, 220
encoding, 41-42
eye-witness testimony, 219-220, 223
exercise, 28, 162, 236, 247-249
faces, 5
false memory, 41, 190, 214-240
fear, 152
   see also anxiety
FIG system, 14
   for numbers, 14, 71-72
   room method, 14, 70
flavinoids, 54
food, comfort, 163
freeze behavior, 87
Freudian slip, 149
genetics, 18
Gettysburg address, 77
glia, 9, 283
habituation, 42
hallucinations, 188
heart rate, 47, 168
hippocampus, 25, 43, 49, 55-56, 115, 125-127, 133, 150, 152-153, 159, 162, 170-171, 192, 193, 255, 258, 259, 273, 282-289
hormones, 113, 151, 155, 230, 261-262, 279
Huntington's Disease, 198
hypertension, 272, 273
hypnosis, 188, 189, 224

hypothalamus, 150
imprinting, 116-120
imaging, mental, *see mental pictures*
interference theory of learning, 120, 217
IQ and intelligence, 1, 96, 121, 123-124, 237-239
jokes, 77
Key Ideas,
   aging, 271-302
   association, 104-105
   attention, 61-63
   consolidation, 140-142
   emotions, 175-177
   false memories, 241-242
   general, 33-35
   retrieval, 209-211
   sleep, 265-267
learning styles, 93, 95
learning to learn, 90, 95-96, 120
magnesium, 56
magnetic resonance imaging, *see MRI scans*
medial forebrain bundle and reward, 51
memory
   amnesia, 49
   classical conditioning, Pavlovian, 20, 25-26, 43, 78, 128, 165, 194, 207, 282-283

consolidation, 17, 108-144, 246, 248, 253, 254, 260
cramming, 80, 139, 252
creativity and, 3
crutches, 31, 207
cues, 13, 44, 89, 97, 154, 186-195, 200-208
declarative, *see explicit*
drugs and, 48-58, 120-122, 153-154, 282-285
event dependent, 39
explicit, 20, 109, 190, 193-198, 258, 260
extinction, 79-80, 138, 206-207
habituation, 79
implicit, 20, 23-25, 67, 123, 128, 188, 193-198, 220, 223, 288
interference, 191, 200-201, 203
kinds, 19
motor learning, *see implicit learning*
pegs, *see FIG systems*
place preference and, 51
priming, 25, 26, 115, 193-199
procedural, *see implicit*
recognition memory, 187, 195
rehearsal, 29-30, 39, 100, 137-138, 166, 259
repression, 146, 158
rote, 58, 67

serial position effect, 41
short-term (and working memory), 17, 39, 109, 123-125, 148, 191, 192
sound-a-likes and, 73
spatial, 24-25, 162
tip-of-the-tongue, 198
vitamins, and, 54-56
mental pictures, 14, 46, 68, 69, 71, 125
mind/brain relationship, 2, 16
motivation, 146, 149
Mozart effect, 47, 163
MRI scans, 49, 85, 137-138, 192, 197, 248-250, 261, 286
multi-tasking, 28
music, 47, 162-163, 197
names of people, 4, 5, 74, 89
nervous tics, 81
neurons (nerve cells), 19, 49, 57, 69, 85, 161-162, 288, 289, 293
odors, 42, 200
optic nerve, 69
organization, 95
Parkinson's Disease, 198
PET scans, 23, 53, 136, 256, 278, 290
positive reinforcement, 50-52 *see also reward*
positron emission tomography, *see PET scans*

protein synthesis inhibitors, 138
psychosomatic disease, 165
remembering
    what you read, 98-100
    what you hear, 100-101
retrieval, 186-207
reward, 146-149, 166, 170
science, 8
self-esteem, 4, 170
sensitization, 132
seven-plus-one rule, 93, 125
sleep and dreaming, 28, 207, 245-270
sleep learning, 251
state-dependent learning, 97-99, 172, 196, 200, 205, 267
stomach ulcer, 81
stress, 22, 28, 80, 154-155, 158, 161, 220, 226, 235
stroke, 293
students, 58
synapses, 9, 50, 115-116, 131, 133, 273, 279, 287, 290
television, 44
unconscious mind, 17, 19-22, 26, 188-191
violence, 157
visceral function, 80-81, 150,
vitamins, 282
worry, 165

```
QP406 .K535 2004
Klemm, W. R. (William
Robert), 1934-
Thank you brain, for all you
remember : what you forgot
was my fault
```